MATTHEW FOX

MODERN SPIRITUAL MASTERS SERIES

MATTHEW FOX

Essential Writings on Creation Spirituality

Selected with an Introduction by

CHARLES BURACK

ORBIS BOOKS
Maryknoll, New York 10545

Maryknoll, New York 10545

Fathers and Brothers

Founded in 1970, Orbis Books endeavors to publish works that enlighten the mind, nourish the spirit, and challenge the conscience. The publishing arm of the Maryknoll Fathers and Brothers, Orbis seeks to explore the global dimensions of the Christian faith and mission, to invite dialogue with diverse cultures and religious traditions, and to serve the cause of reconciliation and peace. The books published reflect the views of their authors and do not represent the official position of the Maryknoll Society. To learn more about Maryknoll and Orbis Books, please visit our website at www.orbisbooks.com

Library of Congress Cataloging-in-Publication Data

Names: Fox, Matthew, 1940- author.
Title: Matthew Fox : essential writings on creation spirituality / selected with an introduction by Charles Burack.
Description: Maryknoll, NY : Orbis Books, [2022] | Series: Modern spiritual masters series | Includes bibliographical references. | Summary: "Essential writings by Matthew Fox, theologian and leading proponent of 'creation spirituality.'"-- Provided by publisher.
Identifiers: LCCN 2021035175 (print) | LCCN 2021035176 (ebook) | ISBN 9781626984554 | ISBN 9781608339181 (epub)
Subjects: LCSH: Theology. | Spirituality--Christianity. | Creation.
Classification: LCC BX5995.F65 A5 2022 (print) | LCC BX5995.F65 (ebook) | DDC 283--dc23
LC record available at https://lccn.loc.gov/2021035175
LC ebook record available at https://lccn.loc.gov/2021035176

Contents

Sources and Permissions

Grateful acknowledgement is made to the following publishers for permission to reprint from the published material. Excerpts are identified by these abbreviations:

AWE   *The A.W.E. Project: Reinventing Education, Reinventing the Human.* Copyright © 2006 Matthew Fox. Published by Copperhouse, an imprint of Wood Lake Publishing, Inc. Used by permission.

CB   Commentary by editor, Charles Burack.

CCC   *The Coming of the Cosmic Christ: The Healing of Mother Earth and the Birth of a Global Renaissance.* Copyright © 1988 Matthew Fox. Used by permission of HarperCollins Publishers.

CM   *Christian Mystics: 365 Readings and Meditations.* Copyright © 2011 by Matthew Fox. Reprinted by permission of New World Library, Novato, CA, www.newworldlibrary.com.

CNF   *Confessions: The Making of a Postdenominational Priest, Revised and Updated.* Copyright © 2015 by Matthew Fox. Published by North Atlantic Books. Reprinted by permission of North Atlantic Books.

CR   *Creativity: Where the Divine and the Human Meet.* Copyright © 2002 by Matthew Fox. Published by Jeremy P. Tarcher, 2004. Used by permission of Tarcher, an imprint of Penguin Publishing Group, a division of Penguin Random House LLC. All rights reserved.

CSLG   *Creation Spirituality: Liberating Gifts for the Peoples of the Earth.* Copyright © 1991 by Matthew Fox. Used by permission of HarperCollins Publishers.

HBMV   *Hildegard von Bingen's Mystical Visions.* Translated by Bruce Hozeski. Introduced by Matthew Fox. Published by Inner Traditions International and Bear & Company. Copyright © 1986. http://www.Innertraditions.com. All rights reserved. Reprinted by permission of publisher.

HBST   *Hildegard of Bingen: A Saint for Our Time.* Copyright © 2012 by Matthew Fox. Namaste Publishing. Reprinted by permission of publisher.

HSM   *The Hidden Spirituality of Men: Ten Metaphors to Awaken the Sacred Masculine.* Copyright © 2008 by Matthew Fox. Reprinted by permission of New World Library, Novato, CA, www.newworldlibrary.com.

IHB   *Illuminations of Hildegard of Bingen* by Matthew Fox. Published by Inner Traditions International and Bear & Company. Copyright © 2002. http://www.Innertraditions.com. All rights reserved. Reprinted by permission of publisher.

JN   *Julian of Norwich: Wisdom in a Time of Pandemic—And Beyond.* Copyright © 2020 by Matthew Fox. Published by iUniverse.

LR   *The Lotus and the Rose: A Conversation Between Tibetan Buddhism and Mystical Christianity* by Matthew Fox and Lama Tsomo. Copyright © 2018 Lotus & Rose LLC. Published by Namchak Publishing Company LLC. Reprinted by permission of the publisher.

ME   *Meister Eckhart: A Mystic Warrior for Our Times.* Copyright © 2014 by Matthew Fox. Reprinted by permission of New World Library, Novato, CA, www.newworldlibrary.com

MF   Commentary by Matthew Fox.

MG   *Manifesto for a Global Civilization* by Matthew Fox and Brian Swimme. Published by Bear & Company, 1982.

MME   *Meditations with Meister Eckhart.* Edited by Matthew Fox. Published by Inner Traditions International and Bear & Company. Copyright © 1983. http://www.Innertraditions.com. All rights reserved. Reprinted by permission of publisher.

NG   *Natural Grace: Dialogues on Creation, Darkness, and the Soul in Spirituality and Science.* Copyright © 1996 by Matthew Fox and Rupert Sheldrake. Published by Doubleday. Used by permission of Doubleday, an imprint of the Knopf Doubleday Publishing Group, a division of Penguin Random House LLC. All right reserved.

NR   *New Reformation: Creation Spirituality and the Transformation of Christianity* by Matthew Fox. Published by Inner Traditions International and Bear & Company. Copyright © 2006. http://www.Innertraditions.com. All rights reserved. Reprinted by permission of publisher.

NU   *Naming the Unnameable: 89 Wonderful and Useful Names for God . . . Including the Unnameable God.* Copyright © 2018 by

Matthew Fox. Homebound Publications. Reprinted with permission of the publisher.

OB *Original Blessing: A Primer in Creation Spirituality* by Matthew Fox. Copyright © 1983 Bear & Company. Republished by Jeremy P. Tarcher, 2000.

ORMW *One River, Many Wells: Wisdom Springing from Global Spiritual Traditions.* Copyright © 2000 by Matthew Fox. Used by permission of Tarcher, an imprint of Penguin Publishing Group, a division of Penguin Random House LLC. All rights reserved.

OS *Occupy Spirituality: A Radical Vision for a New Generation.* Copyright © 2013 by Adam Bucko and Matthew Fox. Published by North Atlantic Books. Reprinted by permission of North Atlantic Books.

OSE *Order of the Sacred Earth: An Intergenerational Vision of Love and Action.* Copyright © 2018 by Matthew Fox, Skylar Wilson, and Jennifer Berit Listug. Appears with kind permission from Monkfish Book Publishing Company, Rhinebeck, New York.

PA *The Physics of Angels: Exploring the Realm Where Science and Spirit Meet* Copyright © 1996, 2014 by Matthew Fox and Rupert Sheldrake. Appears with kind permission from Monkfish Book Publishing Company, Rhinebeck, New York.

PC *Passion for Creation: The Earth-Honoring Spirituality of Meister Eckhart* by Matthew Fox. Published by Inner Traditions International and Bear & Company. Copyright © 2000. http://www.Innertraditions.com. All rights reserved. Reprinted with permission of publisher.

PRR *Prayer: A Radical Response to Life.* Copyright © by Matthew Fox. Published by Tarcher/Putnam, 2001; originally published as *On Becoming a Musical, Mystical Bear: Spirituality American Style* by Harper & Row, 1972.

RW *The Reinvention of Work: A New Vision of Livelihood for Our Time.* Copyright © 1994 by Matthew Fox. Used by permission of HarperCollins Publishers.

SCC *Stations of the Cosmic Christ.* Copyright © 2016 by Marc Andrus and Matthew Fox. Published by Unity Books. Used with permission of Unity Books, unity.org.

SJ *Sheer Joy: Conversations with Thomas Aquinas on Creation Spirituality.* Copyright © 1992 by Matthew Fox. Republished by Ixis/Dover Press, 2020. Reprinted with permission of publisher.

SNC   *A Spirituality Named Compassion: Uniting Mystical Awareness with Social Justice* by Matthew Fox. Published by Inner Traditions International and Bear & Company. Copyright © 1999. http://www.Innertraditions.com. All rights reserved. Reprinted with permission of publisher.

SS   *Sins of the Spirit, Blessings of the Flesh: Lessons for Transforming Evil in Soul and Society, Revised Edition.* Copyright © 2016 by Matthew Fox. Published by North Atlantic Books. Reprinted by permission of North Atlantic Books.

TTA   *The Tao of Thomas Aquinas: Fierce Wisdom for Hard Times.* Copyright © 2020 by Matthew Fox. Published by iUniverse.

WG   *A Way to God: The Creation Spirituality Journey of Thomas Merton.* Copyright © 2016 by Matthew Fox. Reprinted with permission of New World Library, Novato, CA, www.newworldlibrary.com.

WP   *Wrestling with the Prophets: Essays on Creation Spirituality and Everyday Life.* Copyright © 1995 by Matthew Fox. Published by Jeremy P. Tarcher, 2003.

WS   *Western Spirituality: Historical Roots, Ecumenical Routes* by Matthew Fox. Published by Inner Traditions International and Bear & Company. Copyright © 1981. http://www.Innertraditions.com. All rights reserved. Reprinted by permission of publisher.

WWW   *Whee! We, Wee All the Way Home: A Guide to Sensual, Prophetic Spirituality* by Matthew Fox. Published by Inner Traditions International and Bear & Company. Copyright © 1981. http://www.Innertraditions.com. All rights reserved. Reprinted with permission of publisher.

Other Books by Matthew Fox

Creation Spirituality and the Dreamtime (coedited with Catherine Hammond) (Morehouse Publishing Company, 1992)

Hildegard of Bingen's Book of Divine Works with Letters and Songs (Bear & Company, 1987)

In the Beginning There Was Joy: A Celebration of Creation for Children of All Ages (Crossroad Publishing Company, 1995)

Letters to Pope Francis (Level Five Media, 2013)

The Pope's War: Why Ratzinger's Secret Crusade Imperiled the Church and How It Can Be Saved (Sterling Ethos, 2011)

Religion USA: Religion and Culture by Way of Time Magazine (Listening Press, 1971)

Acknowledgments

I feel honored and grateful that Matt chose me to edit his essential writings. My introduction reflects how much I admire him and his invaluable contributions. He is a dear colleague and friend—and a true inspiration—and I have learned so much from him! I am also grateful for the wondrous experience I had teaching at both the University of Creation Spirituality (UCS) and Naropa University, Oakland (NUO). The innovative educational experience at UCS and NUO was transforming not only for students but also for faculty and staff. I was deeply transformed by my seven years with both schools—some of the best years of my life!

I am also deeply thankful to my beloved wife, author, and eldercare professional extraordinaire, Mary Ann Konarzewski, for assisting with the creation of this book. She made the process much more enjoyable!

Introduction

Matthew Fox is the passionate prophet—and pied piper—of creation-centered spirituality. A radical priest, visionary theologian, and ecumenical mystic, he has devoted five decades to exploring the creation spirituality traditions in Christianity and other world religions, as well as demonstrating their relevance to the significant challenges of our times. These traditions affirm the inherent sanctity and creativity of the universe and all its inhabitants, and they assert that a central human mission is to cocreate a world of justice and compassion, beauty and peace, love and gratitude. Fox has also proposed that the latest scientific vision of an evolving, 13.8-billion-year-old universe offers an inspiring, new Creation story that is relevant to our spiritual times.

His three dozen books, as well as his countless talks, workshops, conferences, courses, and cosmic masses, have reached a worldwide audience and not only transformed lives and communities but also challenged church doctrines, dogmas, and practices. His prolific writings brilliantly address vital issues from spirituality and science, culture and politics, ecology and education, gender and work, and offer fresh insights and approaches. In many of his writings, he shows how premodern wisdom can help illuminate and resolve postmodern problems. His innovative educational programs, which have drawn students with diverse backgrounds and professional callings, are a unique contribution to holistic, interspiritual education. He believes that every person is graced with the capacity to be a mystic, an artist, and a prophet, and that all of us are called to actualize our sacred gifts in unique ways—and in doing so to enrich, sanctify, and celebrate life.

Fox has received great acclaim for his work from a wide range of luminaries. Cultural historian and religious scholar Thomas Berry proclaimed that "Matthew Fox might well be the most

creative, the most comprehensive, surely the most challenging
religious-spiritual teacher in America." Visionary economist and
activist David Korten concurred that Fox is "one of the great
prophetic voices of our time," and Bishop John Shelby Spong
opined that "History will name Fox one of the great Christian
spirits of our age." Interreligious pioneer Father Bede Griffiths
stated that "Matthew Fox's creation spirituality is the spirituality of the future, and his theology of the Cosmic Christ is the
theology of the future." In a similar vein, Bishop William Swing,
president of the United Religions Initiative, declared that Fox's
ecumenical work "will inspire many people to imagine that religions have a common vocation as friends instead of adversar-
ies." Rabbi Zalman Schachter-Shalomi, cofounder of the Jewish
renewal movement, stated that Fox's interspiritual work "opens
the treasures of the Great Traditions and retrieves for us the
relevant inspiring sources." Jungian analyst and author Clarissa Pinkola Estes said that Fox "anoints modern Souls with a
medicine he finds in the old and venerable Holy voices," and
biophysicist Beverly Rubik, founder of the Institute for Frontier
Science, declared that Fox's work helped her to see "Nature in
a new way as the explication of divinity, my soul was stirred to
do something new."

The power, originality, and inclusivity of Fox's work is demonstrated by the strident and sometimes vehement attacks he has
received from those—mostly right-wing Catholics and fundamentalist Christians—who have condemned his writings and his
actions as "dangerous," "deviant," and "heretical." Indeed, his
progressive views—particularly on original blessing, feminism,
the Motherhood and Childhood of God, homosexuality, Native
American spirituality, and the four spiritual paths of creation
spirituality—were met by condemnation from the Vatican and
led to Fox's eventual expulsion from the priesthood. Ever irrepressible and committed to spiritual activism and education,
Fox became an Episcopal priest and now considers himself a
"postdenominational priest." In recent decades he has thrown
his "lot in with the younger generation and in particular those

committed to the making of good work through birthing post-modern forms for traditional Western worship" (CNF 301).

In his exploration of the creation spirituality of the great medieval mystic, theologian, and preacher Meister Eckhart, Fox was able to identify four primary, interconnected spiritual paths, each with a set of associated themes. All four paths are ways that people "befriend" divinity in and beyond the world (OB 31). The first two paths are of ways of being, while the second two are ways of doing. The first path, the Via Positiva, is befriending divinity through experiences of awe and delight in the cosmos. It includes numinous experiences of prayer, meditation, sensuality, nature, relationship, and community, as well as gratitude for life and celebration of the essential goodness of existence. The second path, the Via Negativa, is communing with the divine through experiences of silence and also through loss, suffering, darkness, and the emptying out of the self. It includes encountering the infinite Godhead that transcends form and substance. These two paths help us to realize and unfold our mystical capacity for holy intimacy. The third path, the Via Creativa, is companioning with spirit through creative activity, especially through contemplative approaches to the arts. This path helps us to discover and enact our artistic capacity to birth beauty, grow soul, and fashion order out of chaos. The fourth path, the Via Transformativa, is collaborating with the divine by using one's creative energy to transform self and society through acts of compassion and justice. As divinized coworkers, we realize our prophetic capacity to interfere with evil in all its many forms and to come to the aid of the impoverished, the oppressed, and the marginalized. We work together to build a caring, global civilization.

The four paths are interconnected and are more like facets of a single prism or aspects of a complex symphony. Thus, our experiences of sacred joy and sorrow can inspire holy acts of creativity and justice—and inspired art-making and activism can evoke numinous experiences of bliss, grief, peace, and wonder.

EARLY LIFE

Fox emphasizes that his calling is about his work, not about him. Nonetheless, his long, rich life offers important insights into his work—and into the wisdom and passion, courage and conviction, love and strength, needed to realize one's calling as a mystic, artist, and prophet.

Matthew was born Timothy James Fox in Madison, Wisconsin, on winter solstice 1940. During Tim's early years, his father, George Fox, was an assistant football coach at the University of Wisconsin, and his mother, Beatrice Sill, was "a liberated woman long before her time" who "took two hours every afternoon for herself" to read and participate in a bridge club or book club or sewing club "no matter how many kids, diapers, or pregnancies [7 in 11 years]" (CNF 51). George had "an amazing streak of feminist consciousness" and wanted both his sons and daughters to receive a college education. He came from an Irish Roman Catholic family and received an Augustinian education. Beatrice was raised Episcopalian: her mother had been born Jewish and then converted to the Episcopal Church after marrying her father. After a few years of marriage, Beatrice decided to convert to Catholicism to create a greater sense of religious unity in the family.

The Fox family was "not ethnic Catholic," but rather "catholic" in the sense of "universal" and "ecumenical" (CNF 56). His parents rented a room to international graduate students. The conversations at mealtimes felt like "being at the United Nations." These experiences were seeds that came to fruition in his adult exploration and affirmation of "deep ecumenism."

Young Tim enjoyed sports and nature. During a family trip he witnessed Niagara Falls and experienced "the power and majesty of it all"—an experience that "radically opened up" his soul. A few months later, he contracted polio, which ended his participation in sports for a while. Despite the fact that the polio could have cut short his life, he felt no fear. Indeed, his father, who had always admired physical courage, said that he was amazed by his son's moral courage. When, some years later, Tim told his father of his "decision to try out for the priesthood," his father said with pleasure, "Do what you feel called to do. Remember what Jesus said, 'You have not chosen me but I have chosen you'" (CNF 61).

Tim realized that he had to let go of his father's "unspoken agenda" for him to become a serious athlete. Polio taught Tim a profound life lesson about solitude: "It was okay to be alone and to not be in control. Trust is important. And waiting is part of life." This was a profound lesson in the Via Negativa. Eventually, therapy returned movement to his legs, and within a year he was playing sports again, but this time "felt deeply grateful . . . to the universe itself" (CNF 59). Never again would he take his legs for granted. To this day, he tells people that "mysticism is about 'not taking for granted.'" His vocation, he said, began with his polio experience. He became a more serious, conscious, and sensitive human being.

In public high school, Tim's favorite subjects were English and history, and he found that his "mystical life . . . was enlarging as I read literature." He also liked history because it "was like a stage on which greatness strode," and his awe and respect for various historical figures, like Abraham Lincoln, inspired a desire to "emulate them in some way." In addition to his early interest in religion, he became interested in law, which would lead to politics. While attending daily Mass, he discovered "a world of mystery" and was especially enthusiastic about Mary's feast day readings from the wisdom literature of the Hebrew Bible—Proverbs, Song of Songs, Sirach. His love of wisdom— from whatever source—has been a central force in his life and work. Between his junior and senior years, he read Tolstoy's *War and Peace*, and his soul was blown wide open by the "panoply of life" that was presented—"it was all sacred." He developed a desire to pursue "soul work." Later, he would say that he owed his "long-held belief that spirituality and art go together to the influence that Tolstoy's art" had on his journey.

Tim loved the retreats encouraged by his parish priests, and during one retreat he read Thomas Merton's *Seven Storey Mountain* and became interested in becoming a monk like Merton. His parish priest recommended that he explore the Dominicans, the order to which all of his parish priests and lay brother friends belonged. They "seemed happy and serious and about something important" and combined meditation with work in the world teaching and preaching. This blending of inner and outer work would become a central theme of his book *The Reinvention of Work* (1993). After making a retreat with the Dominicans during his senior year, he decided to try out joining the order.

BECOMING A PRIEST

As a "Dominican wannabe," Tim was required to attend two years of college and enter a novitiate program. He attended Loras College in Dubuque, Iowa, and loved his studies, worship, and sports. Team sports gave him "something of a mystical experience," and his appreciation of "body awareness" would later play an important role in his understanding of creation spirituality—which honors the blessings of the body, which "unite[s] us to cosmic history."

Tim entered the novitiate and began his formal training near Winona, Minnesota, where he was "greeted with the name 'Brother Matthew.'" He found the initiation ceremony, which symbolized "a leave taking from 'the world,' quite adventurous and possibly even romantic. It seemed like a great challenge lay ahead of us." Early in his training, Fr. Clancy gave him some advice that always remained with him: "Set your standards high . . . There will be moments in the order when you will be scandalized and disappointed. Don't go the way of everybody else if your conscience tells you otherwise" (CNF 22). Much later, he would be inspired by Thomas Aquinas's admonition that "Conscience is more to be obeyed than authority imposed from the outside"—the same admonition that fortified Rev. Martin

Luther King Jr. when he was put in a Birmingham jail for civil disobedience and social justice activism.

At the end of his novitiate year, Matthew took a three-year vow and then started Dominican studies in Chicago. One day during meditation he "had an experience of my own nothing-ness" and later "confided to a friend-adviser that I wanted that experience to be the cornerstone of my life" (CNF 27). This experience of the Via Negativa "made letting go much easier." He explained that "our nothingness is metaphysical and not psychological . . . we come from nothing—thus our uniqueness—but our existence is not worth nothing. Indeed, we are all special because we could be just nothing!" (CNF 27).

The teachers that Matthew found most profoundly influential were those who encouraged him, "by example or by interaction," to think. He was especially impressed when "Doc" Powell real-ized at the end of the semester that his own sociological thesis was "wrong and unprovable." Matthew recognized with admi-ration that "Here was a man living out the Dominican vocation to 'truth' who had the guts to admit to his students that his own search had been a mistake" (CNF 28).

Tim was aware of the changing world events and the ush-ering in of a new era in church and society. Pope John XXIII succeeded Pius XII, "who stood for a kind of ascetic spiritual-ity." The new pope was "launching his revolution by way of the Second Vatican Council, and we saw signs of the effects of his vision all around us" (CNF 29). More liberal theologians, like Hans Küng, M. D. Chenu, and Yves Congar, were being "reha-bilitated," and they were reading the writings of French priest, scientist, and philosopher Pierre Teilhard de Chardin. Reading the Pope's encyclical *Pacem in Terris* (Peace on Earth) was "a mystical and prophetic experience for me" because it presented "a vision of authentic ecumenism . . . addressed to all persons of good will, not just the clergy or Catholics or Christian or believers" and "calling the nations to disarmament and peace" (CNF 29). This was also a time of social and political revolution.

Dr. Martin Luther King Jr. and the civil rights movement were coming of age, and the Vietnam War was escalating.

At the end of that year Matthew gladly made his solemn (final) vows "to John XXIII and his vision" (CNF 31). During the ceremony, an image came to him that he would never forget and that would take years to fully understand: "a bare foot, bloody and moving through mud and rain." To him it signified "the warrior side, the rigorous side, of the vocation I have come to know and to live." He graduated with a BA and MA in philosophy; his Master's thesis examined Kant and the proof for God's existence. He then was ready for a three-year stint of theological studies at the Dominican House of Studies in Dubuque.

In his third year of philosophy, Matthew's confessor encouraged him to "consider becoming a hermit." At first astonished and amused, Matthew was "haunted" by this recommendation and eventually requested that he spend a summer at a hermit colony on Vancouver Island. His provincial was displeased with his request, calling it "this crazy scheme of yours"—because he had known Dominicans who "had run off to the Trappists and had gone kind of crazy" and said "you may never be ordained"—but eventually relented. Matthew saw this as an important moment in his development, realizing "I left the priesthood before I entered. For that reason, I have always had a relationship with the priesthood that was nonpossessive and therefore somewhat playful. The priesthood was something I let go of early on" (CNF 33). On the train journey west to Vancouver Island, Matthew started a journal, and decades later was surprised to discover that the journal contained many of the themes of creation spirituality, such as panentheism (All in God and God in All), life as the ultimate sacred experience, the relation of contemplation to action, and the importance of listening, silence, and love. Matthew also articulated his calling: "The Dominican vocation is to be in constant communion with God. This is what it is to preach and preach Christ. . . . This is my vocation. It is my happiness. (Or rather, He is). It is my holiness" (CNF 38).

Upon return to the priory in Dubuque, Matthew took on new responsibilities, such as editing the student magazine *Reality*. Considering it "stodgy," he and the other staff decided to end the magazine and start a new one, *Listening*, which published articles and interviews with some of the best Catholic thinkers behind the Second Vatican Council. Matthew wrote an editorial about Merton's "reawakening of the Christian conscience on today's critical issues: marriage and its meaning, politics as a service, civil justice, modern warfare" (CNF 40). He wrote another editorial asserting that "the Playboy philosophy illustrate[s] that Christianity has neglected a theology of sex that is real for our society" (CNF 41). He would explore sacred sensuality in his book *Whee! We, Wee All the Way Home: A Guide to the New Sensual Prophetic Spirituality* (1980).

Matthew continued to have mystical experiences while praying, chanting, meditating, studying theology, and being outdoors but was dismayed when none of the priests he sought for spiritual direction had similar spiritual experiences and so could not help him understand his. Moreover, there was not a single course on spirituality or the mystics. Interested in exploring spirituality in his dissertation, he wrote about "The Prayer of Jesus in the New Testament and Its Significance for a Contemporary Theology of Prayer." His most important lesson was the relationship of culture and prayer. Unsure of where to further pursue doctoral studies in spirituality and unable to receive informed advice from his teachers and from the president of the school, he wrote to Thomas Merton, who recommended that he go to the Institut Catholique (Catho) in Paris.

THE PARIS YEARS

His "Paris years," from 1967 to 1970, were powerfully transforming. He was inspired by the "sense of history," the "sense of the artist," and "the power of culture," especially the cultural revolution that was underway (CNF 72–73). The "one pressing, urgent question that superseded all other concerns" for him was "what is the relationship—if any—between prayer and social justice?" (CNF 75). He felt that this was the "most foundational issue" for him and his generation: "In the midst of the social revolutions, such as the civil rights movement and the anti-Vietnam War protests, this question kept haunting me. It seemed to be the nexus where culture and spirituality or culture and healthy religion met" (CNF 75). His classes at the Catho were very helpful in addressing this question.

From Père Chenu, who became his major mentor, he was able to answer his "question of questions: How do I relate spirituality to culture, prayer to social justice, politics to mysticism. He named the creation spirituality tradition for me" (CNF 79–80). Chenu demarcated the creation spirituality tradition from the "fall/redemption" tradition. The fall/redemption tradition is patriarchal, elitist, ascetic, and dualistic; emphasizes original sin; and worships God as Father exclusively (OB 316–17). In contrast, creation spirituality is feminist, aesthetic, and dialectical; emphasizes original blessing; and worships God as Mother, Father, and Child. Matthew's encounter with this suppressed tradition gave his life a new focus and direction as well as a "notoriety" that he never could have predicted. It would be his "task to study creation spirituality more deeply and to begin a cultural translation of it—a process in its own right with unforeseen consequences" (CNF 80). Matthew was inspired not only by Chenu's approach to theology but also his activism. Chenu tested theology "in the field" and was a theological adviser to the Vatican Council. He both inspired and supported the liberation theology movement in Latin America.

Matthew's work on his dissertation was both a critical study of culture and religion and "truly a baptism into my intellectual radicalization." In his study of the 1958 issues of *Time* magazine, he discovered that "there was far more of 'authentic religion' in the film reviews and arts section than in the religion section, which was invariably preoccupied with institutional religion—buildings, bishops, and so on" (CNF 88). He also discovered that American industry and advertisers "were using religious language to carry out their ideological convictions." Working on the dissertation, which was enthusiastically received by his doctoral committee, helped him to realize "I am a writer. This is the happiest I have ever been" (CNF 89). Looking back on his dissertation two decades later, Matthew would also realize how fundamental the dissertation was to "all my agendas, hidden and not so hidden, of the subsequent twenty-four years. The passion for justice, for relating Marx to Jesus; the interest in prayer as both celebration and honest critique of evil; the revolt against psychologizing and privatizing religion; the faith in artists to be our spiritual leaders; the labeling of living versus dying religion and the ambiguous role that ethnic religion plays in all that; the hypocrisy and decadence of which religion is capable; the false religions of American culture from consumerism to nationalism and anticommunism" (CNF 91).

TEACHING AT LOYOLA AND BARAT AND WRITING ABOUT SPIRITUALITY

For Matthew, the 1970s was a decade of teaching and writing. In late summer of 1970, he returned to the Aquinas Institute in Dubuque. By 1971, most of his Dominican friends had left the order. That summer he taught in the Institute of Pastoral Studies at Loyola University in Chicago and self-published his dissertation as *Religion USA: Religion and Culture by Way of Time Magazine*. By the fall, he completed a book about prayer that he originally planned to title "Spirituality American Style," but had "a memorable dream of a dancing, musical, mystical bear" and having "learned to trust my dreams more than institutions and other literal structures," he changed the title to *On Becoming a Musical, Mystical Bear: Spirituality American Style*, which was published in 1972 (and republished in 2001 as *Prayer: A Radical Response to Life*) (CNF 105). Matthew asserted that prayer was "radical" in a double sense: it says Yes to life, which is mysticism, and says No to injustice, which is prophesy. He deliberately substituted the word *Life* for *God* because the latter carried "so much baggage from our religions woundedness that it seldom conjures up the great mystery that divinity is and that prayer is meant to tap into" (CNF 107). The book also invoked "the artist as an instructor in life and therefore in spirituality." He believed that the word *spirituality* was "a word worth redeeming."

In response to a woman who remarked that he "must write a practical book that outlines the how-to of prayer" more than does "the bear book," he began writing *Whee! We, Wee All the Way Home: A Guide to Prophetic, Sensual Spirituality* (1976) in which he distinguished between natural and tactical ecstasies (CNF 108). The former are, for example, "experiences in nature, art, friendship, sexuality, work, and suffering," while the latter are "rosaries, celibacy, fasting, and the like." *Whee* stood for ecstatic experiences, *we* for "our symbolic consciousness which develops when we move from I to We," and *wee* for "our prophetic struggle" in which "we are reminded of how small an individual is, taking on large powers and institutional 'dragons,' in the struggle for justice."

One of Matthew's students at Loyola was a Sacred Heart sister from Barat College in Lake Forest, Illinois. She informed him of a job opening there, and he was hired as the chair of the religious studies department. At Barat his female colleagues and students helped to deepen his "feminist awareness," and he invited various prominent feminist theologians, such as Rosemary Ruether and Mary Daly, to teach or give talks. In his 1975 preface to the paperback edition of his book on prayer, he said he looked forward to a possible men's movement someday because "an alteration in a woman's view of herself will eventually result in an alteration of a man's view of women and of himself." He also pointed out that creation spirituality is feminist "insofar as it equates the artistic quest with the spiritual quest, as it insists on a mystery-oriented, participatory relationship to creation, as it questions drastically the phallic definition of prayer that most of us have inherited, and as it opts for the yeses as well as the nos in life" (CNF 111). Matthew would offer a new vision of men's spiritual identity and vocation in *The Hidden Spirituality of Men: Ten Metaphors to Awaken the Sacred Masculine* (2008).

In 1974, Matthew invited a newly ordained female Episcopal to say Mass. Eight months later he was summoned by Cardinal Cody, who told him that "I am writing to the Congregation for the Doctrine of the Faith, your master general, and the pope to put you on trial and remove you from the priesthood" because Matthew was "concelebrating mass with an Anglican priestess" (CNF 112). Mathew corrected him, saying that he did not "concelebrate" with her because that would have been "the height of chauvinism, my saying move over, woman, I'm going to do this right." After hearing out Matthew, Cardinal Cody said, "I have saved you." Cody also disapproved of Matthew's book about "sensual spirituality," and Matthew responded that Thomas Aquinas said all knowledge comes through the senses. Cody was upset that Matthew did not have an "imprimatur," but Matthew retorted that "since the Second Vatican Council we don't need imprimaturs. Critical reviews in Catholic journals will do" (CNF 113). Cody shouted, "But how will I control theologians without an imprimatur" and confessed that he could not control any of the priests in his diocese. Matthew left the meeting "deeply encouraged: It had not been a radical theologian a la Hans Küng but a conservative cardinal and protestor of the status quo who had revealed to me that the control game was dying" (CNF 113–14).

From his Jewish students at Barat, Matthew learned that Jews talk about the temptation and fall of Adam and Eve but don't talk about "original sin." This "distinction between the Fall and original sin" deepened his "realization of how un-Jewish much of Christianity is" (CNF 111). One student introduced him to the religious philosophy of Rabbi Abraham Joshua Heschel, whom he grew to love for his leadership in social justice and ecumenical dialogue and for his deep and poetic "spirituality of awe, wonder, grace, and prophesy—a creation-centered spirituality indeed."

Matthew was significantly influenced by his oldest brother, Tom, who was a pioneer in education. At Barat College, Matthew experimented with various educational methodologies, especially with what he would later call "extrovert meditation" or "art as meditation"—a contemplative approach to creative exploration and expression. He was delighted to discover that his students were powerfully, and often lastingly, affected by this "hands-on education."

After a national poll by the Catholic bishops, Matthew was invited to do a study on "Spirituality and Education" and found that all of "the most promising-looking programs in spirituality around the country" were "lacking in feminism, art, social justice, and a biblically based or Jewish-based understanding of spirituality." As a result of the study, he "laid out a basic blueprint for a spirituality institute that would 'teach the spirituality of Jesus in our time'." Six categories of courses included mystical traditions, artist as spiritual voyager, professions as spiritualities, various seminar topics, workshops that develop skills for spiritual practice, and special events. These ideas were the seeds for what would become the Institute in Culture and Creation Spirituality (ICCS) at Mundelein College

Because the president of Barat vetoed his idea of establishing an Institute, Matthew decided to look for another university to implement his vision. From 1977 to 1983 he focused on creating and implementing his vision of ICCS as a master's program at Mundelein College in Chicago, despite "stiff opposition" from some Mundelein faculty and administrators. ICCS's goal was to "train mystics and prophets," which involved developing "intuition and intellect; right and left brain; mind, heart, and body" and awakening the chakras (CNF 126–27). The faculty included dancers, artists, musicians, ritualists, as well as scientist Brian Swimme, Jungian John Giannini, and others. He soon discovered that the "art as meditation" classes proved to be "a kind of truth serum" and "the missing link between spirituality and social justice" (CNF 126).

In the summer of 1976, Matthew and several friends were in a car accident caused by a pickup truck. Seriously injured and in great pain, he "learned you can live with pain—but it takes a lot out of you." It was another lesson in the Via Negativa. With the encouragement of Native Americans Sister Jose Hobday and Fr. Ed Savilla, Matthew attended his first sweat lodge. It was both an "eye-opening" and "heart-opening" experience. Although the experience was quite challenging physically and mentally, he emerged from the lodge with his sore back feeling fine and his spirits soaring. From then on, sweat lodges and native dancing "have played a deep and essential part in my spiritual practice" (CNF 144). He learned from native people—and from feminists—about "the recovery of power, healthy and authentic power" (CNF 144). Sister Jose alerted him to the "positive side of the word *power*."

While Matthew was recovering from the car accident, the compassionate support of his friend and housemate Brendan Doyle and their new puppy, Tristan, turned out to be a seed for his next book, *A Spirituality Named Compassion* (1979), a work that shows how compassion can transform self and many sectors of society and that would be significantly influenced by Meister Eckhart's linkage of compassion to justice and celebration. During this period, Matthew had read the Hindu scholar Coomaraswamy's book on art and spirituality and encountered an essay on Meister Eckhart and was "startled to see entire sentences in Eckhart that were in my *Whee! We, Wee* book" (CNF 119). Although he was "unnerved" by this discovery, months later he "let go of my fear and said to myself: Here I might have a brother!" and obtained his first book on Eckhart. While Matthew was under anesthesia during a back operation to relieve his pain from the accident, Meister Eckhart came to him. They didn't talk but "walked together on a beach. It was the most transcendent dream of my life. From that time on, I knew he and I had a rendezvous together" (CNF 119). After leaving the hospital he found Eckhart's works in Latin, where he discovered a uniquely "rich treatment of the theological concept of compassion." In the concept of compassion, Matthew "found another way to name and deepen that basic theme I had been wrestling with continually since before my days in Paris: the relation of justice and mysticism" (CNF 120).

Eckhart would prove to be the most cited mystic in Matthew's writings. At this time, he wrote extensively about Meister Eckhart in the 500-page tome *Breakthrough: Meister Eckhart's Creation Spirituality* (1980, republished in 2000 as *Passion for Creation: The Earth-Honoring Spirituality of Meister Eckhart*) and in *Meditations with Meister Eckhart* (1983), a brief collection of quotations intended to make Western mystics "available to a wider audience in a poetic, right-brain format." In *Western Spirituality: Historical Roots, Ecumenical Routes,* which he edited in 1981, Matthew had for the first time written about finding the four paths of creation spirituality in Eckhart's spiritual theology. This was a "big step" for him because for years, he had been trying to "extricate myself and Western spirituality from the quagmire of the three paths of Plotinus and Pseudo-Denys, namely those of Purgation, Illumination, and Union," which had put a "stranglehold on our spiritual lives" (CNF 136).

Matthew began studying medieval mystic Hildegard of Bingen when he discovered that her work had a profound impact on Meister Eckhart. Matthew characterized Hildegard as "a true renaissance woman and genius at music, art, healing, and intuition" (CNF 139–40). He "plunged" into her work and began lecturing about her. She offered a rich feminist and ecological spirituality informed in great measure by her many mystical visions. Matthew published *Illuminations of Hildegard of Bingen* in 1985 and *Hildegard of Bingen's Book of Divine Works: With Letters and Songs* in 1987.

Around this time, Matthew was introduced to the work of two individuals who would shape his understanding of art as meditation: M.C. Richard's book *Centering*, which emphasized expressing our divine "creative being," and Otto Rank's *Art and the Artist,* which saw the artistic journey as a spiritual journey.

According to Rank, artists want to leave behind a gift, and their biggest obstacle is the fear of death.

Matthew's progressive views on homosexuality put him on the radar of the Vatican. He gave a lecture at a conference in Seattle that was later published as "The Spiritual Journey of the Homosexual and Just About Everybody Else." He suggested that the four paths of creation spirituality "help name the homosexual's journey in a special way." For example, early in life gay people "must 'let go' [Via Negativa] of society's definition of 'normal' sexuality," which may account for their greater reliance on their creativity and hence their disproportionate involvement in the arts" (WP 243–65). Matthew's talk proved to be "the beginning of my trouble with Rome" because there was "a gang of disgruntled Catholics (Catholics United for the Faith, or CUFF) who kept track of all comings and goings at the conference and who mailed a thick batch of materials about me to Rome following my presentation. I was then on Rome's hit list" (CNF 142). CUFF is "an ideological group of thugs who attack by lies and innuendo anyone to the left of Attila."

ICCS MOVES WEST TO HOLY NAMES COLLEGE

Matthew wanted to expand the seven-year-old ICCS program, but Mundelein College had no physical room for expansion—for example, to accommodate art-as-meditation labs. His friend and colleague Brian Swimme was eager to heed "the call of the west" where "science and mysticism were dialoging." Fortunately, Sister Lois MacGillivray, the President of Holy Names College in Oakland, heard of their continuing interest in coming west and was able to secure the support of the board of regents. Matthew too felt "lured" to California not only by this science-mysticism dialogue but also by "the East-West connection; the flexibility of Holy Names College; . . . [and] the sacred wilderness that still lived in the west" (CNF 147).

Before leaving for California, Matthew had a dream indicating that this new phase in his life and work "promised a

deepening of the spiritual journey, a deeper dive into the cave,
into the ancient mysteries of goddess and Gaia lore" (CNF 147).
Matthew hired Starhawk, a Wicca practitioner, feminist thinker,
activist, and ritualist to join his faculty as well as Luisha Teisch
to teach African Dance as meditation. Starhawk was recommended by feminist theologian Rosemary Ruether as "an artic-
ulate spokesperson for the women's movement." Fortunately,
Holy Names saw ICCS as part of its Catholic mission, which
helped it to "be strong when opposition and attacks came"; and
to its "credit and honor . . . it never backed down . . . to this
day" (150–51). At this time Matthew had a dream that he was
"descending with my mother into ancient and wonderful cham-
bers of goddess love and Egyptian mythologies" (CNF 151). He
interpreted the dream as a warning that "one does not leave
topside and go down under without paying a price. . . . To seek
the goddess below is seen as a threat to those honoring the God
above exclusively" (CNF 151).

At Holy Names College, Matthew was joined by six faculty
members from Mundelein College. He also hired many adjunct
faculty who lived in the Bay Area or who flew in from other
parts of the country to lead seminars and workshops. While still
in Chicago, he completed his book *Original Blessing*, which he
subtitled *A Primer in Creation Spirituality*. It appeared in 1983,
his first year in Oakland. It was the "culmination of all that I had
learned in teaching at ICCS. . . . It was my thank-you note to the
many persons at Mundelein College who had supported me and
ICCS in those good years" (CNF 145). In the book he identified
the themes associated with each of the four paths and illustrated
these twenty-six themes with examples from diverse religious,
philosophical, literary, and scientific sources, from ancient
times to the present. He would explore these themes in all of
his subsequent writings and would use the four paths model to
address the major issues of our day. The book has sold more
than 360,000 copies and has been translated into several languages. Whiteheadian philosopher and process theologian John
Cobb said this about the book: "Gradually the book is assuming

the status of a classic. In due course, it will take its place in the history of spirituality and indeed in the history of theology."

ICCS drew diverse students who ranged in age from the twenties to the seventies. Over its eighteen years of existence at Mundelein and Holy Names colleges, ICCS would graduate over eight hundred students and offer workshops to more than eight thousand participants. Friends of Creation Spirituality (FCS) was established as a nonprofit organization that sponsored five-day summer workshops around the country and world. Over the years, Matthew has given thousands "of talks, workshops, and retreats" and finds speaking to be "a communion reached between myself and the listeners in which I feel buoyed and communicated to, so that I become a listener even while talking" (CNF 165). In 1985, ICCS launched a magazine entitled: *Creation: Earthy Wisdom for an Evolving Planet*. It included both articles and interviews with prominent thinkers, artists, scientists, and clergy, such as Howard Thurman, a "creation-centered African American mystic and theologian" who had an important influence on Dr. Martin Luther King Jr. (CNF 161).

ESCALATING TROUBLES WITH THE VATICAN

Nineteen eighty-seven was a decisive year because Matthew "felt a definite and perceptible shift in attitude" when he was on the road speaking about creation spirituality. The response of his listeners shifted from "Yes, but . . ." to "More, more. Tell us more" (CNF 167). He thought that "Something was shifting in the American soul—even that word, *soul*, was becoming a topic of discussion again." However, as openness to creation spirituality increased, so did opposition. Extreme right-wing Catholics vehemently protested the second "cosmic mass" created at ICCS. Held in November, the Mass was dedicated to "a Thanksgiving for the Body." After the Mass, protesters sent angry letters to Cardinal Ratzinger, then head of the Congregation for the Doctrine of the Faith (CDF), "telling him that we were worshiping body parts and extolling genitals at mass!" (Prior to 1908, the

CDF was called "the Holy Office of the Sacred Inquisition.") Buck Ghosthorse, a Native American ICCS faculty member, said he had "never met a group of people who would attack others at worship" (CNF 161). Matthew saw the Christian fundamentalist movement of the 1980s as "the opposite of creation spirituality. Fundamentalists do not want to be bothered with mysticism or cosmology . . . because Jesus has all the answers, and by Jesus they mean their projection onto Jesus" (CNF 163). He believed that "Fascism and fundamentalism go hand in hand" because they represent institutionalized violence and "pray to a theistic God . . . who is above and over us" (CNF 163).

In 1988, Matthew published *The Coming of The Cosmic Christ*, which emphasizes the divine presence, light, or image in all things. He stressed that focusing on the Cosmic Christ "does not mean we ignore or throw out the historical Jesus. Quite the opposite" (CNF 169). Jesus was the exemplar par excellence of Cosmic Christ mysticism and awakened this mysticism in his followers, so much so that "they did not hesitate to put words into Jesus's mouth . . . that they felt he ought to have said, might have said, or would have said had he known what they had experienced" (CNF 170). Matthew believes that the Cosmic Christ is implicitly recognized by other creation spirituality traditions but is given different names, such as *Divine presence, Buddha nature, image of God, eternal Soul (Atman)*, etc.

Shortly after Pope John Paul II appointed Cardinal Joseph Ratzinger to spearhead the CDF, Matthew discovered that "the spirit as well as the letter of book-burning" was back. Indeed, not long after arriving in California, Matthew received a letter from his provincial in Chicago that the Vatican had received complaints about his books on prayer, sacred sensuality, and original blessing. The Master General of the Dominican order requested that a theological commission be set up to review the three books. The commission concluded that Matthew "does not see himself as formulating a totally new spirituality, but rather rediscovering a traditional spiritual insight that has been lost, or at least obscured, within the historical life of the Church" and that "there should be no condemnation of Fr. Fox's work . . . but rather an invitation to our brother to an ongoing dialogue with his peers in the various disciplines of theology" (CNF 180).

Despite the additional support of Matthew's new provincial in Oakland, Fr. Don Goergen, the Vatican was not satisfied with the commission's report and requested a new report. Matthew believed that the commission's "finding that I was not in heresy did not fit the Vatican's opinions and purposes" (CNF 182). Between December 1985 and April 1988, Cardinal Ratzinger sent a series of letter to the Master General of the Dominican order that challenged the commission's commendations of Matthew's work and questioned its capacity to render an effective judgment. Ratzinger urged the Master General to use his "good offices to assure that Fr. Fox's present assignment as Director of the Institute for Creation Spirituality at Holy Names College . . . be terminated and that he be instructed to cease from further dissemination of the central thesis of his book, *Original Blessing*" and "that he dissociate himself from" Starhawk (CNF 184). Included with one letter was a document critiquing *Original Blessing* as "dangerous and deviant" and "not in touch with authentic spirituality" and "far from the doctrine of the Magisterium." Matthew's provincial wrote a detailed defense against the accusations, and Matthew made some concessions: he stepped down as ICCS director and took on the title of "founding director" and promised to submit his book manuscripts to two Dominican theologians for review before publishing, but that did not suffice. He was asked to go silent for a year.

A YEAR OF SILENCE

Going silent meant "no teaching, lecturing, workshop leading, or preaching" and "ceasing all my public work except quiet research behind the scenes" (CNF 186). Although initially inclined to resist, Matthew acceded, realizing it was an opportunity to have his first sabbatical in nineteen years of teaching. He also resolved to generate a creative response by writing an

Open Letter to the "Cardinal Inquisitor" in which he asked, "Is the Catholic Church today a dysfunctional family?" and "Is the Catholic Church reverting to fascism in our times?" (CNF 187). At a press conference, Matthew stated that "The Vatican seems incapable of understanding the spirit or the struggle of the Americas—of liberation theology in Latin American and of creation spirituality in the first world" (CNF 190). Moreover, "I believe that Cardinal Ratzinger's theological objections to my work are unbelievably thin" and that "power, rather than theology, is the real issue in this case. . . . The very act of silencing theologians instead of engaging them in dialogue is a sign of institutional violence" (CNF 191). A letter-writing campaign was also launched in which more than five thousand people wrote letters to the Vatican on Matthew's behalf.

During the year of silence, beginning December 15, 1988, Matthew did a retreat in the Canadian woods near Toronto, followed six months later by a "Native American–style" vision quest under the guidance of his friend and colleague Buck Ghosthorse. The vision quest proved to be inspiring, invigorating, and reaffirming. Buck emphasized that spirituality builds the strength and courage to combat evil successfully—evil forces that prey on fear and hatred. During that year, Matthew also read and traveled a lot, visiting South America for the first time and meeting with liberation theologian Leonardo Boff and with Dominican bishop Tomas Balduino in Brazil, where he "experienced a church that knows what solidarity means" (CNF 213). He also traveled to Nicaragua and met with the minister of culture, Ernesto Cardenal. A month after returning from his Latin American journey, Matthew wrote in his journal that "I feel my new book on liberating first worlders being born soon," and in 1991 published *Creation Spirituality: Liberating Gifts for the Peoples of the Earth*. It is "my thank-you to my brothers and sisters in the south and my expression of solidarity with them" (CNF 218). Matthew also traveled to the south of France to visit the goddess shrines and then went to Italy, where, standing in front of St. Peter's at the Vatican, he realized "I am not a Roman

Catholic as much as a twelfth-century French Catholic" (CNF 222). In the Vatican, he experienced "Marble, marble everywhere. . . . All is cold marble. All is man-over-nature. . . . Man the measure of man. The future of the church does not lie here—in marble" (CNF 222). In contrast, while standing in Crete before six-thousand-year-old statues of "a woman priestess leading a circle dance of worshipers," he made "deeper resolves to keep ICCS going no matter what the opposition" (CNF 224).

Back in California, he spent the last week of his silencing in Bodega Bay working on *Sheer Joy: Conversations with Thomas Aquinas on Creation Spirituality*, which would be published in 1992. On the eve of the end of his silencing, he was translating Aquinas's commentary on Isaiah and was struck by chapter 62, "Do not keep silent in Zion." Aquinas stated that "The saints are not silent" because of their burning desire, commitment to truth, and duty to preach the good news. Matthew reflected, "Surely this passage played some role in my later refusal to allow my work to be permanently silenced by leaving Oakland" (CNF 227).

At the end of the year of silence, Matthew received no notice from the Master General that he was free to speak again, but when he spoke with his provincial, he was told to just start talking again. He came out of silence in January 1990 at a five-day program in Melbourne, Australia. In America his first public speech was delivered at a Call to Action gathering, in Chicago, of Catholics committed to change within the church. He opened with the statement "As I was saying fourteen months ago. . . . when I was so rudely interrupted. . ."—words that came to him in a dream and that created quite a sensation in the audience, which cheered on their feet for ten minutes (CNF 229). He resolved he would never go silent again.

EXPULSION

In 1993, Matthew was given an ultimatum to return to Chicago or be expelled from the Dominican order. He had been cooperative and compromising throughout his years of struggle with the Vatican and "did all I could do short of betraying my conscience" (CNF 230). His conscience would not let him abandon his work at ICCS. His provincial's attitude had dramatically changed toward him; he told Matthew he was "not worth defending any longer" and ordered him to "abort the work at ICCS and the magazine and the support community in California and go back to Chicago"—an order that he could not obey (CNF 185). Later, when his provincial was interviewed by the *New York Times* following Matthew's dismissal, he explained it this way: "The church and country moved right, but Matt Fox did not."

On August 8, 1992, Matthew received a letter from the Master General dated June 20 (the Master General's last day in office) that he had sent Matthew's papers for dismissal from the Dominican order to the Congregation of Religious. In November, Matthew received a letter of support from Brazilian theologian Leonardo Boff saying that "The Divine is bigger than the Church, and human rights are more important than ecclesiastical discipline. Don't let them take away your liberty and your creative capacities . . . Have the courage to follow new paths even if it means giving up the ministerial and clerical priesthood for the lay priesthood of Jesus" (CNF 234).

Later that year he met Fr. Bede Griffiths, who offered to review and write the preface of *Sheer Joy*. Griffiths also told Matthew, "Don't worry about the Vatican. It will all come tumbling down overnight someday, just like the Berlin Wall" (CNF 236). Matthew found that working on the Aquinas book "was a kind of therapy for me." He loved Aquinas's "deep sense of cosmology" and his "strong stance on the primacy of conscience" and was inspired by his teachings on magnanimity and courage (CNF 236–37, 239). On March 3, 1993, while he was at work on *The Reinvention of Work: A New Vision of Livelihood for Our Time* (1995), Matthew received the official letter from his provincial that he was dismissed from the order. Matthew reflected that the

Dominican order was informing him that "it was time to reinvent my work. Rome had spoken" (CNF 235).

A POSTDENOMINATIONAL PRIEST

After Matthew was dismissed by the Vatican, the first thing he did was "sit down and meditate." In that meditation he realized that "the Vatican had made me a postdenominational priest in a postdenominational era" (CNF 272). For him "postdenominational means to belong to one and many" (CNF 274). The postdenominational era is holistic, pluralist, and ecumenical. In the summer of 1993, he wrote in his journal that "the times call for me to stand up as an ecumenical priest. . . . Thus I shall continue to pray and celebrate ritual with all those who care to pray and celebrate with me" (CNF 275). He transformed his priestly vows of poverty, obedience, and celibacy into a renewed commitment to sustainable living, reinvigorating democracy and small communities, and revering all of his relationships. He decided to stay a priest because he believed "something useful might still be forged from that tradition" and that the priesthood could be reinvented, "making of it a source of authentic spiritual renewal and leadership" (CNF 286). He considers a healthy priesthood to be "a midwife of grace" and believes that we all possess the archetype of the priest and are called to form a "priesthood of workers."

In February 1994, Matthew had a dream that moved him to tears. In the dream he was standing outside an old rusty gate when he heard the statement "Everyone is here for a purpose. God has a role for everyone," followed by a question "Has my role been to make creation spirituality known?" He was brought to tears because of the "simplicity" and "clarity" of the message and its suggestion that "maybe my life and life work have had some meaning after all" (CNF 271).

During a press conference two months later, he and Bishop William Swing announced his switch to the Episcopal Church. The night before the press conference, he had a dream in which he heard Jesus's advice to "Shake the dust from your feet"; Jesus was speaking about entering a house, wishing peace upon it but not getting peace in return. The dream "pretty much summarized my struggle with the Roman Catholic Church at this time in history" (CNF 277). Later that month he preached his first sermon as an Episcopal priest in Grace Cathedral in San Francisco.

PLANETARY AND COSMIC MASSES

In October 1994, Matthew co-led "the first Planetary Mass in America" in the basement of Grace Cathedral. The "posse" was himself and "thirty-six dedicated young people from the Nine O-Clock Service (NOS) of Sheffield, England" (CNF 288). The theme of the "rave" Mass was the Word of God as the light through which all things came to be. The Planetary Mass was supported by Bishop Swing, who agreed with what Matthew called "a preferential option for the young" and "letting the youth lead—not without elders, but with elders who are still young at heart and young in spirit" (CNF 320).

Over the next two and a half decades, Matthew would cocreate and co-lead—sometimes with rabbis, monks, lamas, and other ministers—more than a hundred Cosmic Masses in Oakland and around the United States and the world. He has been supported by many talented and committed individuals. Although Christian in origin, the Masses are intended to be interspiritual. Some of the themes have been The Black Diaspora, Green Man, Black Madonna, Return of the Divine Feminine, Trees, Flowers, Celtic Story, Drinking from the Source, Pink Triangle, Healing Racism, and Angels among Us (CNF 368). Every Mass is a unique spiritual journey through the Four Paths, accompanied by multimedia, music, and dancing. Matthew understands the creative renewal of ritual as "A nonviolent revolution. The return of celebration"—a "healthy worship" that "awakens a critical moral and ecological ethic that leads to action" (CNF 295). This renewal is also "an exercise in orthopraxis . . . the conviction that we must walk our talk. . . . Instead of debating the development of doctrine, it is time to implement the development of polity" (CNF 295). In 2016, Matthew collaborated with Bishop Marc Andrus to publish *Stations of the Cosmic Christ*, a practice to balance the traditional ritual of the Stations of the Cross.

LEAVING ICCS AND LAUNCHING THE UNIVERSITY OF CREATION SPIRITUALITY

In the fall of 1995, the new president of Holy Name College, along with the academic dean and the acting director of ICCS, called Matthew in and said it was time to "institutionalize" ICCS. To which Matthew replied, "that would be like drying water, wouldn't it?"—and concluded that "we have outlived our welcome" at the college (CNF 321).

Still passionately committed to running ICCS's curriculum in a new setting, Matthew realized it was best to start a new university, which would require "some chutzpah and some good luck and lots of allies" (CNF 327). With the support of generous grants, he launched the University of Creation Spirituality (UCS) in 1996 and was joined by thirty-one of the thirty-three ICCS faculty members. Indeed, one of the reasons he founded UCS was to keep the amazing faculty together. Matthew also invited other teachers to join the faculty. Descriptions of the many talented teachers, administrators, and staff who have worked with Matthew over the years can be found in his *Confessions*.

His friend Ben Yee, a self-taught architect and builder, helped to design and construct the space on the second floor of a building on Broadway Avenue in downtown Oakland. In the middle of the space was a large area for public gatherings of up to 250 persons, which was surrounded by classrooms, each named after "spirit guides of our university," including Meister Eckhart, Sister Jose Hobday, Buck Ghosthorse, Sojourner Truth, Rabbi Abraham Joshua Heschel, and Mahatma Gandhi. The library was "graced" with Hildegard of Bingen's name, and the art-as meditation room was named after Mechthild of Magdeburg.

There was also a kind of chapel called the "sacred cave" because "it had no windows and was quite mysterious" (CNF 331). A steep, carpeted stairwell led from the street level to the university. On one wall was a floor to ceiling painting created by Native American artist Ellen Flowers, which depicted cosmological events from the Big Bang to the creation of galaxies and stars and Earth and the evolution of life. It followed exactly and proportionately the scientific evolution of time—humans arriving beyond the light switch at the top of the stairs. To enter the university, you ascended from the beginning of time to the present moment. It was Matthew's intention to bring "the universe back to university," which was "at the core of my educational project" (CNF 331). At the top of the staircase, one realized how brief the evolution of life is in comparison with the evolution of the entire cosmos, and how even briefer is the evolution of human existence: just a sliver of time—a tiny, tiny fraction of the mural—compared to the fourteen-billion-year-old universe. On the opposite wall were paper placards with quotes from creation-centered mystics and scientists, such as "Just to be is a blessing. Just to live is holy" (Heschel), "Imagination is more important that knowledge" (Einstein), and "Isness is God" (Eckhart).

Unlike ICCS, UCS offered a doctor of ministry program in which students were encouraged to reinvent and "bring a sense of spirituality" to their professions and to see their work as an important ministry that travels all four paths of creation spirituality. In its first two years of operation, there were over four hundred applicants from around the world. Each weeklong seminar began with a morning "body prayer" followed by an academic seminar in the morning, an art-as-meditation course in the afternoon, and a process group at the end of the day. The body prayers came from different spiritual traditions and involved song, chanting, and dance. The process group helped students to integrate their daily learning experiences.

Not wanting to abandon a regionally accredited master's program, Matthew was advised to find a sponsor school that could grant immediate accreditation of a master's program based on creation spirituality. The first sponsor of the master's program was New College of California in San Francisco. When New College was told by the Western Association of Schools and Colleges to shut down all its new programs, Naropa University became the sponsor.

During the nine-year period when Matthew was president of UCS, he continued to write regularly. He collaborated with biologist Rupert Sheldrake to publish two books in 1996 that record their conversations about science and spirituality: *The Physics of Angels: Exploring the Realm Where Science and Spirit Meet* and *Natural Grace: Dialogues on Creation, Darkness, and the Soul in Spirituality and Science.* Also in 1996 he published his memoir, *Confessions: The Making of a Post-Denominational Priest*, which was updated in 2015. Ecological activist and Buddhist teacher Joanna Macy remarked that "The unfolding story of this irrepressible spiritual revolutionary enlivens the mind and emboldens the heart—must reading for anyone interested in courage, creativity, and the future of religion."

In 1999, Matthew published *Sins of the Spirit, Blessings of the Flesh: Lessons for Transforming Evil in Soul and Society.* He not only challenged traditional religious assumptions about evil as located in matter and the body but sought to "redeem" the word *flesh*. He explored the different forms of evil by making use of Aquinas's understanding of sin as "misdirected love" and innovatively relating the seven cardinal sins of Christianity—which he sees as "sins of the spirit"—to the Indian chakra system of subtle energies. In 2002, he published *Creativity: Where the Divine and the Human Meet*, which draws together the many insights he gained over decades of engaging in creative living and working. In 2004, he wrote his most extensive work on deep ecumenism: *One River, Many Wells: Wisdom Springing from Global Faiths* (2004). There he identifies eighteen common themes in all the world's creation-centered traditions such as light, the feminine face of divinity, creativity, joy, suffering, beauty, compassion, meditation, and spiritual warriorhood.

After nearly a decade as president of UCS, Matthew decided that the university would benefit from new leadership. He gave up his position as president, and eventually Jim Garrison was hired as the new president. Garrison renamed the school Wisdom University. The two men had a significant falling out, and Matthew's connection to the university was terminated.

UCS and ICCS inspired hundreds of students to reinvent their work and their lives. Bernard Amadei, a professor of engineering at the University of Colorado, started Engineers without Borders, whose members go to places like Belize, Haiti, the Amazon, Afghanistan, and Africa to "teach people to create solar-generated irrigation projects and much more" (CNF 343). Gina Rose Halperin, an artist, teacher, minister, and chaplain, created The Chaplaincy Institute, which has trained hundreds of interfaith ministers and chaplains. Deidre Combs, who had a thirteen-year career in high tech, became a consultant, coach, and teacher of cross-cultural approaches to transforming conflict and has written three books. Carol Pearson became president of Pacifica Graduate Institute and also held positions as a senior administrator and professor at various universities. Connie Kaplan, who had a background in television production, became a spiritual teacher, dream worker, and author of three books on the spirituality of dreams. Sister Dorothy Stang returned to the Amazon to continue her work as a missionary among the peasant farmers. Her work was opposed by "landowners and corporate-fueled politicians . . . not friendly to the rights of the peasants or the rainforest," and she died a martyr, "shot by two hired gunmen while walking in the forest" (CNF 341). At her funeral, one of the peasants said, "We are not burying you, Sister Dorothy, we are planting you."

YELLAWE

After leaving UCS, Matthew contemplated the question "what next?" and "received a message at this time that went something like this: 'If you feel so strongly about the pedagogy you have developed over the past thirty-one years, why not take it to where it is needed the most, to the inner city and to high school students who are dropping out in untold numbers?'" (CNF 353).

Matthew formed an alliance with "Professor Pitt," a talented African American rapper, martial artist, and filmmaker who had "lived on the streets of Oakland for some time." They collaborated to "reinvent education by bringing creativity to the fore" (CNF 353). Supported by several generous grants, Matthew and Professor Pitt developed a pilot project called "YELLAWE." For two years, YELLAWE allied with the Oakland charter school Oasis High School. Students in YELLAWE, an acronym for "Youth and Elder Learning Laboratory for Ancestral Wisdom Education," made films using Apple iMovie about whatever they were passionate about. They also needed to include some of the "10 Cs" (which are ways of naming common values for a public school curriculum) in the film: cosmology/ecology, contemplation, chaos, creativity, compassion, community, critical thinking, ceremony, character, and courage (CNF 354). The students created films that were "diverse, inspired, and personal in nature," and the quality of their work was "impressive." Matthew was struck by "how much beauty these kids carry around inside of them but how few outlets they are given by school and often at home to express that beauty" (CNF 355). When Professor Pitt and his wife moved to Los Angeles after the first year of the program, Ted Richards was hired as codirector. Richards went on to found the Chicago Wisdom Project, which offers programs for high schoolers, middle schoolers, and "young adult alumns of juvenile detention facilities," and he wrote the book *Creatively Maladjusted: The Wisdom Education Movement Manifesto* (CNF 356). Subsequently, YELLAWE was taught at McClymonds High School and Fremont High School, both in Oakland. Matthew wrote about YELLAWE in *The A.W.E. Project: Reinventing Education, Reinventing the Human* (2006).

CONTINUING TO PROTEST THE VATICAN

Shortly after Cardinal Ratzinger was elected Pope Benedict XVI in spring 2005, Matthew affixed ninety-five theses to the door of the Wittenberg Church where Luther had posted his theses. Five years later, after the publication of *Original Blessing* in Italian, Matthew pounded his ninety-five theses on "Cardinal Law's Basilica in Rome" (CNF 379). Like the event in Germany, this one received media coverage. Cardinal Law was formerly the archbishop of Boston who passed from parish to parish a "pedophile priest who abused 150 boys" (CNF 379). Shockingly, Law was not only promoted by Pope Benedict XVI to run the ancient Maria Maggiore basilica in Rome "but was also appointed to be on the board that appoints bishops the world over." Matthew critiqued Cardinal Ratzinger/Pope Benedict XVI in *The Pope's War* (2011), exposing the corruption, coverups, powerplays, anti-Semitism, and authoritarianism in the church. Two years later, he offered counsel to Pope Benedict's more compassionate and openminded successor in *Letters to Pope Francis* (2013).

BOOKS, BOOKS, AND MORE BOOKS

We have seen that it is an understatement to say that Matthew is a prodigious author. During his five decades of professional writing, he has written, on average, one book every year and a half—all this while directing programs and teaching many classes, being a university president, raising money, traveling, recruiting talented faculty and students, hiring and firing people, and finding buildings for the Cosmic Mass! In each book, his thorough and original scholarship is evident, and he loves to dialogue—and dance—with inspired thinkers, creators, and activists, living and dead, modern and ancient. Other people's insights spark or extend his own—and his insights further develop theirs and offer new implications and applications. Some of his books are explicitly structured as dialogues: the two books with Rupert Sheldrake; *The Lotus and the Rose* (2018) with Buddhist teacher Lama Tsomo; and *Occupy Spirituality: A Radical*

Vision for a New Generation (2013) with spiritual activist Adam Bucko, which discusses the principles of an engaged spirituality. His big book about Thomas Aquinas, *Sheer Joy*, is also structured as a series of deep dialogues: Matthew raises questions, presents answers from Aquinas's works, and then responds to those texts, interpreting meanings, offering contemporary applications, and then asking new questions. All of these dialogues inevitably employ dialectical thinking that leads to new insights, syntheses, and applications.

Matthew's love of the artist is also evident in his professional writings. He knows a great story when he sees one and can tell a riveting story with flair and passion. His love of language is not only obvious in his joyful wordplay but also in his passion for etymologies. He probes the meanings of words back to their linguistic origins in ancient languages, and these origins often hold hidden insights. Matthew is also a poet, who laces his scholarly works with poetic prose and original poems. His children's book, *In the Beginning There Was Joy* (1995), is a Dr. Seuss–like poetic telling of the Creation story. Several rap poems that he delivered at various gatherings in Oakland appear in *Confessions*.

In the past decade he continued to write about some of his favorite creation mystics. He published *Hildegard of Bingen: A Saint for Our Times* in 2012, *Meister Eckhart: A Mystic-Warrior for Our Times* in 2014, *A Way to God: Thomas Merton's Creation Spirituality Journey* in 2016, and *The Tao of Thomas Aquinas: Fierce Wisdom for Hard Times* in 2020. *Christian Mystics: 365 Readings and Meditations* (2011) collects and comments on quotations from many of his beloved mystics. His latest book, *Julian of Norwich: Wisdom in a Time of Pandemic—And Beyond* (2020), demonstrates how Julian's spiritual insights, visions, values, and loving relation to Creator and Creation offer inspired guidance on how to live well during a time ravaged by a lethal virus. Julian also shares a wondrous understanding of God and Christ as Mother.

In *The Order of the Sacred Earth* (2017), Matthew and his coeditors, Skylar Wilson and Jen Listug, assemble the declarations, poems, and reflections of a host of individuals from diverse backgrounds and professions who are devoted to eco-spiritual activism—honoring and protecting our precious planet. Psychiatrist and author M. Scott Peck has described Matthew's "daring, pioneering work" as capable of "stimulating us to the kind of resurrection of values and practices required for planetary salvation." He may well be right.

HOW THIS BOOK WAS CO-CREATED

The creation of this book was a collaborative effort. Matthew and I agreed on each stage of its development. At Matthew's request, I created the initial outline, which we discussed and modified several times throughout the course of this project. Also at his request, I did the initial selection of passages, and he made deletions and additions. He also condensed some passages, and occasionally added a sentence or two to clarify or update an issue or to create a smoother transition, so some of the selections are adaptations, rather than exact transcriptions, from the original texts. In the interest of making this book as reader friendly as possible, we dispensed with the scholarly apparatus of footnotes, endnotes, bracketed insertions, etc. Sources are cited for all selections. When a series of selections are drawn from the same section of a book, we put the source after the last selection. The list of sources appears at the front of the book. We hope you will be inspired to read some of Matthew's other books. His voluminous oeuvre contains countless gems of wisdom and insight, many of which could not make their way into this slim volume.

The different parts of this book can be read in any order. Chapter 1 gives an overview of creation spirituality, including Matthew's discovery of the tradition, the Four Paths, Original Blessing, Cosmic Christ, and other principles. Chapter 2 presents various dream and visions that were important to Matthew's life and work. Chapter 3 focuses on the dialogue between creation spirituality and contemporary science. Chapter 4 explores Christian creation mystics from medieval times to the present. Chapter 5 addresses spiritual practice and creativity, with a particular emphasis on prayer, meditation, and ritual. Chapters 6–10 examine various aspects of the Via Transformative, demonstrating how creation-centered paths, principles, and approaches can be applied to the central issues of our day: sensuality, evil, youth, eldering, education, work, gender, social and political activism, eco-justice, the media, the Catholic Church, and deep ecumenism. The book closes with a letter from Matthew to young seekers.

I hope you find the book as inspiring and illuminating as I do. And I pray that it stirs you to actualize the mystic, the artist, and the prophet that live in you.

1

The Creation Spirituality Tradition

WHAT IS CREATION SPIRITUALITY?

Like Falling Off My Horse: Père Chenu Names the Creation Spiritual Tradition

In the fall of 1967, Fox began his studies at the Institut Catholique de Paris, where Père M. D. Chenu, O.P., named the crucial distinction between creation spirituality (CS) and fall/redemption religion. That distinction and the emphasis on culture in spirituality formed the foundation of Fox's future work. (CB)

The CS tradition, as the name indicates, considers creation—nature, the cosmos, Earth, all of existence—to be sacred. CS mystics affirm that our first experience of the Divine is our wondrous experience of the universe. The tradition does not put humans first; rather, the prime reality is the totality of creation, just as in the first chapter of Genesis, and just as in contemporary science with its new creation story of the 13.8-billion-year unfolding of the universe, and just as in the works of the pre-modern mystics who offered a psychology of microcosm/macrocosm, and just as we need to do to save Mother Earth as we know her. CS is the oldest tradition in the Bible (the J source) and constitutes the very tradition from which the historical Jesus derives—namely, the wisdom tradition. Therefore, it is feminist and welcoming of science since wisdom is feminine and the job of scientists is to teach us about nature. It is also prophetic since "wisdom is a friend of the prophets," and justice is needed

to save Earth and its many species, including our own human
communities. (MF)

I loved Paris. I could walk forever the streets of the Latin Quarter. There were Saint-Severín; Saint-Julien-le-Pauvre; Notre
Dame (even if Thomas Aquinas once said, during the construc-
tion of it, that he would give the entire cathedral for just one
lost book of theologian Gregory of Nyssa); the monument at the
end of the Île de la Cité to the deported ones of the Holocaust;
Shakespeare & Company, where T. S. Eliot, Hemingway, Joyce,
and so many other great writers had hung out . . . I used to
walk the Latin Quarter imagining what it must have been like
in Aquinas's day or Abelard and Heloise's day, when the university was just coming into existence and ferment was everywhere.
The museums drew me regularly, especially the Rodin museum,
which was within walking distance of where I lived my first year
in Paris, and the Jeu de Paume, where the impressionists were
displayed . . .

   In addition to a sense of history, Paris gave me a sense of the
artist. Little children accompanied their parents to art museums
and appeared just as curious and enthralled with the paintings
as the adults were—this was new to me. When my mentor Père
M. D. Chenu would one day say to me, "Remember, the greatest tragedy in theology in the last three hundred years has been
the separation of the theologian from the poet, the dancer, the
painter, the dramatist, the potter, the filmmaker," I knew what he
was talking about. I too had ceased writing poetry the moment I
entered higher education. Now, in Paris, the poet began to return
to my soul. There was permission in the air to be an artist. Here
I learned that art is not about getting a degree or even being a
genius. Art is about the way we see our world, and let it see us.
I had to leave my own country to learn this lesson, but it was a
lesson I have never forgotten . . .

   Being immersed in an ancient, fascinating, rich culture and
seeing things in a whole new way with a new language and
new customs and new food and new values were all part of my

awakening in Paris. They were all part of learning about culture and religion, culture and spirituality—an awareness that
was deepened considerably by my Master's thesis in theology
on Jesus's prayer in the New Testament. As an American in
Paris, I was learning about the relativity of my own culture: its
language, its history, its interpretation of history (someone in
America had taught me that we had invented cars and cinema
and all kinds of things that Europeans would have other opinions about), its global politics, its war in Vietnam, its racism, its
mythologies. . . .

I made my way to the school of my choice, the Institut
Catholique de Paris, or the "Catho" for short. The Institut was
begun in the nineteenth century, but the theology faculty, where
I enrolled, traces its history back to the original University of
Paris in the twelfth century. I love the French system of education at the doctoral level, since it emphasizes *thinking* and is
only minimally concerned with exams, pleasing the faculty, and
memorizing . . . I thank Thomas Merton many times over for his
advice to come here.

I came to Paris with one pressing, urgent question that superseded all other concerns for me: what is the relationship—if
any—between mysticism and social justice? I felt that was the
most foundational issue for me and possibly for my generation. In the midst of social revolutions such as the civil rights
movement and the anti-Vietnam War protests, this question kept
haunting me. It seemed to be the nexus where culture and spirituality or culture and healthy religion meet. But there was very little that I could find in the traditional literature that answered the
question for me. I remember how excited I was to see a book by
Père Jean Danielou with the wonderful title *Prayer as a Political
Problem*. My heart sank as I read it, however. Unfortunately, the
title was the only worthwhile part of the book. His politics were
rightest, and his grasp of prayer was anything but magnificent. I
began reading Louis Cognet's four-volume series on the history
of Christian spirituality from the Bible to the twelfth century,
taking copious notes and following the leads in his footnotes to

other books. I realized that it would be a process, wrestling with my fundamental question about prayer and justice, spirituality and culture. . . .

My classes at the Catho were a large part of that process, though sometimes I felt like we were taking two steps forward and one back; or two back and one forward. From Père Michel de Certeau—a young and vibrant though slightly nervous Jesuit who came to class in dark glasses, having recently been in a serious automobile accident—I took a seminar on the seventeenth-century Jesuit Père Jean-Joseph Surin . . . I was keen on relating spirituality to politics, and seventeenth-century France would be the last place to look for such a connection. On the other hand, by becoming so steeped in the spiritual pathology of that period (Madame Guyon, one of the Parisian gurus of the period, had the name "Jesus Christ" carved on her breasts—for whom to see, I was never sure!), I was seeing the Via Negativa of modern spirituality: how *not* to do spirituality.

In my first year, Louis Cognet offered a course on "Bach's spirituality," and though my French was too lean to understand much of the technical language, I would sit in the back of the room taking in by osmosis what I felt was an important subject. I remember saying to myself that there was no theology school in all of North America where one can listen to someone lecturing on the spirituality of Bach. Even though I wasn't getting the details, I was truly in a good place just being there.

Cognet himself offered a three-year lecture course on the entire history of Western spirituality. These classes were especially valuable to me. His knowledge plus his sense of humor made the time pass swiftly, even when it was deep winter, and he had to compete with the one radiator that kept singing out of tune and releasing enough heat to overheat the entire school. In his final year of lectures, he covered the pressing theological issues of the sixties: the role of Karl Marx, who was "far more influential on religion than Père Henri Lacordaire" in the nineteenth century; the role of Freud in psychology—the analyst is often the priest in our society; subjectivism of seventeenth-century Protestant and Catholic spirituality as passé today; secularization; atheism. He felt the "death of God" theologians were asking the basic spiritual questions of our time, including those of language itself. He urged us to go beyond the pessimistic theology of Augustine and its Neoplatonic suppositions. Cognet cited Dietrich Bonhoeffer for his emphasis on the essential role of justice in our spirituality, thus putting an end to pietistic religion. God becomes engaged by *creation*—not just by the incarnation. This would prove a dominant theme in my development of a creation spirituality.

Cognet, who published ten books on Christian spirituality and was an accomplished organist and photographer, as well as a scholar and priest, died suddenly of a heart attack in his early fifties, a year after I graduated. I will never forget his final lecture, in which he laid out the principles that must guide a new spirituality for our times. He said that we need a spirituality that includes the body, justice making, a sense of history and evolution, therefore a spirituality of matter that is cognizant of science. In his final lecture Cognet challenged me deeply when he said that:

> all we need to know is that there is a real drama going on, and we're in it and so is God— we don't know how it will turn out. The reign of God is already here since salvation is not somewhere else. Terrestrial values are real values—justice, generosity, kindness are already salvation. The Beatitudes are right now: justice has to be reached on this earth. To work for it is the church's duty. There must be a vertical as well as a horizontal relationship to God for these things to happen, say what you will. The task can fail— evolution can contradict itself. The risk is real.

In retrospect, I see that much of my work has indeed been in response to Cognet's challenge in that lecture . . .

The two most influential doctoral seminars I took were from Abbé Marchasson and Père M. D. Chenu. Marchasson was an older priest, an historian whose expertise was nineteenth-century French history. He had devised a method (the French were very big on *methods*) for examining nineteenth-century French newspapers to derive from them the philosophy behind the culture . . . After several weeks in his class, I began to ask myself: What am I doing here? Why did I take this class? Then the great French word hit me: *la méthode*! Method. Yes, the methodology was interesting, and it held promise if I was serious about studying culture and spirituality. Why not take the method used here and apply it to contemporary America?

With this in mind, I sat down with Marchasson and made my proposal to him: I would do my doctoral study on some influential American publication, employing his methodology to discern the ongoing suppositions in that culture toward religion/spirituality. "Ah, yes," he said, "you can take this method to the New World." *The New World*, I thought. I had never looked at America that way before. For me it had been my *only* world, and currently, with the riots and rebellions and the bloody mess in Vietnam, it appeared anything but new.

Then there was my encounter with Père Chenu. Seventy-six years old, big, bushy eyebrows, excited, dynamic, funny, political, warm, affectionate—he became my mentor. He was the reason I remained a Dominican. He had what I hoped to see in all Dominicans: life, passion, political consciousness, wisdom. And above all, the French *passion for ideas*, an intellectual life, an intellectual history, that served a greater cause. It was Père Chenu who kept me in the order—not because we ever talked about it but because of his example. From the French, and from Père Chenu in particular, I learned respect for the power of ideas and for those who carry them.

While I owed to Abbé Marchasson a methodology that gave me access to a critical appraisal of religion in my culture, I owed to Père Chenu the answer to my question of questions: how do I relate spirituality to culture, prayer to social justice, politics to mysticism? He named the creation spiritually tradition for me. In encountering this tradition, my entire life would gain a focus and a direction that it never had before. It would also gain a notoriety that I never, in my ecclesial naiveté, could have predicted.

I remember as if it were today that moment in our seminar, in the dimly lit upper room at the Catho with the green velvet cloth on the table, when Chenu named the two spiritual traditions: that of "fall/redemption" and that of "creation-centered spirituality." Scales fell from my eyes; I was bumped from my horse! The most pressing question I had brought with me to Paris—how do mysticism and social justice relate (if at all)—now had a context! So did the issues of dualism and the demeaning of body and matter. Creation spirituality would bring it all together for me: the scriptural and Jewish spirituality (for it was the oldest tradition in the Bible, that of the Yahwist author of the ninth or tenth century before Christ); science and spirituality; politics and prayer; body and spirit; Christianity and other world religions; and soon, the ecological movement. It would be my task to study creation spirituality more deeply and to begin a cultural translation of it. This task would prove to be a process in its own right with unforeseen consequences.

In Chenu's seminar, three-quarters of the students were from Latin America. It was in his work in the worker-priest movement in the forties and fifties that Chenu developed the methodology of praxis preceding theory. He used to say, "I did not do theology in an armchair. I tested it in the field." He would attend meetings of the worker-priests and workers just to listen to their dialogues. He was not there to give speeches, but to listen and offer feedback if asked. It is little wonder that liberation theology's base-community movement found such support in his person and in his methodology. That is one reason why Gustavo Gutiérrez cited Chenu in his classic work *A Theology of Liberation* and why students from Latin America were so drawn to him . . .

Time and again Chenu reminded us that movements of the laity had sparked the church renewal in the twelfth century, "the only renaissance that succeeded in the West," because it came from below and not from above. Laity would lead today's renewal of church life too, he was convinced.

In his seminar on twelfth-century spirituality, he would bring large picture books to class, volumes of the twelfth-century cathedrals. "You can't do theology without art," he would say, and "you can't understand twelfth-century spirituality without appreciating the architecture and the artisans and engineers behind it." In addition to appreciating the artist, Chenu also welcomed *youth*. He never talked down to students when he taught. I never heard him do anything but encourage us young thinkers, exuding enthusiasm and excitement about our questions and ideas. His approach to thinking was one of "Yes, and," not "Yes, but." He had a deeply youthful soul himself; no trace of complacency or cynicism was visible in him. He was a deeply joyful and humorous man. Once, when he was discussing Nicholas of Cusa in class, he gave the basic information about him: a theologian, scientist, mathematician, diplomatic, and "a cardinal in the Roman Catholic Church." Immediately his eyes began to twinkle, and he looked up swiftly to say, "Not necessarily a good reference, you understand." Though Chenu was silenced and forbidden to publish for years under Pope Pius XII, there was no bitterness in the man . . .

Sometimes when I wonder what my role is as theologian, I think of an interview Chenu gave when he was eighty-six years old. Asked "What do you think of the crisis in the church today?" Chenu replied:

> It's a godsend. A theologian has to be immersed in the movement of history. You might say that when something new is beginning, when things start to fall asunder, that's when he's most deeply happy, because then he's given a unique opportunity to observe the Word of God at work in history. The *nowness* of the Word of God, shaking up the world—that's where true theology springs from! . . .

Christians fear change, and so does the Church, insofar
as it is a society of Christians. Afraid of being blamed by
the future, it prefers security to freedom. I prefer freedom.

During our seminar with Chenu in the spring of 1968, all of
Paris was paralyzed by student riots and strikes of civil workers.
The Sorbonne was closed, as were most schools and businesses,
though the Catho was still in session. At the end of one class,
Chenu shut his notebook and said, "We have been talking about
twelfth-century history—here is your chance to make some
history. Go out and join the revolution! Don't come back next
week; come back in two weeks and tell me what you have contributed!" He was seventy-six at the time.   —CNF 72–82

Contrasting Creation Spirituality to Fall/Redemption Religion

All spirituality is about roots. For all spirituality is about living
a non-superficial and therefore a deep, rooted, or radical (from
radix, root) life. Roots are collective and not merely personal—
much less are they private or individualized. To get in touch with
roots is to leave the private quest for *my* roots to get in touch
with *our* roots. Where roots grow and nourish in the bowels of
the earth, things come together, and there a collectivity of energies
is shared. No root that was ruggedly individualistic would long
survive. In the earth's bowels roots feed on the same organisms
as they twist and turn interdependently among one another. The
name that religion gives this collectivity of roots is "tradition."

Tradition is the common nourishing and searching and
growing of our roots. We need tradition as much as we need
one another. It has been said of the late Rabbi Heschel that he
believed in the transmigration of souls because this doctrine
"contains a profound religious truth. For one to know oneself,
one must seek to understand one's past, one's heritage, the religious tradition from which one emerges . . . The human soul is
born with a past." Westerners have been born with a past, and

it is important to get us in touch with those roots once again. For the question arises: How much in touch with our roots are we of the West? Roots, being underground energies, can easily be covered over and covered up. They can become forgotten and even be violently repressed. They can be put on a shelf or exalted on a pedestal where they never truly intersect our own lives and where they dry up and then die. They can become lost and unknown for centuries, and only explorers into the bowels of the earth who journey from the light of day and the ego-separations of daytime to the dark caves of our collectively hidden unconscious can reclaim them.

Christianity is in great danger of forgetting its roots. Much of this is due to the overly weighty influence of nonbiblical philosophies in the history of Christian spirituality—ways of thought like Stoicism, gnosticism, Platonism and Neoplatonism. Much also is due to the political, sexual, and economic dominance of Christianity and Empire, so that much that was authentic in biblical spirituality was twisted or repressed in order to put Christianity at the service of Empire building and Empire maintaining. Thus the passage from Christianity as a way of life (spirituality), which is how the early Christians saw themselves in the *Book of Acts*, to Christianity as a religion. Thus too the passage from creation spirituality, which sees life as a blessing, to the dominance of redemption motifs, motifs that instead of reminding people that they are of divine stock ("images of God") instruct even the young—especially the young!—in how corrupt they are or ought to consider themselves. Thus the unhealthy and unbalanced sexual dominance of the male and masculine images (for example, that of climbing Jacob's ladder) in Western mystical history.

Western spirituality has two basic traditions—that which starts with the experience of sin and develops a fall/redemption spiritual motif; and that which starts with the experience of life as a blessing and develops a creation-centered spirituality. This book's purpose (*Western Spirituality: Historical Roots, Ecumenical Routes*) is to put Westerners in touch once again with the more neglected of these traditions, namely that of blessing/creation. This tradition will emphasize humanity's divinization rather than humanity's fallenness.

A Christian professor who is a fine and distinguished scholar of the Hebrew Bible said in a lecture recently that creation spirituality must never ignore the redemption tradition. As an abstract statement this declaration is true enough, but as a critical comment on the history of Christian spirituality it utterly misses the point and in fact continues the ongoing repression of the creation tradition. For the evidence is overwhelming that in Christian history the fall/redemption motif, so often championed by dualists like Augustine and Bossuet, has held overpowering sway—it condemned Pelagius and Scotus Eriugena, Thomas Aquinas and Meister Eckhart, and it platonized and thus neutralized Francis Assisi. It practically wrote women off the face of the spiritual map, locking them up whenever possible, virtually ignoring their experience and their writings, with only a few breakthroughs visible such as Catherine of Siena or Teresa of Avila. In the over-emphasis on salvation history and the silence vis-à-vis the history of nature, society, and creativity, it has ignored rich and badly needed roots in scriptural and historical spiritual development—to say nothing of ecumenical spirituality. It has put the body down and called this repression holy; it has encouraged private conversions and sentimental pieties that have nothing to say to what Nicolai Berdyaev calls *theosis* or a "cosmic and social religion"—thus it renders sacraments and ritual trivial. It has substituted a private "righteousness" for biblical justice; it has taught sin consciousness rather than peoples' capacity for the divine; it has more often fostered curses than blessings. It isolates: it isolates individuals from themselves, for example as regards their own passions, and it isolates individuals from one another. It thus very readily becomes a tool for dividing and conquering that sacralizes and legitimizes those who would lord it over others, whether in state or church. It has remained silent about that ultimate way of life that Jesus taught and died for—namely, compassion, and when has it consented to include compassion as a part of spirituality at all, it has sentimentalized this biblical name for the divine which in fact is about setting captives free. It has failed to resist docetism and the dehumanizing of Jesus and the incarnation event. In its dualistic view of the world, it puts salvation history against history, supernature against nature, soul against body, redemption against creation, artist against intellectual, heaven (and hell) against earth, the sensual against the spiritual, man against woman, individual against society and condemns all those with a cosmic vision (creation after all *is* cosmic) as pantheists. Its one-sided spiritual theology does not even have the term pan*en*theist in its vocabulary.

In short, I suggest that it is not creation spirituality that needs to bend over backwards to include the redemption tradition, since the latter is just about the only tradition most Christians have been exposed to; rather, it is the redemption spirituality that should quit its hegemony for a while, practice something of the detachment it preaches to others, and listen and learn from those who represent the creation-centered tradition and are trying to live it. Creation spirituality, far from ignoring redemption, actually involves itself in reunderstanding the meaning of redemption in different cultural and historical periods. This is clearly the case in Latin American Liberation Theology, which is clearly a species of creation spirituality. Creation spirituality is dedicated to what biblical scholar Dr. Helen Kenik, in her essay "Toward a Biblical Basis for Creation Theology," demonstrates to be justice as the act of preserving creation and passing it on as a blessing to others. The nature/grace dualism that haunts the Western psyche is reinforced by the hegemony of redemption spirituality *over* creation spirituality, of grace *over* nature, as if nature itself is not graced. Moreover, the fall/redemption tradition has become distorted itself to the extent that it ignores the gracefulness of creativity and creation. Just as creation-centered thinkers do not ignore redemption motifs, so too must the redemption-thinkers begin to include creation in their consciousness in a deep way in order to redefine what is meant by redemption in the West.

Nor are cries for "reconciliation" between the two traditions to be heeded at this time in Christian history. For, as Krister Stendahl has pointed out, a reconciliation that comes too soon is nothing but a surrender by the powerless to the powers that be. When unequals reconcile, what obtains is capitulation, not reconciliation. Reconciliation is for equals, not for those still bound in a powerful/powerless situation. The fact is that creation spirituality remains an unwanted step-child in Western Christianity whose mainstream has invested so heavily and so long in an Augustinian original sin and redemption motif and a patriarchal consciousness of empire-building. Instead of reconciliation at this date, what is needed is more and more scholarship that uncovers the wonders and beauties of creation spirituality on the one hand and more and more persons willing to throw themselves into living it on the other. For only out of this living will a lost tradition be refound and reborn.   —WS 1–5

A Spiritual Paradigm for Our Times

I believe that the creation-centered spiritual tradition represents the appropriate spiritual paradigm for our time. I also believe that this tradition and the living of it represents a Copernican revolution in religion. Copernicus moved people from believing that Earth was the center around which the universe revolved to believing that Earth moved about the sun. In religion we have been operating under the model that humanity, and especially sinful humanity, was the center of the spiritual universe. This is not so. The universe itself, blessed and graced, is the proper starting point for spirituality. Original blessing is prior to any sin, original or less than original . . . Chapter one of Genesis begins with a cosmology—a celebration of the goodness of the universe and earth with all its creatures. Chapter two gets into human fallenness. The time has come to let anthropocentrism go, and with it to let the preoccupation with human sinfulness give way to attention to divine grace. In the process sin itself will be more fully understood and more successfully dealt with. The eco-crises of our time are witness to the failures of religion and spirituality to contextualize our understanding of the sacredness of creation. Our narcissism as a species haunts us to this day. We, along with Mother Earth, are paying the price for an anthropocentric religion. —OB 26

Furthermore, all scholars today agree that the historical Jesus derived from the wisdom tradition of Israel. But the wisdom tradition is the creation spiritual tradition of Israel. It is about finding the divine in nature and in the creativity of humanity. It would see fitting to establish a Christian spirituality on the foundation of Jesus's own spiritual heritage.

It is useful to compare the two spiritual traditions of the West. (MF)

Fall/Redemption versus Creation-Centered Spirituality

Fall/Redemption	Creation-Centered
Key spokespersons: Augustine; Thomas á Kempis; Bossuet; Cotton Mather; Tanquerry; Pat Robertson; Jerry Falwell, etc.	Key spokespersons: Yahwist author; wisdom writers; prophets; Jesus; Paul; Irenaeus; Benedict; Hildegard; Francis; Aquinas; Mechtild; Eckhart; Julian; Cusa; Teilhard; Chenu; Feminists; liberation theologians; Artists; musicians; poets
Faith is "thinking with assent" (Augustine)	Faith is trust
Patriarchal	Feminist
Ascetic	Aesthetic
Mortification of body	Discipline toward birthing
Control of passions	Ecstasy, Eros, celebration of passion
Passion is a curse	Passion is a blessing and the "seat of virtues" (Aquinas)
God as Father	God as Mother, God as Child as well as Father

Fall/Redemption	Creation-Centered
Suffering is wages for sin	Suffering is birth pangs of universe
Death is wages for sin	Death is a natural event, a prelude to recycling and rebirth
Holiness is quest for perfection	Holiness is cosmic hospitality
Nostalgia for a past state of perfection and innocence	Imperfection is integral to all nature
Keep soul clean	Make soul wet so that it grows, expands, and stays green (Hildegard, Eckhart)
Begins with sin	Begins with Dabhar, God's creative energy
Original sin is starting point	Original blessing is starting point
Introspective in its psychology	Cosmic (microcosm/macrocosm) in its psychology
Emphasizes introvert meditation	Emphasizes extrovert meditation, i.e., art as meditation
Miracle is outside intervention contravening the law of nature	Basic miracle is the wonder of existence, isness, creation
Anthropocentric	Ecological, cosmological
Sciences of nature are unimportant	Science, by teaching us about nature, teaches us about Creator
Dualistic (either/or)	Dialectical (both/and)
Suspicious of body and violent in its body/soul imagery; "Soul makes war with the body" (Augustine)	Welcoming of body and gentle in its body/soul imagery; "soul loves the body" (Eckhart)
Humility is to "despise yourself" (Tanquerry)	Humility is to befriend one's earthiness (*humus*)
In control	Letting go—ecstasy, breakthrough
Pessimistic	Hopeful
Climbing Jacob's ladder	Dancing Sara's circle

Fall/Redemption	Creation-Centered
Elitist	For the many
Particular	Universalist
Personal Christ and/or Christ of the empire	Cosmic Christ intimate to all beings and to the whole universe
Emphasis on Jesus as Son of God but not on Jesus as prophet	Emphasis on Jesus as prophet, artist, parable-teller, and Son of God who calls others to their divinity
Personal salvation	Liberation and healing of all people and the cosmos
Build up church	Build up Kingdom/Queendom
Kingdom = church	Kingdom = cosmos, creation
Human as sinner	Human as royal person who can choose to create or destroy
Struggle to clean one's conscience	Struggle to make justice of injustice and to balance the cosmos
Time is toward past (lost perfection) or future (heaven): unrealized eschatology	Time is now, and making the future (heaven) begins to now: realized eschatology
Spiritual journey follows three Paths: Purgation, Illumination, Union (Plotinus)	Spiritual journey follows four paths: Via Positiva, Via Negativa, Via Creativa, Via Transformativa
Eternal life is after death	Eternal life is now
Contemplation is goal of spirituality	Compassion, justice, and celebration are goals of spirituality, contemplation is a means
A spirituality of the powerful	A spirituality of the powerless, the *anawim*
Emphasizes the cross	Considers the cross significant for the Via Negativa but also emphasizes joy at creation, the resurrection, the coming of the Spirit, creation, co-creation

Fall/Redemption	Creation-Centered
Tends toward christolotry and docetism with an underdeveloped theology of the Creator and the Holy Spirit	Trinitarian in full sense of celebrating a Creator God, a prophetic Son of God, and the Holy Spirit of divine transformation
Emphasizes obedience	Emphasizes creativity
Righteousness	Justice
Duty	Beauty
Guilt and redemption	Thanks and praise
Purity from world	Hospitality to all of being
Apolitical, i.e., supportive of status quo	Prophetic, i.e., critical of status quo and its ideologies
Soul is in the body to guard it	Body is in the soul and the soul enlarges (Eckhart: "God is delighted to see the soul enlarge.")
Nothingness as psychological experience	Nothingness as metaphysical experience
Humanity is sinful	Humanity is divine *and* capable of choosing both good and sinful
Faith is in intellect	Faith is in imagination
Suspicious of the artist	Welcomes the artist since all are called to be co-creators with God
Theistic	Panentheistic
Begins with Genesis 2: human sin	Begins with Genesis 1: the goodness of creation

—OB 316–19

FOUNDATIONAL PATHS AND THEMES OF CREATION SPIRITUALITY

One of the most transcendent dreams of my life occurred when I was undergoing an operation on my back two years after a serious car accident in 1976. During my operation, Meister Eckhart, in a Dominican habit, came to me, and we walked together on the beach. No words were exchanged between us. I knew, on awakening from the operation, that Eckhart and I were destined to spend some serious time together in the future. It was shortly after that that I discovered his rich commentary of Jesus's teaching, "Be you compassionate as your Creator in heaven is compassionate," found in Luke's gospel (6:36). I inserted his teachings into my book on A Spirituality Named Compassion *and wrote my first article on him, which appeared in* Western Spirituality.

Thomas Aquinas says that experience is the basis of spirituality but that to teach spirituality one also needs concepts that assist us to name those experiences and thus be able to share them with others.

Basic to understanding and living creation spirituality are the four paths, as well as the experience of original blessing, the Cosmic Christ, realized eschatology, panentheism, and trust, which is discussed below. These concepts help name the experiences that underlie the creation spirituality lineage. (MF)

The Four Paths of Creation Spirituality

The four paths of creation spirituality first emerged for me on examining my own experiences and on encountering Eckhart. It is one thing to talk about the Via Positiva and Via Negativa, but if you put them together, they are like an electric charge—the positive and negative make sparks. They make a third thing—the Via Creativa. And that in turn gives birth to a fourth thing: Compassion, Justice, Celebration.

My first writing on Eckhart was also my first writing on the four paths, which I published in my book, *Western Spirituality: Historical Roots, Ecumenical Routes* (1979). I called the article "Meister Eckhart on the Fourfold Path of a Creation-Centered Spiritual Journey." The naming of the journey in four paths constitutes the very backbone or structure of creation spirituality.

When I lectured on these paths at the Graduate Theological Union some forty years ago, a Jewish rabbi approached me at the end of my talk. He was from Switzerland and a student of Gershom Scholem, the great scholar of Jewish mysticism, and he was thrilled. "You are the first Christian I have heard who consciously threw out the three paths (of Plotinus)—what you are talking about is truly Jewish. Now Judaism and Christianity can finally start communicating again," he told me excitedly. I was deeply pleased with this affirmation of the Jewish and therefore biblical roots of creation spirituality.

Creation spiritualty is a tradition and a movement. The backbone of the creation spirituality tradition is its naming of the spiritual journey. It is important to be able to name the journey so that people can share in a common language. By naming the journey, we are assured that we shall not get stuck in any one of the paths, which can easily happen since each of the paths is deep and powerful in itself.

The Four Paths as a Paradigm Shift

The four paths of the creation spirituality journey represent a distinct paradigm shift from the way in which the spiritual journey was formerly described in the West. Plotinus (205–270) identified only three paths: purgation, illumination, and union. Creation spirituality rejects as inadequate this way of naming the spiritual journey. It is not biblical, and Plotinus, a Neoplatonist philosopher, did not know the Bible at all. His paths leave out delight and pleasure, creativity and justice; the goal is not compassion or justice-making but contemplation and the turning away from the earth and all that relates to it.

The four paths of creation spirituality tell us *what matters.* We are told in Path One that awe and delight matter; in Path Two that silence, darkness, suffering, and letting go matter; in Path Three that creativity and imagination matter; and in Path Four that justice and celebration, which add up to compassion, matter. When the four paths are understood in light of the new cosmic story, then a whole civilization can be born because, while the four paths tell us what matters, the new creation story tells us why it matters—because it has taken 13.8 billion years to bring all these experiences of delight and suffering, of birth and justice-making, to this point in history.

The Four Paths also address the question, Where will God, where will the experience of the divine, be found in our time? Creation spirituality responds: The divine will be found in these places:

In the Via Positiva. In the awe, wonder, and mystery of nature and of all beings, each of whom is a "word of God," a "mirror of God that glistens and glitters," as Hildegard of Bingen put it. This is Path One.

In the Via Negativa. In darkness and nothingness, in silence and emptying, in letting go and letting be; and in the pain and suffering and grief that constitute an equally real part of our spiritual journey. This is Path Two.

In the Via Creativa. In our generativity we co-create with God: in our imaginative output, we trust our images enough to birth them and ride them into existence. According to Eckhart, we actually birth God or the Christ by our creative work in the world. This is Path Three.

In the Via Transformativa. In the relief of suffering, in the combatting of injustice, in the struggle for homeostasis, for balance in society and history, and in the celebration that happens when persons struggling for justice and trying to live in mutuality come together to praise and give thanks for the gifts of being and being together. This is Path Four. Which spirals back to Path One again.

The Four Paths as Four Commandments

One way of grasping the Four Paths is to understand them as Four Commandments that can energize us for the journey. The journey is a spiral journey, for we move from path to path and back again in an ever larger and expanding spiral our whole lives long. The journey is *not one of climbing a ladder, but of spiraling in and out.*

1. Thou shalt fall in love at least three times a day (Via Positiva)
    At first glance, this commandment sounds threatening to one's
marriage or relationship, or vow of celibacy, but that's because
our anthropocentric culture has taken the immense mystical
experience of "falling in love" and applied it exclusively to finding a mate. In fact, we could fall in love with a galaxy every day
and, since there are two trillion of them according to the latest
science, still bequeath many quite virginal on our deathbed. Or
we could fall in love with a star, of which there are 500 billion in
our galaxy alone. Or a species of wildflower, of which there are
at least 10,000 on this planet. Or birds, or fishes, trees, flowers,
plants, animals. Or with another human being—preferably one
different from oneself or suffering differently, such as a homosexual if one is proud of being heterosexual. Or black if one is
white, and vice versa. We could fall in love with music, poetry,
paintings, dance. If we fall in love with one of Mozart's works
each week, we would have seven years of joy. How could we
ever be bored?
    Yes, creation has much to do with falling in love. The creation
spirituality journey begins with awe, wonder, and falling in love.
The first commandment, the Via Positiva, is that of praise that
flows for beholding the awe of our being here. "Praise precedes
faith," says Rabbi Heschel.

2. Thou shalt dare the dark (Via Negativa)
    Meister Eckhart says that "the ground of the soul is dark."
This implies that there is no moving from superficiality to
depth without entering the dark—and every spiritual journey is about moving from the surface to the depths. Eckhart
calls God "superessential darkness"—so there is no encountering divinity merely in the light. The divine is to be met in
the depths of darkness as well as in the light. We call this the
apophatic divinity. "Daring the dark" means entering nothingness and letting it be nothingness while it works its mystery on
us. "Daring the dark" also means allowing pain to be pain and
learning from it.

In the pathway that is the Via Negativa, we enter the shadow, the hidden or covered-up parts of ourselves and our society. In doing so, we confront the cover-up that often accompanies evil in self or society. "It is part of an unjust society to cover up the pain of its victims," notes theologian Dorothee Soelle. This commandment requires that we not only let go of cover-up and denial, but that we actually enter into the darkness that pain is all about. Since both despair and apathy arise from the cover-up of pain, this journey of letting go is also one of going deeper than the despair, apathy, bitterness, and cynicism that can create such resentment in our souls and society.

The mystics talk of the "dark night of the soul," which we all taste because we are all mystics. We can move beyond despair and numbing. Joanna Macy advises us to "experience the pain. Let us not fear its impact on ourselves or others. We will not shatter, for we are not objects that can break." The darkness is deeply communitarian, for "we are in grief together." It is when the heart is broken that compassion can begin to flow through it.

A return to the dark is also a return to our origins; we were all conceived in the dark, lived our first nine months in the dark, and dwelled from all eternity in the dark heart of the Godhead that preceded the creation of fire and light. The dark mystery of the Godhead calls us all to dare the dark.

Part of darkness is the absence of words and images and the presence of silence. Solitude, silence, and contemplation are part of the Via Negativa also. Silence beckons us from the dark. "What preceded the Word?" asks the poet and potter M. C. Richards. The poet Rilke wrote: "Being silent. Who keeps innerly silent, touches the roots of speech." And Meister Eckhart tells us that "nothing in all creation is so like God as silence."

Path Two builds up our muscles of receptivity and subtraction, letting go and letting be, our being at home in the dark.

3. *Do not be reluctant to give birth (Via Creativa)*

All four paths of creation spirituality find their apex in Path Three, the Via Creativa. Paths One and Two lead up to it (we create out of what we have beheld of light and darkness) and Path Four flows out of the Via Creativa, since we put our moral imaginations and creativity to service and compassion.

The basic spiritual discipline in creation tradition is decidedly not asceticism, but the development of the aesthetic. Beauty, and our role in co-creating it, lies at the heart of the spiritual journey. Eckhart reminds us that "we are heirs of the fearful creative power of God." Art as meditation becomes the basic prayer or practice in the creation spirituality tradition.

Our culture often intimidates us when it comes to becoming the artists we are meant to be. This commandment cuts through that intimidation. Since the masochist in us is the one who says, "I can't do it, I can't create," Path Three breaks through masochism. Because the masochist needs a sadist, one who says, "You can't, but I can," Path Three also confronts sadism. As Nicaraguan poet Ernesto Cardenal puts it, "People do not consume culture; they create it." A culture is an environment where creativity is honored as a great value where it happens around and through the people.

The *imago dei,* or image of God, in all persons is necessarily the image of the Creator. To give birth is to enter the Creator's realm, the work of co-creation, as we assist nature and history in carrying on the creativity of the universe and bring even more awe into the world. In fact, Eckhart says that what we birth in the world is nothing less than the Christ.

4. Be you compassionate as your Creator in heaven is compassionate (Via Transformativa)

You may recognize this commandment as coming directly from Jesus's Sermon on the Mount in Luke's Gospel (6:36). It represents the summation of his teaching. Matthew's gospel is often translated as "Be you perfect as your Creator in heaven is perfect" (5:48). However, the word *perfect* fails to convey the true sense of the word in Jesus's language. A better translation would be *ripe* or *mature* or *full.* In the Jewish consciousness, such ripeness or fullness would consist in being compassionate as the Divine One is compassionate. Thus, to be "perfect" is to be compassionate.

The creation spiritual journey culminates in compassion—which is both justice-making and celebration. Justice and joy equally make up our spiritual journeys. The capacity to experience our interconnectedness brings forth both the joy and sorrow that we undergo with others. In compassion, "peace and justice kiss," as the psalmist put it (Ps. 85:10) Compassion names the response that flows from our interdependence.

To be compassionate is also to be prophetic. In Path Four all are anointed as prophets. The prophet interferes with the injustice, the unnecessary pain, that rains on the earth when humans neglect justice and compassion.

It is important to recall that justice is a cosmic category as well as a human one. All creation is ruled by justice or homeostasis, the quest for balance and equilibrium that is intrinsic to all nature. Compassion is not about feelings of righteousness or pity. It is a matter of humans joining the dance of all creation in the quest for sustainability and balance. "What happens to another, whether it be a joy or a sorrow, happens to me," says Meister Eckhart.

—CSLG 17–23

Original Blessing

I have come to study other religious traditions, including biblical ones, and have learned how rare a concept "original sin" is among these faiths. Islam rejects original sin (even though they keep the story of Adam and Eve); Judaism rejects it (even though they created the story of Adam and Eve); Native Americans reject it (one Catholic sister who is Native American told me that when it comes time for baptism, Native Americans memorize by rote the catechism about original sin to please the officiating clergy but cannot believe in it); Buddhism rejects it: Eastern Orthodox Christians do not emphasize original sin either. It was Saint Augustine who first used the term in the fourth century A.D. Jesus himself, being a Jew, never heard of the concept. How strange that a religion would sustain itself on a theory that its "founder" never even heard of. There must be a reason for a religion sustaining itself on a theory that was invented four centuries after its "founder" died. And there is. The church inherited the Roman Empire in the fourth century, and to run an empire efficiently one needs theories like original sin to keep the citizens and soldiery in line.

What I call "original blessing" can also be named "original goodness" (Aquinas), "original grace" or "original wisdom" (Hildegard). It begins with the goodness that 13.8 billions of years of the universe's grace has revealed and shared with us. It is about the blessing that the universe is and has been over its fruitful history. Since writing *Original Blessing/* (1983), I have discovered the remarkable work of the twelfth-century nun and visionary, Hildegard of Bingen, who employs the phrase "original wisdom." She says we are all born with original wisdom and that life's task is to set up this tent of wisdom, which comes to us small and folded up as children. This rich image is mirrored in the work of a contemporary Buddhist nun, Pema Chödrön, who writes: "This is our birthright—the wisdom with which we were born, the vast unfolding display of primordial richness, primordial openness, primordial wisdom itself." She recommends meditation practice through which we "realize that we don't have to obscure the joy and openness that is present in every moment of our existence. We can awaken to basic goodness, our birthright." In Buddhism, our true nature has been called "Buddha nature," "original mind," and "luminous." This language is like the teaching of the *Cosmic Christ* in the Christian mystical tradition. This Christ dwells in all beings, but we need to return to our origins to find the Christ there. Buddhist teacher Pahmasambhava writes: "In its true state, the mind is self-radiant . . . immaculate, transparent, timeless, unimpeded . . . [Our] self-born wisdom is undoubtedly indestructible, unbreakable, like the ever-flowing current of a river . . . [It] is as vacuous and clear as the (cloudless) sky" . . .

Since "blessing" is the theological word for "goodness," original blessing is about original goodness. The forces of fear and pessimism so prevalent in society and religion need to be countered by an increased awareness of awe and goodness. This goodness is inherent in the beauty, wisdom, and wonder of creation. Goodness and creation go together as do goodness and God . . . When this becomes the starting point of spirituality once again, hope will return also. We will see everything differently, including Divinity itself. Blessing awareness motivates us to be grateful and hopeful—and generous in our actions. The issue at stake is nothing less than *biophilia* (love of life) displacing *necrophilia* (love of death). Psychologist Erich Fromm implies that there is no exit from evil without biophilia being learned on a daily basis when he writes: "Necrophilia grows as biophilia is stunted." Original blessing is a commitment to putting biophilia first. Biophilia is a synonym for eros, which in turn is a synonym for wisdom. Are we up to this task of putting biophilia first? It will require a new depth and breadth of falling in love with life and its many beauties. It will mean meditation and cleansing our perception in order to see the world differently. It will mean learning and celebrating the new creation story from science. It will also mean detoxing our souls of necrophiliac tendencies derived from toxic religious teachings and toxic ideologies including patriarchy. It calls for a great *unlearning*. This is possible given the new cosmology from science and given the recovery of our best mystical traditions from around the world. But time is running out. Necrophilia and biophilia are indeed engaged in a great battle. Praise and goodness need resurrecting.

—OB 5–8

Cosmic Christ

A few years ago I referred to the term "the Cosmic Christ" in a television show being taped under the direction of a Methodist minister. She asked, "What is 'the Cosmic Christ?' I've never heard the phrase before." This woman was a well-read and recently educated minister, having been ordained about five years. I have since learned that very few graduates of Christian seminaries—Protestant or Catholic—have been exposed to the theology of the Cosmic Christ. Why is this concept so foreign to Christianity today?

Lutheran scholar of church history Jaroslav Pelikan believes it is the result of the Enlightenment. "Enlightenment philosophy deposed the Cosmic Christ," he writes. One might expect that, when rationalism and patriarchal mindsets drive out mysticism, intuition, imagination, and above all cosmology, the Cosmic Christ would be banished as well. In an anthropocentric era of culture, education, and religion, there is no need of a Cosmic Christ. Such a concept is an embarrassment. If Newton is correct and our universe is essentially a machine, who needs a Cosmic Christ? There is no mystery in a machine-line universe. The concept of "mystery" itself is reduced to the level of an "unsolved problem." Mystery as the dark silence behind all being and the deep, unfathomable presence that grounds all being, is banished.

Instead of the Cosmic Christ, the Enlightenment challenged Christian theology to go in search of the "historical Jesus." The quest for the historical Jesus has dominated christological studies for two centuries . . .

I believe the issue today for the third millennium of Christianity—if the earth is to survive into the next century—is the *quest for the Cosmic Christ*. The movement from the Enlightenment's quest for the historical Jesus to today's quest for the Cosmic Christ names the paradigm shift needed today. Albert Einstein said that we are moving into the "third era of religion," that being a *cosmic religion*. One that celebrates cosmos, science, and conscience. One cannot explore the meaning and power of the Cosmic Christ without a living cosmology, a living mysticism, and the spiritual discipline of art as meditation. *The holy trinity of science (knowledge of creation), mysticism (experiential union with creation and its unnameable mysteries), and art (expression of our awe at creation) constitute a living cosmology . . .*

What has been accomplished in the period of the quest for the historical Jesus is by no means lost in our pursuit of the Cosmic Christ. Twenty-first century scientific revelations instruct us in understanding the dynamic character of the Cosmic Christ by teaching us the radically dynamic and creative nature of our universe from the very first millisecond of its existence. A theology of the Cosmic Christ must be grounded in the historical Jesus, in his words, in his liberating deeds (cf. liberation theology), in his life and orthopraxis. The Cosmic Christ is not a doctrine that is believed in and lived out *at the expense of the historical Jesus.* Rather, a dialectic is in order, a dance between time (Jesus) and space (Christ); between the personal and the cosmic; between the prophetic and the mystical. The dance is a dance away from anthropocentrism.   —CCC 76–79

The Cosmic Christ in Israel

The Cosmic Christ was present in the Hebrew Bible principally as cosmic wisdom. Preexistent wisdom is celebrated in Israel on numerous occasions. In the book of Job, the penetrating question is asked, "Where does wisdom come from?" (Job 28:12, 20), and in Baruch wisdom is celebrated as the divine attribute by which God governs the world (Bar. 3:9-4:4). Wisdom is personified in Proverbs (1:20–33; 8:1–36; 9:1–6) in passages such as the following: "Wisdom calls aloud in the streets, she raised her voice in the public squares; she calls out at the street corners, she delivers her message at the city gates" (Prov. 1:20–21). "Yahweh created me when his purpose first unfolded, before the oldest of his works. From everlasting I was firmly set, from the beginning, before earth came into being . . . When he fixed the heavens firm, I was there" (Prov. 8:22–26).

The Cosmic Christ is present in the prophets and in certain messianic expectations. As Rabbi Heschel puts it, "what concerns the prophet is the human event as a divine experience. History to us is the record of human experience; to the prophet it is a record of God's experience." The experience of God as integral to human history is the experience of the suffering, the pathos, the anguish, and the anger of God who suffers when innocent victims suffer from injustice. This is surely an instance of the Cosmic Christ as the universal suffering one . . .   —CCC 83–85

In the Christian tradition, the Cosmic Christ is the light in all things as well as the light in the entire cosmos. Microcosm and macrocosm hold the divine presence. Christ is "the pattern that connects," as Paul puts it. For Hildegard, the Word of God is everywhere and in everything: "God's Word is in all creation, visible and invisible." . . . Meister Eckhart 150 years later would say, "Every creature is a word of God and a book about God." Yes, a book about God, a revelation, a Bible. As Aquinas put it, "revelation comes in two volumes: nature and the Bible."

—HBST 11, 15

The Cosmic Christ finds a parallel archetype in the concept of tselem *or the image of God in Judaism. Rabbi David Seidenberg has written a major work,* Kabbalah and Ecology: God's Image in the More-Than-Human World, *which demonstrates how Judaism honors all beings as images of God. Indeed, he too speaks of the "pattern that connects" being the image of God in all things.* (MF)

Realized Eschatology

Realized eschatology is the teaching found in Johannine theology and the late theology of Paul that eternal life begins in the present life. Says Eckhart: "Just think what an amazing and blessed life the person 'on earth' has in God himself—a life 'as it is in Heaven.'" Commenting on the Our Father prayer, Eckhart says that Christ "has ordered the earth itself to become heaven, saying: 'Your will be done on earth as it is in heaven.' And the kingdom too will come whether here by grace or in the future by glory." . . . Commenting on 1 Jn 3:1, Eckhart declares: "It is in this life that a person is begotten as a Son of God and that he or she is born to eternal life." Realized echatology recognizes that the future has already begun.   —WS 217, 245

Panentheism

Panentheism rejects theism (we below, God above) and recognizes God in all things and all things in God. It is the way the mystics envision our relationship to the divine. Mechtild of Magdeburg said, "The day of my spiritual awakening was the day I saw and knew I saw all things in God and God in all things." And Julian of Norwich's very definition of faith is this: "Faith means trust that God is in all things and all things are in God." Eckhart said: "God created all things in such a way that they are not outside himself, as ignorant people falsely imagine. Everything that God creates or does he does or creates in himself, sees or knows in himself, loves in himself." Eckhart cites time and again—and even at his trial—a favorite scriptural locus of panentheists, that of Acts 17:28: "God in whom we live, move, and have our being." Panentheism honors the intimacy of the divine to creation, while also respecting divine transcendence or beyondness.   —WS 218

Trust Is the Real Meaning of Faith

The world that the Creator has made "is a world that is thoroughly worthy of trust," according to biblical wisdom scholar Gerhard Von Rad. Another scholar of wisdom literature, Roland Murphy, says that the two most important factors in learning wisdom are "an openness to experience and nature and a basic trust." Indeed, "the reason for this openness is trust." The New Testament word most often used by Jesus and translated as "faith" and which Augustine understood as "intellectual assent" in fact means "trust" (*pisteuein* in the original Greek). Jesus time and again assures people that "your trust has healed you." Says Hildegard, "Trust shows the way." Says Eckhart: "You can never trust God too much. Why is it that some people do not bear fruit? It is because they have no trust either in God or in themselves."   —OB 83, 81

2

Dreams and Visions

DREAMS

Dreams have played an important role in my life and work, offering vision, insight, healing, and creative possibilities. Reverend Jeremy Taylor, who taught dreams as an art-as-meditation class with us for years, says that all dreams come to heal. Carl Jung says dreams are the surest access to the divine self, and that has often been my experience. Here, and in other sections of this book, I share briefly some of my most significant dreams. Some of them are what Native people call "big dreams," that is, dreams for the community at large. (MF)

On Being Invited to Holy Names College

Shortly after receiving the phone call in Spring 1983 from the president of Holy Names College inviting us out to Oakland to establish the Institute for Culture and Creation Spirituality there, I had a remarkable dream. I was riding a roller coaster–like train with my mother at my side. It was exhilarating and joyful, and we went down, down, down into ancient places and amid ancient sites: We went into Egypt (a flight into Egypt?) among temples and pyramids and ancient gods and goddesses (Isis, the black Madonna?). Yet I knew it was also a journey to California that was depicted. In the dream my mother lost one of her red shoes, and I had to go looking for it. Intimations of the "yellow brick road" journey that I felt was ahead of me out west perhaps.

But also a deeper exploration awaited us into what Frederick Turner calls the "aboriginal mother love" that characterizes native religions. Freedom, exhilaration, and the exploration of new but ancient underworld places—all this was in the dream, and all this awaited me in California and beyond. My horizons regarding culture and religion were sure to expand. It was in Oakland that Lakota teacher Buck Ghosthorse showed up, having driven cross country with his wife and all their belongings, and following an instruction from dreams over a ten-year period to "work with white people." His contributions teaching and leading rituals, such as sweat lodges for our students and faculty, were immense. We became good friends.   —CNF 146

"Your Mother Is Dying"

About 1985, I had a dream that I realized was an important one, a "big dream" meant not just for myself as an individual but for the whole community. It was a Saturday night, and I was leading a retreat at Kirkridge Retreat Center in Bangor, Pennsylvania. I was exhausted, and my defenses were down. The climax of the dream contained this refrain: "Your mother is dying." But my literal mother was not dying. She was healthy and kicking.

So I asked the question: Is our mother dying? . . .

The first meaning of the warning, "Your mother is dying," can be taken in reference to Mother Earth. That the earth is our mother is a deeply held truth among native people of the Americas, Africa, Asia, and Europe . . .

Is our Mother Earth dying? Consider Bhopal; Chernobyl; Love Canal; Times Beach, Missouri; the Rhine River, where one thousand tons of chemicals, including eight tons of pure mercury, were spilled—the river where Hildegard of Bingen and Meister Eckhart, the two greatest creation mystics of Western Europe, lived and preached their message of compassion and interconnectivity with creation. And today, of course, climate change with all that means, including coronavirus, droughts, floods, hurricanes, wild fires, the extinction of millions of species, and more. Yes, our Mother is dying.

A second meaning to the dream is that the mystical brain is dying. A crucial dimension of the imbalance in the West is the stunted growth of our mystical awareness and the under-development of the mystical brain. The right lobe of the brain accomplishes the synthetic, sensual, intuitive, and mystical tasks . . . Western civilization, which dominates the globe today, has invested almost exclusively in left lobe education, which accomplishes rational and analytic verbal processes in politics, economics, religion—even many seminaries ignore the intuitive brain, home of mysticism.

A third meaning of the dream is that creativity is dying. Carl Jung said that creativity emerges "from the realm of the Mothers." The maternal is the place of new birth, of new wombs, of new stories, of new beginnings, and new possibilities.

A fourth meaning is that wisdom is dying . . . Wisdom appears universally in cultures and religions as a feminine, maternal figure . . . Wisdom requires the right brain as well as the left, for it is born of both analysis and synthesis. Wisdom requires imagination and nurtures it.

A fifth meaning is that youth are dying. "Mother" is a word that defines a relationship after all—a mother does not stand alone. She is, by definition, in relationship to a child . . . We have increasing evidence of youth dying as we learn more about the numbers of suicidal youth, drugged and alcoholic youth, depressed and apathetic youth, unemployed and apparently unemployable youth, youth who have been victims of physical, sexual, education, and religious abuse, and youth who are murdering others, often in mass shootings—think Sandy Hooks and Columbine and Parkland. Youth are victims, but very often young men are the perpetrators. Both are dying.

A sixth meaning to our mother dying is that native peoples, their religions, and cultures are dying. Theirs are the oldest religions on earth, whether in the Americas, Africa, ancient Europe, Australia, Polynesia, or Asia. In these religions one finds deep memories of what essayist Frederick Turner calls "aboriginal mother love." These religions arose in cultural periods that were very often matrifocal . . . The extermination and devastation caused by colonialism and imperialism brought about immense trauma that is still with these peoples to this day, a holocaust of ineffable proportions occurred.

A seventh meaning is that mother church is dying. Mother church is deeply entangled in the lethal embraces of matricidal patriarchy. Fundamentalism is a planetary phenomenon in religions today. Worshipping a punitive father God, such fundamentalism is built on a deep-seated fear triggered by the breakup of cultural patterns . . . Religious fundamentalism exemplifies identification with the oppressor—the very hatred of mother that caused it is embraced and intensified by fundamentalism. Fundamentalism is patriarchy gone berserk . . .

An eighth meaning is that mother love (compassion) is dying. The Hebrew word for compassion is derived from the word for womb. Womb love, mother love, creative love are all part of the power we know as compassion . . . The ancient tradition of God as mother and the goddess in every person is lost. And the sense of nature as sacred is lost when nature is dying.

The dream said "your mother is dying," but it did not say "your mother is dead" . . . There is still hope, there is still something we can do to turn things around (*metanoia*), to convert and change our ways. What does it take to bring the healthy mother back to balance with the healthy father in us all? I believe the answer lies in a deep mystical awakening that is truly planetary, that draws out the wisdom and the mystic, the contemplative and the justice-maker, from the wisdom traditions of all religions and cultures. Such a mystical and activist awakening would surely birth that "peace on earth" for which creation longs.

This dream became the first part of my book on *The Coming of the Cosmic Christ* because that book names the sacredness imbedded in all creation and how we can recover an awareness of that sacredness.   —CCC 13–34

Outside the Rusty Gate

In February 1994 I had a dream following my reception as an Episcopalian priest that moved me to tears (something that happens rarely in my dreams), and I recorded it:

Ash Wednesday, February 16, 1994

Dream last night (I cried in the dream)—I'm at an old gate, outdoors, made of iron. It is like a cemetery gate, and I hear the statement (have I been teaching it?): "Everyone is here for a purpose. God has a role for everyone." And then I hear a question: "Has my role been to make creation spirituality known?" With that I cry because of the simplicity of it and the clarity of it and (I think) because it says something about my life and its many choices, including the recent one to become Episcopalian and the Vatican's choice to dump me. And also because it suggests that maybe my life and life work have had some meaning after all.

In reflecting on this dream, I suspect that being "outside the old gate" means being outside the church as I have known it and also outside the modern culture. Both of these structures are getting very old—indeed the gate is a cemetery gate, thus a dying church and a dying modern structure. There is grief work to do—ashes to bless ourselves with—as we want to give them a decent burial. Yet my vocation remains alive—I am here *for a purpose,* and there is continuity in my work, that of making creation spirituality known. Indeed, *all* our vocations are *alive* . . .

The gate is an iron gate, and it is rusting. This speaks to me of the modern age, which is industrial and whose metaphor in the nineteenth-century was the iron horse, that engine that spanned the continent but destroyed the buffalo and the indigenous peoples' way of life and so much more. Now that era is a cemetery, a rust belt, and we are asked to let the dead bury the dead and move on. The key to our moving on from the modern era will be our heart work—the grief and the joy that come from doing the true work for which we are here.

I recognize the iron gate in the dream as being the gates that surround the Luxembourg Garden in Paris, located midway between the Latin Quarter and the Catho. The order and the institutional church rejected what I had learned beginning in my Paris days. The fact that I am expelled from the garden has obvious archetypal meanings; yet the garden is no longer a garden but a cemetery; and the gate is no longer beautiful and polished but is rusting. All this speaks to me of death and rebirth; of letting go and moving on; of grief work and—with the words that accompanied the dream—hope for the future. For my existence in the garden was for the same purpose as my existence beyond the garden. I am no longer protected by the *cloister* in the garden it represented, as in my novitiate days. But the vocation continues. The tears were grief—for all that might have been (what if the Dominicans, instead of turning on me, had sent another brother out to work with me?). But the tears were essentially tears of joy and relief and beauty. For they did not flow because the gates were closed; they flowed at the moment when the voice said, "Your vocation has been to make creation spirituality known." Joy is deeper than sorrow. In spite of the expulsion, my vocation continues. Inside or out, my vocation goes on. Everyone's does.
—CNF 271–72

Adrienne Rich, a Silver Sea, and a Very Feminist Dream

During my "sabbatical year" of silence from the Vatican, I stopped by Marshfield, Massachusetts, where the ocean had kept me in the order nineteen year earlier. I asked the ocean for a dream that night to help guide my way—something I very seldom do—and a special dream did indeed emerge. It was that same ocean, I was on that same beach, and it was nighttime. A silver moon shone from a silver sky on the all-silver ocean. And out of the ocean there emerged Adrienne Rich in a silver wet suit. She said nothing, but she pointed at her knee.

It was a very transcendent dream—still, quiet, and totally bathed in silver. Clarissa Pinkola Estes says that silver represents an archaeological layer in the old wild feminine, and the color bespeaks the spirit world and the moon. The knee represents prayer (*genou* is the French word for "knee," and from it we get the word *genuflection*). So it bespeaks the sacred and recovering the sacred and reverence for creation with the help of the moon and the feminine.

In addition, the knee connects us to the earth, pulls us *down* to our lower chakras, and is also part of our *flexibility*. Flexibility was one of the lessons this same sea had instructed me in years ago when I was making my decision whether to stay in the order. Adrienne Rich, of course, is one of the premier feminist poets and thinkers of our time and certainly one of the most important poets in my life. Emerging from the sea as she did, she represented the Magna Mater, the great mother of the sea, the return to our origins in *la mère, la mer* (mother, sea). Sophia, lady wisdom, also seemed to be speaking in the dream. The beauty of the dream and its simple message seemed to be encouraging me not to abandon my work in bringing the feminine and the mystical back to religion and culture. Including wisdom back to education. The dream healed.   —CNF 220–21

VISION QUEST

Animals as Other Christs

During the year of his silencing by the Vatican, Fox underwent a vision quest under the guidance of his friend and mentor, Lakota teacher Buck Ghosthorse. He recounts some of that happening from a journal he wrote after the ritual. (CB)

Notes from My Vision Quest

I chanted and prayed and danced and kept the sacred pipe in my hand, as instructed, at all times. Then I would sit on the log that was in my space of four feet by six feet. The log contained a lot of mosquitoes which one was instructed not to kill, but it was good to be able to sit on it—though I could only look in one direction.

Two redemptions of Catholic piety came to me: One is redeeming the rosary by way of a new (and more ancient?) Hail Mary: "Holy Mary, mother of God, pray for us co-creators now and at the hour of our creativity." I saw the benediction of the "Blessed Sacrament" in a creation-centered form. Every creature is a Blessed Sacrament, including the galaxies, sun, earth, etc. The Divine Names litany applies to each creature as well as to the communion host. Why not devise a ritual that honors a different creature each day—like a host—for each is a Cosmic Christ and a Blessed Sacrament (cf. "original blessing")? . . .

It was after this "theological reflections" that, as the sun began to set in the forest, the light show began. Light as light of Christ, *Lumen gentium,* "light of the nations," became *lumen animalium* and *lumen creatuorum*, "light of creatures," "light of animals and creatures." It was then that I noticed the polar bear in the tree, i.e., a leaf in the shape of a polar bear. Next to it was a bird—several of them and all the leaves were lighting up. Behind a bush there was a rocklike "grotto" that looked Celtic, and lots of little people were gathered beside it. Behind this were tree trunks that became snakes and a chimpanzee on its knees. I saw at the back of the forest an immense structure forming a kind of backdrop to the scene. It was like a castle or museum, and then I realized it was both. It was the Vatican covered with moss, deserted. It was "back there"—while all this action of life and light was taking place here, in the foreground, in our forest.

Every place I turned there were forms to be seen: leaves of animals, each one lit up and shining (Cosmic Christ?)—deer, monkeys, a dinosaur, crocodiles, elephants, pandas, bears. Near to me was another tree stump that became—was I seeing it right? Yes, absolutely—a crèche, a manger. Joseph was there with his staff and the animals and all. "Francis, get a load of this," I commented—since he is credited with inventing this object of veneration. How peaceful and, above all, amazing this illuminated forest seemed, and how natural that Mary and Son should be in a tree right alongside a deer and how on the other side there would be a manger. I said, "My whole Cosmic Christ book is coming alive." This is quite a show . . .

An icon appeared that was distinctly African—two black figures standing together—framed, it seemed, as in an icon of the Madonna figure. They seemed to be two male adults. Trans-African, Druid-goddess, and Celtic represented along with Christian and Native American. We were having all the fun in this enchanted forest, and the Vatican structure, highly fortified and heavy with moss like an abandoned museum or fortress, was not close enough to the earth to join us. A theological thought occurred after the Thanksgiving ritual: Is not all prayer of petition in reality a prayer of Thanksgiving? For we only petition on behalf of what we in some way cherish as blessing—but this is Thanksgiving. When we petition without thanks, we are mere spiritual consumers . . .

As the night wore on toward the morning, I was surprised to see dead leaves shaped like ugly and sinister masks with big teeth. A menacing sign of a threatening presence nearby that did not, however, enter my prayer space. . .

Buck explained to me afterward that he and his elders felt I would be attacked by negative forces from the Vatican, and that is why I was given the special eagle-defense prayer stick. . . . Buck says that humans create evil forces out of their hatred, but that all of it can be defeated by prayer and courage. These evil forces prey on fear . . . Thus, the importance of spirituality—to build the strength, the big heart (courage)—based on faith, i.e., trust, which is the opposite of fear—that combats evil successfully.

He also interpreted my wild night this way: That all the spirits of animals who had ever lived on this land for millions of years were coming to support my work. "The two-legged ones may not always support you, but the animals do," he said.

—CNF 206–11

3

Science and Creation Spirituality

A NEW COSMOLOGY AND SCIENCE OF FIELDS, SOULS, AND ANGELS

We cannot do creation spirituality without those who study nature and creation, namely, scientists. I have been blessed to have worked with scientists and learned from scientists over the years. I worked with cosmologist Brian Swimme for many years both at the Institute in Culture and Creation Spirituality program at Mundelein College in Chicago and then at Holy Names College, Oakland, California. While in Chicago, we wrote together the book, Manifesto for a Global Civilization, *from which the following excerpts are taken.*

I also had the privilege to write two books with British biologist Rupert Sheldrake and to teach with and learn from many other scientists, including Beverley Rubik, Thomas Berry, Joel Primack, Nancy Abrams, Ralph Abraham, Paul Carr, Lester Brown, and numerous writers. (MF)

DIALOGUE WITH BRIAN SWIMME

A Parts Mentality versus Wholeness Mentality

For three centuries the West has labored under a mechanical understanding of the world. We have understood the universe as a place where inert particles interacting with one another form the basis of the world itself. Because science was structured on the assumption that the world could be analyzed in terms of

these relatively autonomous parts or particles, and because science showed itself as tremendously powerful, the West recre-
ated all of its forms of life in response to the fundamental
assumptions of science. Economics, religion, social sciences,
medicine, politics and governments, every aspect of culture eventually reflected the underlying mechanical understanding of the
world that grounded science. The West fragmented into all the
micro-specialties that splinter our universities even today. With
a worldview based on a parts-mentality, we humans created a
parts culture, a fragmented and centerless attempt at the fullness
of civilization.

But through the work of Albert Einstein, Max Planck, Werner
Heisenberg, Erwin Schrodinger, Niels Bohr, and Paul Dirac, we
have come to understand that the world is, at its most primal
level, *an undivided whole*. We have uncovered the inadequacy
of the parts-cosmology, have broken through this limited and
limiting perspective to an understanding of the wholeness that
grounds all of reality. The work of these and many other theoretical physicists has shattered the structures of our worldview
and created the foundations of another world radically distinct
from the past one. Whereas it was the core of classical scientific
theory to speak of parts-in-interaction as the beginning points
in any discussion of the world, this is now understood as at best
a high-level abstraction. Rather, twentieth-century quantum
physics reveals the undivided wholeness of the experimental situation as the ground for scientific understanding. The creative
achievements of theoretical physics in our century establish one
undivided world as the starting point for scientific analysis.

A fundamental symbol for the classical scientific worldview
was the billiard table with the billiard balls glancing off one
another. A fundamental symbol for the world that has emerged
from twentieth-century theoretical physics is that of the musical
symphony. Though careful understanding of quantum physics
demands an understanding of its mathematics, the symbol that
best grasps the new worldview implicit in the mathematics is the
symphony, the world itself as symphony. With the symphony,

we are compelled to begin with the wholeness of the music alto-gether before we attempt any analysis or discussion of the music. Indeed, to speak of the late motif of the second movement of Beethoven's ninth as if this late motif could *be discussed in its entirety, in its fullness,* and *in all its meaning* without considering the whole from which it has been abstracted is an absurdity. In an analogous manner, to attempt to speak of the electron in an experiment as if this electron could be discussed and understood in its full meaning without consideration of the whole experi-mental situation is without scientific validation. The experimen-tal situation is an indivisible whole, and to speak of an electron is to speak of an aspect of the wholeness, an aspect that has its meaning only in relationship to this whole.   —MG 10–12

Mind as Computer versus Based in the Human Spirit

The understanding of mind in the classical scientific age is that of the electronic computer; the understanding of mind in the emerging era is found in the ineffable depths of the human spirit. For what has been established is that the ground of truth *is not* and *cannot be found* in the axioms on the page. The judgment of truth is not bound within any system however complex, is not found within any machine, however richly interconnected it might be. The ground of truth and the ground of the creative act that leaps beyond all theoretical systems is the human spirit. An emerging symbol for the human spirit is *a well of creativity* from which truth gushes forth and becomes manifest in the creations of the human being.

The understanding of the emerging era is that the stunning power of creativity of the human being is rooted in the divine plenary emptiness that is inseparably interinvolved with the human spirit. We create the global civilization taking this under-standing as our grounding of the human person. We begin with the understanding of the human spirit as interinvolved with the dark plenary creativity of the divine word, and we remake our world and our relationships in our world as well as ourselves from this foundation.   —MG 15–16

Cosmogenesis

Everything that exists boasts a 13.8-billion-year history. Everything that exists contains within itself the entire history of being in our world. The sun, the Earth, the tree in the backyard, one's fingernail, the Elizabethan drama, the mathematical theorem: each existent in the cosmos has a 13.8-billion-year family history. Each existent has for its first memory that primeval fireball that initiated the entire cosmic drama at the beginning of time. In the future, our orientation toward any existent thing will be that this thing-in-process has been 13.8 billion years in the making.

We understand that the cosmogenesis is a 13.8-billion-year-old dance that began with the primeval fireball; that its first epochal moment was its coalescing into the great systems of galaxies; that it erupted into billions of living beings after the careful nurturance of the Earth; that it deepened its creation with the incomparable emergence of the human person and its language; that it extended this creativity into the shamanic tribal era of humanity with its magic and its cults and its rites; that it gathered itself into the focused and stable formation of the great axial civilizations; that it soared into a frenzy of creativity with the emergence of the scientific-technological era; and that it is now unfolding in a radically new manifestation of the compassionate global civilization. But this is not the whole story.

We need to develop the story beyond the limits of the mechanical worldview of scientific materialism. The new story will not overlook the fact that the human person carries within herself the full 13.8-billion-year history of the cosmos. . . . As the most intricate and most profound and most dangerous being in creation, the human being can no longer be neglected in our attempts to fathom the meaning of the cosmos itself. Only in the new story will we grasp the full truth that we are microcosms that reflect and realize the full macrocosm itself.

It is difficult to imagine that the sciences could lapse into triviality, and yes this happened once before in western history when Augustine's repudiation of the scientific mind contributed to science's vanishing from European civilization for over a thousand years. As Albert Einstein said: "the most important function of art and science is to awaken the cosmic religious feeling and keep it alive."

—MG 22–24

THOMAS BERRY ON THE NEW COSMOLOGY

In 1992 Brian Swimme collaborated with Thomas Berry to publish The Universe Story, *a wondrous history of the cosmos and a new creation story from science.* (CB)

> *Now, in our modern scientific age, in a manner never known before, we have created our own sacred story, the epic of evolution telling us, from empirical observation and critical analysis, how the universe came to be, the sequence of its transformations down through some billions of years, how our solar system came into being and how the earth took shape and brought us into existence. . . . This is our sacred story.* (Thomas Berry)

Fox comments: Thomas Berry celebrates our new, and collective, sacred story, one that permeates the globe at this time, one that is truly universal, and one that derives form science. He emphasizes in other places how important sacred stories have always been to human tribes in order to ground them in morality and in celebration. Today, the "tribe" is no longer just local. It is our entire species. Our whole species shares this common story. . . . Are we busy creating rituals and ceremonies to tell these deep stories of belonging once again? Are we developing a common ethic from them, a common morality?   —CM 359, 362

DIALOGUES WITH RUPERT SHELDRAKE

Fox has held numerous dialogues with British biologist Rupert Sheldrake, and together they have written two books, Natural Grace: Dialogues on Creation, Darkness, and the Soul in Spirituality and Science *and* The Physics of Angels: Exploring the Realm Where Science and Spirit Meet. (CB)

Has the Concept of Field Replaced the Concept of Soul?

Sheldrake: The modern field concept has replaced the old soul concept as a matter of historical fact. . . . Electromagnetic fields have replaced the old electrical and magnetic souls. In biology, morphogenic fields, the organizing formative fields of the embryo and of the developing organism, have replaced the vegetable soul of Aristotle and the medieval philosophers.

I think the concept of fields helps to eliminate or even demystify some of the aspects of the older use of the word *soul.* . . .

It seems to me that in the Christian tradition the energetic principle would be the spirit, which is always portrayed in terms of movement, change, the blowing wind, the breath, the fire, the flying bird—these are all moving images. And the field would be the formative principle, the logos, the formative aspect of creation. Have you ever thought of fields in these terms?

Fox: Well, I have in fact, just before you suggested that spirit would be the right metaphor. Theologically, that's exactly what I was thinking. Again, . . . we have a very underdeveloped theology of spirit in the West. And part of our theology of spirit comes from John, who says, "The spirit blows where it will" (John 3:8)—the chance, chaotic dimension of surprise that you alluded to earlier. For me the contemporary word for transcendence is not *up*—there is no up in a curved universe, Buckminster Fuller points out. There's only in and out—and for me the word *transcendence* means surprise. And that's what the spirit brings. And the spirit flows through all religions, all cultures, and all of us. It's not easily controlled. An awakening of the spirit is something our ecclesiastical bureaucracies are a little afraid of. But I think it's what a renaissance is all about.

Sheldrake: The spirit, then, is a source of creativity. By contrast, the morphic fields that I'm talking about are essentially habitual. They are formative principles based on what's happened before. They are carriers of habit, the carriers of inheritance, good and bad. The way I see the Universe in terms of modern science is an interplay between the habit principle, represented by fields, and the creative principle, represented through the ongoing flux of things that's always bringing about surprises. Indeed, our own lives seem to be an interplay of habit and creativity. Perhaps this fits in with what you've just said.

Fox: Very much so. Another word that we use for *habit* is *tradition*. But there's a danger of spelling it with a capital *T* instead of a small *t*. I was in Cardiff speaking on Celtic spirituality in a large Protestant church, and after the event a young man in his twenties came up and said, "You know, I go to church here and it's the first time I've ever seen the place filled. About thirty people come here on Sunday and it's so boring. Ritual's something they do to you. How can we reinvent ritual here?" I said, "You have to begin by removing all the benches and reimaging the field as curved because that's the kind of universe we say we believe in. You need to get the breath moving because you can't pray without the body and the breath. The body and the heart go together." "Well," he said, "this church is 150 years old; it has a tradition, and they wouldn't tolerate moving the benches." But I told him that the Universe is 13.8 billion years old, and soon the human community has to make a decision: the hundred fifty years of human tradition or 13.8 billion years of creation's tradition. "You may lose half your congregation, but you may gain a whole generation of worshippers who are eager to be invited to pray with their bodies in more curved spaces." This names the field and brings forth that morphic memory, because when we pray in circles, the circles of our ancestors and circles of our curved Universe, we are rousing and awakening that memory and the resurrection that comes with that: a new life.

—NG 36–39

On Darkness and Light

Sheldrake: Darkness is the polar opposite of light. Light and darkness are correlative terms, and there's a polarity between them.

There are two senses in which light involves darkness. The first is perhaps the less interesting and flows from what we know of the spectrum of electromagnetic radiation. The part of the spectrum we can actually see is a very narrow band, the visible spectrum. Then we go over into the infrared and radio waves at longer wavelengths . . . and the ultraviolet, X-rays, and gamma-rays at shorter wavelengths. There's a vast amount of radioactive activity going on, every room is full of all sorts of radiation which we can't see. . . .

The center of the pupil is black because the inside of the eye is black. You can see light because that which receives the light is dark. If the inside of the eye weren't black, the light that went in would scatter all over the place, and we wouldn't be able to distinguish the light that was coming in from that which was reflected within the eyeball. Cameras are painted black inside for the same reason. It's the contrast between the blackness of the eye and incoming radiation that enables us to see.

In fact, darkness is contained within light itself. This is shown by the phenomenon of diffraction. If you have two slits, for example, and the light goes through the two slits, then when the light rays interfere, you get a series of light and dark bands. . . .

Fox: This has me thinking about the relationship between cosmos and psyche because, as I hear you speak, I keep hearing the resonances of the whole mystical tradition. As Eckhart puts it, "The ground of the soul is dark." I'm reminded of the mystical tradition that the Godhead is dark, that it cannot be seen by its actions. The Creator, Redeemer God is active, and the results are visible. But the Godhead from which all things begin is supremely dark. It's "a not-active superessential darkness that will never have a name and never be given a name" (Eckhart). It's a great mystery.

In many ways, what keeps appearing in what you're saying here is *mystery.* The whole universe or ninety-five percent of it is a dark matter and dark mystery. This is like our psychic life, which comes through once in a while with memorable dreams at night. I always ask, "Where do dreams come from?" I recently asked a good friend of mine who wrote a very powerful book on dreams: "Without using the word *unconscious,* tell us where dreams come from." He responded, "I think dreams come from the Universe" . . .

Another theme that is translatable into mystical language is that of illumination—the idea that we are illuminated, that we are enlightened, that the light in us increases and, paradoxically so, as we go more deeply into the dark, as we sink. This is the *Via Negativa*, that illumination comes at the end of the bottoming out in the darkness experience. The psychic experience of the dark night of the soul and suffering as darkness, something that we do not have control over, something we can't really name but which is big within us, the great mystery again. Our culture would try to intervene with quick remedies, whether it's drugs or palliatives of some kind. A lot of our addictions are efforts to intervene with the darkness that's happening. But the mystical traditions would all say there's something deep to be learned by making the journey into the darkness . . .

Some mystics recommend letting go of all images: images imply light; we see images only in the light, and some images in some way reflect light, so they all are luminous in some way and hopefully even numinous from time to time. One method, one path, into spiritual depths is to let go of all images, even our most cherished ones, including visual and audio images, and to sink into the silence. . .

I would say that there's a big difference between the darkness of sleep and dreams and the darkness of meditation. Maybe dreams come halfway, a kind of shadow between that and the radical letting go of all images that Eckhart was saying we are capable of in meditation. I think the exact expression of Eckhart is found more in Zen, this letting go of all images. When he says, "I pray to God to rid me of God," he names our capacity for emptying. And touching the apophatic divinity which is that side of the Godhead that is darkness and mystery.   —NG 131–44

Too Much Light and Insomnia in the Modern World

Sheldrake: Just one further point about sleep. One of the characteristic diseases of the modern world is insomnia. Sleeping pills are a major industry, and places like Los Angeles seem to be filled with insomniacs.

This may be related to your point about the modern world being saturated with light. We have lights blazing in our cities twenty-four hours a day. I've never heard of insomnia being a big problem in third world countries.

Fox: Maybe insomnia in Los Angeles and other cities of the overdeveloped world is the price we pay for the Enlightenment, also known as the Age of Reason. We have light on demand, light twenty-four hours a day. It's as close as your television set: you can watch "The Tonight Show," then old movies, and then it's time to go to work. Maybe this is really the Enlightenment coming to its logical conclusion. While, obviously, we can acknowledge the accomplishment of the Enlightenment in discovering a lot of facts and truths about nature, we're just beginning to realize the price we pay. Insomnia may well be only one price we pay for banishing darkness.

We invented this light machine, that's what television is, there's no question. That's why you can't avoid it. Your solution for your children is not to have one. If it's there, no matter how good the will and intelligence, if a light machine is on in the room, we're all going to be drawn to it, instead of paying attention to our stillness, or having intelligent conversation and family gathering, or whatever.   —NG 148–49

Angels as Fields

Sheldrake: Insofar as we think of whatever affects us as being mediated through messengers or invisible connections, or angels, then something of what's happening to us and what's happening to the world will be conveyed back through the angelic field to more inclusive layers of organization to more inclusive fields of consciousness.

Fox: The image of fields is so much healthier to me than the basic image we get of a ladder. The field is three-dimensional.

Sheldrake: Angels operate in fields of activity, coordinating and connecting. Material bodies are mutually exclusive—you can't have two billiard balls in the same place at the same time—but fields can interpenetrate. For example, the room in which we're sitting is filled with the earth's gravitational field, which is why we're not floating in the air. Interpenetrating the gravitational field is the electromagnetic field, through which we see each other, which is also full of radio waves, TV transmissions, cosmic rays, ultraviolet and infrared rays, all sorts of invisible radiations.

These also don't interfere with one another. Radio waves interfere with one another only if they are at the same frequency. But all radio programs and TV programs in the world can co-exist, interpenetrating the same space and not canceling one another out or denying one another. Even if we take only the fields that orthodox science currently recognizes—quantum-matter fields, electromagnetic fields, and gravitational fields—they all interpenetrate. And so the idea of angels as field-like allows us to see how they too can interpenetrate.

Fox: What I like about the word *field* is that it is an everyday word. *Field* has a sense of space to it. It feels like an invitation to play: one plays in a field. Also, things grow in a field. A field is generative; it is a place of life and activity. It's also about having your feet on the ground. It's matter, it's earth, it's life bubbling up from below. It's an honoring of the lower chakras. I think fields are a wonderfully rich metaphor for bringing angels down to earth, and yet they are three-dimensional. So I want to honor the word *field* and its non-scientific connotation. It too speaks to us of something every-day and something welcoming.

We can also rediscover the meaning of the word *receptive*. In a way, a field is a mirror. It's pulling in the light and converting it into life through photosynthesis and into food. Wonderful things come from fields. Obviously, all food comes from fields. Pastures and orchards and romping places and ball games. Gaia offers us fields of play. She invites people to play in her fields. —PA 42–43

Angels as Connectors

Fox: The angels are connectors, administrators, messengers that touch and connect the microcosm, the human being, and integrate us with the spheres of cosmic forces. —PA 55

Hierarchy as Pattern

Fox: There's something very exciting here. If we go back to Dionysius Areopagite's definition of celestial hierarchy and substitute the word *pattern*, it reads: "Pattern, is, in my opinion, a holy order and knowledge and activity . . ."

I wonder if pattern might not be a more appropriate and more contemporary meaning of hierarchy. We talked about a holarchy, nested levels of wholeness, and wholeness loves pattern. Pattern somehow gets down more to the specific realm, whereas holarchy is the synthesis of it all. Take a developing egg: there's a pattern-forming going on inside it. And as you say, corresponding patterns are found in microcosm and macrocosm, in vortical patterns in a stirred cup of tea and in storms on the sun.

Why is it that we're in such a quest for pattern? Maybe that's what the mind is about. It's either making patterns or discovering patterns. Somehow the mind seeks pattern . . .

Wisdom brings together Logos and Eros, the pattern and the energy. By itself, Logos might become knowledge, but together I think they bring about wisdom. Naming the Cosmic Christ as "the pattern that connects," as St. Paul does, is very provocative and full of meaning.   —PA 57–59

A Power That Flows into Angels and All Beings

Fox: In these passages of Dionysius Areopagite we have a redemption of the word *power*. The angelic orders receive their godlike powers, including their aspiration to goodness, from an infinitely good power. Dionysius celebrates their power to aspire to that ceaseless power.

But this power is not limited to the angels. It's the same power that flows into humans, animals, plants, and the "entire nature of the universe." All things are filled with this ever-flowing power. It's interesting that all beings, including angels, participate in this same energy or power. From this point of view, we are not different from the angels. Dionysius offers the image of power as a maternal embracing—one that extends great security: "There is no single thing in the entire universe which is outside the almighty embrace and safe-keeping of the divine power."

—PA 71

Silence as a Vacuum That Sucks Angels In

Fox: Thomas Aquinas names the angels as "*announcers of divine silence.*" And angels not only do the announcing but help us in understanding announcements. They touch our intellects by the brightness of their own light. . . .

I think this news that angels bring silence is part of our recovering a sacred cosmology. I remember Rusty Schweickart, the astronaut, talking about how it was the cosmic silence out in space that made him a mystic, after having trained for years as a jet-fighter pilot. People who go to the depths of the sea or scuba dive have talked to me about the awesome silence down there. Silence is clearly one of the ways into the heart, into the divine mystery. It's a very special task and a very mysterious one that Aquinas names here in this simple sentence, "Angels are announcers of divine silence."

Sheldrake: Does this mean that one way that we contact the angels is through being silent? It would suggest that whenever we go into a silent space through meditation, insofar as that silence is divine, then the announcement of the divine presence is made through an angel.

Fox: That's right, angels are present. Silence is like a vacuum that sucks angels in. They can't resist sacred silence. But we don't always approach silence through meditation, though that's the obvious route. My experience is that whenever there's an experience of awe, there's an experience of silence as well. In doing ritual, for example, which may not be a silent ritual, when you are doing good prayer, it always raises silence. If that's true, then it's also true that good prayer raises the angels; it makes present the angels.

—PA 92–93

Blind Chance versus Guiding Intelligence in Evolution

Sheldrake: There is a continuing creativity in all realms of nature. Is this all a matter of blind chance, as materialists believe? Or are there guiding intelligences at work in the evolutionary process?

One of the first people to explore this possibility was Alfred Russel Wallace. After he and Darwin together published the theory of evolution by natural selection, Darwin went on to develop a gloomy materialism, which now pervades the thinking of Neo-Darwinism, the orthodox doctrine of academic biology. All of evolution must have happened by chance and through unconscious laws of nature, and it has no meaning or purpose.

By contrast, Wallace came to the conclusion that evolution involved more than natural selection and was guided by creative intelligences, which he identified with angels . . . I am fascinated that these very different conceptions of evolution were expressed by the two founders of evolutionary theory. . . . If you believe there are other forces or intelligences in the universe, then there are other possible sources of creativity, whether you call them angels or not. . . . Our evolutionary cosmology does not have less room for angels but vastly more.

Fox: Yes. I feel very strongly that as a living cosmology comes back, the angels are returning, because they are part of any sound cosmology. Maybe the angels themselves will usher into our cultures some of the imagination that we're calling for. . . . All religious traditions that we know of have something to say about angels—spirits other than human beings.

Buck Ghosthorse, a Lakota spiritual teacher, once said to me, "What you Christians call angels, we Indians call spirits." This is common ground on which all our religious traditions can come together today, in deep ecumenism. Angels are not labeled Buddhist, Muslim, Hindu, Lutheran, Anglican, or Roman Catholic; they are beyond denominationalism . . .   —PA 24–26

Angels as Photons

Fox: I know you were struck in reading Aquinas's statement that angels move from one place to another with no time lapse. You said it reminded you of Einstein's thinking about light. What about the idea of angels as photons, light-bearers?

Sheldrake: When Aquinas discusses how angels move from place to place, his reasoning has extraordinary parallels to both quantum and relativity theories. Angels are quantized; you get a whole angel or none at all; they move as units of action. The only way you can detect their presence is through action; they are quanta of action. And although when they act in one place and then another, from our point of view time elapses while they are moving; from the point of view of the angel this movement is instantaneous, no time elapses. This is just like Einstein's description of the movement of a photon of light. Although we as external observers can measure the speed of light, from the point of view of the light itself, no time elapses as it is traveling. It doesn't get older. We still have light around from 14 billion years ago from soon after the Big Bang in the form of the cosmic microwave background radiation. After all that time, it's still around and still going strong.

So in modern physics there are remarkable parallels to the traditional doctrines about angels, and I think the parallels arise because the same problems are being considered. How does something without mass, without body, but capable of action, move? Angels, according to Aquinas, have no mass, they have no body. And the same goes for photons: they are massless, and you can detect them only by their action.　　　—PA 23

4

Creation Mystics

HILDEGARD OF BINGEN: FEMINIST, MYSTIC, ECO-PROPHET

The creation mystics live out creation spirituality and constitute its most striking lineage. "They go to the edge of consciousness and invite us to accompany them there," notes Fox. Hildegard of Bingen (1098–1181) can rightly be called the "grandmother" of the Rhineland mystic movement that was so richly creation centered. She wrote ten books and the oldest opera in the West. She was a healer and abbess, scientist, theologian, and musical genius. Fox has written three books on her, which include Illuminations of Hildegard of Bingen, *containing twenty-five of her visionary paintings and mandalas;* The Book of Divine Works with Letters and Songs, *containing her last and most mature book along with fifty of her most important letters and ten of her musical pieces. When word was out that Hildegard was to be canonized and declared a Doctor of the Church, Fox wrote* Hildegard of Bingen, a Saint for Our Times: Unleashing Her Power in the 21st Century. (CB)

On Love of Creation

Hildegard waxes ecstatic on the beauty, grace, and sacredness of creation. With her, the Via Positiva is alive and well. She writes: "All of creation is a symphony of joy and jubilation." Notice how Hildegard talks about *all* of creation, which shows how she thinks with a cosmic awareness. All of it is filled with "joy and jubilation." Creation isn't neutral; it isn't just "there." It carries bounty, exuberance, delight, joy, celebration, even jubilation.

Consider what Thomas Berry says in the early 21st century: "In the end the universe can only be explained in terms of celebration. It is all an exuberant expression of existence itself." The great feminist archeologist, Marija Gimbutas, came to the conclusion that the "essence of the goddess civilization was the celebration of life." For Hildegard, the whole universe works together as a "symphony," in that it harmonizes, is interconnected, is celebrative, and is ultimately one.   —HBST 66

Hildegard speaks ecstatically about creation and God's relation to it: "Holy Spirit is Life-giving-life, all movement. . . . Radiant life, worthy of all praise. The Holy Spirit resurrects and awakens everything that is." For Hildegard, "God is life." Indeed, "God lives in every created thing" and "all creation is gifted with the ecstasy of God's light." How different is this from today's science that tells us that every atom in the universe contains photons or light waves?   —HBST 26–28

Hildegard is celebrating the Cosmic Christ, the Word, which she says is "the Light of all lights, and it gives light of itself." . . . Light and love bind us to other creatures as well, for "we, too, have a natural longing for other creatures and we feel a glow of love for them." Do you feel a *glow of love* for other creatures?
—HBST 29–31

Our Struggle for Wisdom

Hildegard pictures our life's journey as a struggle to "set up our tent of wisdom." This refreshing image is a deeply biblical one deriving from the wisdom tradition of Shekinah, the divine presence that accompanies God's people. The tent is a feminine, four-sided divine figure which in her understanding comes folded up in us at the time of our birth as *original wisdom*. Our life journey, therefore, is to set up our tent of wisdom.

But wisdom does not come easily. Much struggle is demanded; confusion, pain, and opposition place themselves in our path. But the "strong soul" perseveres. The strong soul for Hildegard is the virtuous person—virtues are kinds of strengths. There is a strength to merriment, to constancy, to justice, to compassion, that Hildegard not only finds beautiful to behold but essential for personal and communal survival. "Become strong," Hildegarde admonishes. "Oppose the devil like a strong warrior opposes his enemy and you will delight God in your struggle. "Oh, fleeing soul," she counsels, "be strong. Clothe yourself in the armor of light." Wisdom for Hildegard constitutes the very definition of what church ought to be—a gathering of those rejecting the folly of dualism and corruption and war-like attitudes and what we today would call patriarchy in favor of the ways of healing and celebration and cosmos and peace-making.

Wisdom for Hildegard is cosmic—indeed, the keeper of cosmic order, cosmic justice. "With wisdom I have rightly put the universe in order. . . . I, wisdom, bind together heavenly and earthly things as a unity for the good of the people." Wisdom is that bias in creation in favor of goodness, in favor of blessing. Hildegard finds divine revelation and wisdom in all creatures of the universe: "It is God whom human beings know in every creature." Every creature is in fact a "mirror of God," an image of God who is wisdom.   —HBMV xix

The Feminism of Hildegard of Bingen

Hildegard displays at times the fierce energy of both Kali and the Black Madonna. In part, her resilience may have been derived from her Celtic spiritual roots, as one can find this kind of sureness and strength in Celtic women even to this day. It originates from a deep grounding in the Divine Feminine. Hildegard writes about Mary as the "ground of all being." Sometimes we talk about God as ground of all being, but she addresses Mary as ground of all being. This is Goddess talk, the language of the Divine Feminine. It is strong.

Hildegard declares that "God made the form of woman to be the mirror of all his beauty, the embrace of his whole creation." Hildegard underwent a vision in which she ascribes the work of creation to a woman named Love. Her vision echoes the biblical teaching that Wisdom was present at creation. The vision follows:

> I heard a voice speaking to me: "The young woman whom you see is Love. She has her tent in eternity . . . It was love which was the source of this creation in the beginning when God said: 'Let it be!' And it was. As though in the blinking of an eye, the whole creation was formed through love. The young woman is radiant in such a clear, lightning-like brilliance of countenance that you can't fully look at her . . . She holds the sun and moon in her right hand and embraces them tenderly . . . The whole of creation calls this maiden 'Lady.' For it was from her that all of creation proceeded, since Love was the first. She made everything . . . Love was in eternity and brought forth, in the beginning of all holiness, all creatures without any admixture of evil. Adam and Eve as well were produced by love from the pure nature of the Earth."

This amazing vision pronounces on a theology of original blessing.   —HBMV 111–12

The Man in Sapphire Blue: A Study in Compassion

Hildegard paints a mandala of a "man in sapphire blue" which she describes in the following manner: "A most quiet light, and in it burning with flashing fire the form of a man in sapphire blue." We experience in this mandala much that is peacemaking and powerful. The blue colors denote compassion as do the hands of the blue man, extended in a manner of healing and assisting. They are not presented in a vertical and folded manner of stylized piety, but in an extended way. An energy field surrounds the man. Clearly this is a person whose "body is in the soul" and not whose soul is in the body. Notice, too, the aperture at the man's head, so that this powerful healing energy can leave his own field and mix with others—and vice versa. The woven tapestry-like detail of the inner golden circle is reminiscent of basket weaving and the rituals of southwestern Indians, as a Native American told me. In such practices the cosmic web is being celebrated and renewed.

She calls the Creator in this vision a "living" light; the Son, "flash of light"; the Spirit, "fire." She says that this fire of the Holy Spirit binds all things together—"The Holy Spirit streams through and ties together 'eternity' and 'equality' so that they are one. This is like someone tying a bundle together—for there would be no bundle if it weren't tied together—everything would fall apart."

This mandala represents the Divine Trinity. "One light, three persons, one God," she declares. For Hildegard, that God is imaged essentially as curved and circular. This is an ancient tradition in women's religions: Divinity as circle, or circle in motion, that is, spiral. Hildegard writes elsewhere: "A wheel was shown to me, wonderful to behold . . . Divinity is in its omniscience and omnipotence like a wheel, like a circle, a whole, that can neither be understood, nor divided, nor begun nor ended." And again, "just as a circle embraces all that is within it, so does the Godhead embrace all." The imagery of God as circle, God that embraces all, is deeply maternal. "Godhead," which is feminine in both Latin and German, is an all-embracing name for divinity. We celebrate here the curved and all-encompassing power of God. Yet we also celebrate God's nearness, for Hildegard also says: "God hugs you. You are encircled by the arms of the mystery of God." Thus God's power is not an abstract power or a vengeful power but a maternal, loving, and deeply personal power. It is a *compassionate* power. This power cannot in the long run be excluded from our lives or society, for "no one has the power to divide this circle, to surpass it, or to limit it." God is curved—like nature is—and this is part of her feminist awareness.

For Hildegard and for the entire creation-centered tradition, the ultimate power of God, universe, and humanity is *compassion* . . . Hildegard's Christology presented in this picture of the "blue Christ" celebrates Jesus as the revelation of the compassion of God, the incarnation of divine compassion, a human from whom divine compassion shines forth in a special way. It is through him that "the maternal love of the embracing God came" to humankind. Hildegard's identifying compassion with maternal love is insightful when one remembers that the Hebrew word for compassion is the same root word as the word for womb.

But Hildegard, by presenting her Trinity in a mandala form, is revealing still more about divinity. She is revealing how we too are divine and how we, too, are "other Christs" called to bring our compassion from our hearts into our hands and thus serve the world. Her blue Christ has an amazing parallel in Swami Muktanada's vision in the twentieth century of a pearl that morphed into a blue man that in turn healed him of his fear of death and empowered his vocation as a healer and compassion bearer. He called it the most powerful meditation of his life. The Blue Man is an eloquent and affirming archetype for the Sacred Masculine.

—IHB 32–36

Viriditas: *Greening Power*

Hildegard gifts us with a rich concept she calls *viriditas* or "greening power." She talks of "the exquisite greening of trees and grasses," of "earth's lush greening." She says that all of creation and humanity in particular is "showered with greening refreshment, the vitality to bear fruit." Clearly, creativity and greening power are intimately connected here. She says that "greening love hastens to the aid of all. With the passion of heavenly yearning, people who breathe this dew produce rich fruit." Like Eckhart, she was deeply excited by the promise in John's Gospel that we are to "bear fruit, fruit that remains." (Jn. 15.16). She believes that Christ brings "lush greenness" to "shriveled and wilted" people and institutions. She celebrates the Divine Word or Dabhar in this fashion: "The word is all verdant greening, all creativity." She calls God "the purest spring," just as Eckhart would later image God as "a great underground river." For Hildegard, the Holy Spirit is greening power in motion, making all things grow, expand, celebrate. Indeed, for Hildegard salvation or healing is the return of greening power and moistness. She celebrates this in her Opera, *Ordo Virtutum*. "In the beginning all creatures were green and vital; they flourished amidst flowers. Later the green figure itself came down." Thus Jesus is called Greenness Incarnate. "Now bear in mind," she tells us, "that the fullness you made at the beginning was not supposed to wither." She calls Jesus a "green man" in a time when the goddess was returning to culture and along with her, the green man who symbolizes a spiritual warrior defending Mother Earth and celebrating creativity and generativity in men.

What else is *viriditas*? It is God's freshness that humans receive in their spiritual and physical life forces. It is the power of springtime, a germinating force, a fruitfulness that comes from God and permeates all creation. This powerful life force is found in the non-human as well as the human. "The earth sweats germinating power from its very pores," she declares. Instead of seeing body/soul in a warring struggle as did Augustine, Hildegard sees that "the soul is the freshness of the flesh, for the body grows and thrives through it just as the earth becomes fruitful through moisture."

Mary, the mother of Jesus, is celebrated for being the *viridissima virga*, the "greenest of the green branches," the most fruitful of us all. She is a branch "full of the greening power of springtime"— deep overtones of the goddess echo in these teachings. In one of her songs she addresses Mary this way: "You glowing, most green, verdant sprout . . . you bring lush greenness once more" to the "shriveled and wilted" of the world.   —IHB 43–44

Hildegard calls Mary "Mother of all joy."
You have established life!
Ask for us life.
Ask for us radiant joy.
Ask for us the sweet, delicious ecstasy that is forever yours.

This is goddess language. Can patriarchy absorb it? Or do we have here new (but very ancient) wine that, as Jesus taught, can't be contained by the old, brittle, leaky wineskins of patriarchal society or religion?   —HBST 120

Hildegard's Many Contributions to Creation Spirituality

With her recent canonization and being named a "doctor of the church," Hildegard enters the well-guarded and thick patriarchal gates of the Vatican bringing many surprises with her just like the Trojan Horse of old. She brings along the powerful lineage of the creation spirituality tradition, coupled with her fierce commitment to the reality of the Divine Feminine in its various manifestations. Among them are:

- the Cosmic Christ or divine image in all beings
- life and therefore the goddess who is in all of nature
- the "God within" of mysticism
- the motherhood of God
- wisdom
- the circle that is divine power
- Love, the Lady who "made everything" in creation loveable and therefore an original blessing
- the democracy of the Holy Spirit
- the omnipresence of creativity
- the love of Mother Earth
- the fierceness of the warrior
- the work of compassion
- "the king's daughter, justice"
- the Wild Woman
- a relationship that penetrates everything
- keeper of the creative fire
- a church that is *not* defined as hierarchy or institution but as lay people who constitute the "living" and "holy" stones" of mother church and are themselves "houses of prayer" and warriors of virtue.   —HBST 128–29

Hildegard as Eco-Prophet

Hildegard's is a strong voice on behalf of Mother Earth. She thunders, "The earth must not be injured, the earth must not be destroyed." She speaks often of "the web of creation" to which we all belong but humans can rupture. "As often as the elements of the world are violated by ill treatment, so God will cleanse them through the sufferings, through the hardships of human-kind." And, "the high, the low, all of creation God gives to humankind to use. But if this privilege is misused, God's justice permits creation to punish humanity." She urges humanity to "awaken from our dullness and arise vigorously toward justice."
—HBST 41–43

Her passionate defense of Mother Earth derives from her understanding of how much God is present and in love with the earth and all its creatures. "Holy persons draw to themselves all that is earthy," she declares. "As the Creator loves his creation, so creation loves the Creator," and they are related as lover to lover, wife to husband. "Creation is allowed in intimate love to speak to the Creator as if to a lover. "The creation, of course, was fashioned to be adorned, to be showered, to be gifted with the love of the Creator. The entire world has been embraced by this kiss."   —HBST 38–39

The sacredness of nature and earth is everywhere in her writ-ings. Consider this "I am" poem where Divinity speaks:

I am the rain coming from the dew
that causes the grasses to laugh with the joy of life.
I call forth tears, the aroma of holy work.
I am the yearning for good.

Her prophetic voice, wherein she stands up to abbots and bish-ops, clergy and popes, emperors too, exhorting them to resist evil and work harder for justice, is also a lesson for all to take to heart. With Hildegard, we all share a mystical heart of love but also a prophetic call to speak out.   —HBST 34

THOMAS AQUINAS: LOVER OF CREATION

Thomas was born in 1225 near Naples, Italy. His parents placed him in a Benedictine monastery at the age of five with high expectations that he might raise the family fortune by some day becoming abbot at Monte Cassino, the original home of the Benedictine order. But after ten years of a solid education with the monks, sixteen-year-old Aquinas exited the Benedictine monastery and wandered to Naples where a new university (an invention of the late twelfth-century renaissance) had opened its doors in 1224. There he encountered an Irish professor lecturing on Aristotle and science and discovered a new movement called the Dominican Order. Aquinas fell in love with both.

After joining the Dominicans and studying with Albert the Great in Paris and Cologne, he taught theology in Paris and then in Anagni, Orvieto, Rome, and Viterbo in Italy. In 1268, he returned to Paris to wage a fierce battle on behalf of Aristotle, who was being discredited by atheists on the one hand and by fundamentalists on the other. In 1272, he returned to teach in Naples. Throughout these years he wrote prolifically.

In December 1273, he underwent an experience that rendered him mute; he went silent and never wrote another word. He did manage to say that "such things have been revealed to me that all I have written seems to be as so much straw."

Following his death at forty-nine years of age on March 7, 1274, some of his teachings were condemned by the bishops of Paris and Canterbury. However, in 1323 he was canonized a saint. His many books were written all within a twenty-one-year period (1252–73).   —TTA xli–xlii

Fox has written two books on Aquinas. The first, Sheer Joy: Conversations with Thomas Aquinas on Creation Spirituality, *descholasticizes him by interviewing him (with every sentence from Aquinas footnoted). It also contains many passages from Aquinas that have never been translated into English, German, French, or even Italian, giving us a much broader understanding of his thinking. His second,* The Tao of Thomas Aquinas: Fierce Wisdom for Hard Times, *is meant as a practical spiritual guide. Each chapter title is a sentence from Aquinas such as* "'They shall be drunk with the beauty of thy house, that is, the Universe"; "The Greatness of the human person consists in this: that we are capable of the universe"; "Joy is the human's noblest act"; "Religion is supreme thankfulness or gratitude"; "The proper objects of the heart are truth and justice," etc. (CB)

On the Via Positiva: The Nature of God

Aquinas: God is in all things in the most intimate way. Insofar as a thing has existence, it is like God. Just as flaming up comes with fire, so the existence of any creature comes with the divine presence. The first fruit of God's activity in things is existence itself. All other fruits presuppose this one, namely, existence.

Fox: You seem so confident about the absolute holiness and divinity of existence itself. Where do you derive this confidence about the graced mystery of existence?

Aquinas: God is pure existence. The existence of all other things partakes of God's. God is essential existence, and all other things are beings by participation. The essence of God is God's existence. Moses was taught this sublime truth when he asked: "If the children of Israel say to me, 'What is God's name?' what shall I answer them? The Lord replied: 'I am who am; so shalt thou say to the children of Israel: The One who is has sent me to you' (Exod. 3:13–14)."   —SJ 87

Aquinas: God is sheer goodness. . . . Goodness of itself is generous. God is supremely good and therefore supremely generous. . . . There is no loss of the original goodness involved in the sharing [of goodness with creatures].   —SJ 99, 100

Love of Self and Others

Aquinas: Self-love is the form and root of all friendship. Well-ordered self-love is right and natural—so much so that the person who hates himself or herself sins against nature. To know and to appreciate your own worth is no sin.

Fox: What would you say follows from this healthy self-love?

Aquinas: It is natural for human beings to love their neighbor and the truth.

—SJ 99

God's Love and Creation's Goodness

Fox: You seem to find much love in the universe, then, if, as you say, all things act out of love and there is an "original goodness."

Aquinas: The habitual or conditioned appetite for something as for its own good is called love.

Fox: Where does all this love come from?

Aquinas: God, who is the cause of all, on account of an excess of the goodness that is God's own, loves all things. And from love God makes all things, giving them being. And God perfects all things by filling them individually with their own perfections. And God contains all things by preserving them in being. And God converts all things, that is, God orders them toward the Godself as toward an end. . . . Love, by which God loves, is the actual existence of goodness in the things themselves, and on account of this, one says that everything is good, since it preexists causality in the good. . . . For out of the love of God's own goodness it happened that God wished to pour forth and share the divine goodness with others, as far as was possible, namely, through the mode of likeness, with the result that the divine goodness not only remained in God but also flowed out to other things.

—SJ 108

All Delight in God

Fox: God, then, is our enjoyment and our delight?

Aquinas: Delight is not best just because it is delight, but because it is repose in the best. The very sight of God causes delight. At the sight of God, the mind can do nothing but delight. Human's salvation consists in the enjoyment of God, who gives bliss to human beings. How appropriate, then, that Jesus took delight in God, for the originator of a process should be its master. Our ultimate and principal good is to enjoy God. Eternal life consists in enjoying God.

Fox: Do other creatures besides human beings take delight in God?

Aquinas: All things desire God as their end whenever they desire any good whatsoever. Whatever attracts them—be it intellective, sensitive, or unconscious desire—all of it is attractive because of some likeness it has to God.

Fox: A likeness to God?

Aquinas: Every creature participates in some way in the likeness of the divine essence. Every creature represents God and is like God insofar as it possesses some perfection.   —SJ 120

On the Via Negativa: Meditation, Receptivity, and Being Emptied

Fox: To appreciate God's fullness, we also need to be emptied.

Aquinas: Nothing receives what it already has, since as Aristotle remarks, the recipient must be devoid of the thing received. . . . The first requirement, then, for the contemplation of wisdom is that we should take complete possession of our minds before anything else does.   —SJ 208, 210

Fox: Clearly the Via Negativa is a path of *receptivity*. I find your teaching on this way to God to be deeply Zen-like. It is surprising to hear from you, so often depicted as the ultimate rationalist of the West, such Zen-like teachings of the "most perfect" path to God.

Aquinas: Divine wisdom is excellently praised as "irrational," insofar as it exceeds reason; and as "mindless," insofar as it exceeds mind or intellect; and as "stupid," insofar as it exceeds the condition of the mind, namely, wisdom.

Fox: These surprising phrases you use—"irrational, mindless, stupid"—seem to celebrate holy folly and other gifts of what we call today the right hemisphere of the brain.

Aquinas: Divine truth is ineffable to us and exceeds all the reason we have . . . The greatest accomplishment of the human mind is to know that it does not know who God is. —SJ 208, 196

On the Via Creativa: Things Are Godlike and Possess the Dignity of Causality

Fox: I hear you saying that the likeness that things have to God is a likeness not only in being but also in the power of generating.

Aquinas: Things were made like God not only in being but also in acting. Whatever causes God assigns to certain effects, God gives them the power to produce those effects. . . . The dignity of causality is imparted even to creatures.

Fox: It follows from what you are saying that we and God generate together—we are co-creators?

Aquinas: God's power is in every natural thing, since God is in all things by the divine essence, presence, and power. —SJ 255

Working and Creating from the Heart

Fox: Our work, then, must come from our heart?

Aquinas: Always rejoice in the good work that you do. . . . One who knows the cause knows the effect. But the cause of all human effects is the heart.

Fox: Now we are truly speaking of art as meditation—of our returning to our hearts to give birth by centering there. And we encounter the divine in this return to the heart to give birth.

Aquinas: God, who makes the heart, knows it. . . . God knows the heart. Therefore, also its works.

Fox: And we encounter the truth of our experience when we return to our inner self as well?

Aquinas: Contemplation is nothing else than the consideration of truth.

Fox: Thus art as meditation brings forth the deepest desires of our hearts. —SJ 289

On the Via Transformativa: Imitating God through Compassion

Aquinas: Compassion is the fire that Jesus came to set on the earth. . . . Through compassion human beings imitate God.

Fox: "Imitation of God"—that would seem to be what a spiritual path is all about, the living out of our divinity.

Aquinas: To be compassionate is proper to God the Father. . . . God is compassion itself. God's holy name is the name of the divine compassion.

Fox: If compassion comprises our imitation of God, then we really need to delve deeply into the meaning and practice of compassion, don't we? What do we mean when we say to imitate God is to be compassionate?

Aquinas: In every work of God, viewed at its primary source, there appears compassion. In all that follows, the power of compassion remains, and works indeed with even greater force.
—SJ 401, 385

Fox: And so there is no compassion without justice?

Aquinas: God is compassionate. God does not work in opposition to divine justice, but transcends. Compassion is the fulfillment of justice, not its abolition.

Fox: Please elaborate on the meaning of this path of compassion that we are called to travel.

Aquinas: In Matthew's gospel we read: "Blessed are the compassionate for they themselves shall attain compassion." To be compassionate is to have a heart that suffers from the misfortune of others because we think of it as our own. But we are pained by our own misfortune and are eager to repel it, so you are truly compassionate when you are eager to repel the misfortune of others.

Fox: So compassion is our capacity to treat others as ourselves—a sign of our radical interdependence.

Aquinas: Compassion is the fullness of all graces.   —SJ 392

Justice and Joy

Fox: Joy is no obstacle to our just actions.

Aquinas: Pleasure arising from virtuous activities will be more delightful than any other pleasures. One may by the judgment of one's reason choose to be affected by a passion in order to work more promptly with the cooperation of the sensitive appetite. And thus a passion of the soul increases the goodness of an action. . . . Our passions are the very seat of virtues . . . and while it is a great thing to do miracles, it is even a greater thing to live a virtuous life.   —SJ 326

Fox: I hear you saying that an increase of virtue, for example, our love of justice, actually increases our passion.

Aquinas: The more perfect a virtue is, the more does it cause passion.

Fox: And this too constitutes our imitation of God?

Aquinas: Sheer joy is God's, and this demands companionship.

Fox: This would suggest that the very reason the universe exists is for the sake of joy—the divine joy and the joy of all creatures, ourselves included.   —SJ 100

"Joy Is the Human's Noblest Act"

That "joy is the human's noblest act" might amaze us. Really? Is joy our noblest act? Why not fighting for justice or dying for a noble cause? Aquinas reminds us that even justice exists for the sake of joy—a just world is a balanced world and is therefore conducive to joy for the many, not just the few. Justice is not an end in itself, but joy is. To remain in joy through hardship and loss, disappointment and struggle, is no small thing. It demands a deep spiritual life. A depth of soul. Working for justice in order to share the joy renders joy more available to more people.   —TTA 37

Fear Enslaves

Fox: No wonder the prophet is seldom popular! He or she names the fear of the times.

Aquinas: Fear makes people slaves. Love sets them free.

Fox: Sometimes I wonder what price humanity pays for fear.

Aquinas: When they are brought up under a regime of fear, people inevitably degenerate. They become mean-spirited and adverse to many and strenuous feats.

Fox: And so fear discourages magnanimity and the expansion of the soul. Of course, the prophet offers some good news too in the form of hope for liberation.   —SJ 453–54

"Revelation Comes in Two Volumes: Nature and the Bible"

All revelation is not found in a book—it is also found in nature itself, in creation. Aquinas insists that all people should study nature and that our meditation on nature opens up the divine to us. "One meditates on creation in order to view and marvel at divine wisdom."   —SJ 78

Citing the psalmist who sings, "I meditate on all your works, I muse on the work of your hands" (Ps 143:5), he observes that "meditation is indispensable for a well-instructed faith." And since "all creatures confess that they are made by God," it is our job as humans to examine creatures for the revelation of the divine that they carry within them.   —SJ 80–81

We are to read creatures as we do books. Creatures can therefore be objects of the practice of *lectio divina*—and they ought to be. We contemplate them, just as monks contemplate the biblical scriptures. Both are spiritual practices to awaken and strengthen the soul.   —TTA 17, 19

It follows that "a mistake about creation results in a mistake about God." It is difficult to come across any statement that more deeply celebrates the vocation of the scientist's search for truth than this one.

All the mistakes we make about nature steer us away from our understanding of Divinity. Consider the mistake that says homosexuality is "contrary to nature" (which it may be for heterosexuals but not for homosexuals, who constitute roughly 8 percent of any human population). Furthermore, we have counted 464 other species that sport homosexual populations. Or the mistake that the difference between races is anything but a superficial difference. Or the mistake that the sun turns around our earth, or that stars are eternal; or that species have always been here, or that the earth is 6500 years old, or that God punishes us through disease, or that men are active and women are passive, or that men are born to rule, or that there has always been patriarchy, and so on. Yes, "a mistake about creation results in a mistake about God." It follows that an insight about creation may result in insights about God as well.

Aquinas's observation underscores the value and necessity of our searching for truth. "The proper objects of the heart are truth and justice." He says. Justice and truth go together, just as injustice and lies go together.

Humans regularly project onto Divinity our own unexamined shadows, and this renders Divinity often very scary indeed.

—TTA 25–26

"God Is the Artist of Artists"

One of Aquinas's favorite names for Divinity is *artist*. He says, "Every artist loves what they give birth to—the poet loves his poems, the potter her pots, how can God—who is the artist of everything—hate anything?"

—TTA 53

"The First and Primary Meaning of Salvation Is This: To Preserve Things in the Good"

Having lived eighty years on this planet, and having heard quite a few sermons and religious teachers over the years, I remain quite nervous whenever I hear the words "salvation" or "redemption." Perhaps that is because history reminds us that those who are busy "saving" or "redeeming" others are often rather shortsighted regarding their own limitations and those of the ideologies to which they adhere. I am thinking of crusades and inquisitions, of witch burnings and book burnings, of declarations of heresy and all the rest--dark forces of projections and scapegoating done in the name of a punitive deity wrapped in the clothing of orthodoxy and power. The term "lord and savior Jesus Christ," for example, often makes my hair stand on end—savior of what? Of whom? From what? From where? For what end?

But that salvation means *preserving things in the good* gives us a rock solid basis for saving Mother Earth and her many

creatures, humans included. Here lies a deep foundation for an
eco-theology.   —TTA 45

*"Every Being Is a Name for God;
And No Being Is a Name for God"*

By opening up our minds and hearts to multiple names for God,
Aquinas encourages us to let go of stale and tired God-nam-
ing to become young and fresh again in our relationship to the
divine. He also encourages our creativity and that of one's culture (including science) to be creative.   —TTA 79–80

*"Conscience Is More to Be Obeyed Than Authority
Imposed from the Outside"*

Conscience plays a central role in Aquinas's teaching about
morality. We are to develop a conscience and live by it. The passages in Aquinas about conscience always struck me deeply as I
grew up in a very Protestant culture in the 1950s, and heard time
and again that it was Martin Luther who "invented" conscience
as the bottom line in morality . . .

Without diluting Luther's invocation of conscience, consider
these teachings from Aquinas three hundred years earlier:

> Conscience is more to be obeyed than authority imposed
> from the outside. By following a right conscience you
> not only do not incur sin but are also immune from
> sin, whatever superiors may say to the contrary. To act
> against one's conscience and to disobey a superior can
> both be sinful. Of the two, the first is worse since the
> dictate of conscience is more binding than the decree of
> external authority.

He elaborates: "Every judgment of conscience . . . is obligatory
in such a way that anyone who acts against their conscience
always sins." To go against conscience—even a mistaken one—is
to "contravene the law of God."   —TTA 117–18

Aquinas has been rightly praised for introducing the idea of
the *common good* to Western jurisprudence. And the common

good, he teaches, is the basis of all healthy laws. Martin Luther King Jr., in his iconic *Letter from Birmingham Jail*, cites Aquinas for his insistence that bad laws ought not to be obeyed. Conscience reigns. The work of the prophet is "not only to apprehend something, but also to speak or to do something." To stand up and be counted therefore. —TTA 118, 121

"Playfulness, or Fun, Is a Virtue"

According to Aquinas, prophets must undergo practices that refresh one's mind, spirit, and body on a regular basis. Aquinas celebrates the virtue of *eutrapelia,* which he defines as "playfulness" and calls for busy people to make room for it: "Words or deeds wherein nothing further is sought than the soul's delight are called *playful* or *humorous*. Hence, it is necessary at times to make use of them, in order to give rest, so to speak, to the soul." We need to rest the soul just as we must rest the body, and "the soul's rest is pleasure." —TTA 137

MEISTER ECKHART: CREATION MYSTIC, PROPHET, DEEP ECUMENIST

Meister Eckhart (1260–1327) has had a profound influence on Fox's life and work. The medieval German mystic is the most cited author in Fox's writings and is a paragon of the creation-centered tradition. While studying Eckhart's writings, Fox discovered the four paths and many of the themes of creation spirituality.

Matthew has written three books on Meister Eckhart including Passion for Creation: The Earth-Honoring Spirituality of Meister Eckhart *(originally called* Breakthrough: Meister Eckhart's Creation Spirituality in New Translation. *He presents thirty-seven sermons translated from the critical German editions with a commentary after each. Madonna Kolbenschlag, author of* Kissing Sleeping Beauty Goodbye, *called that book "the most important book on mysticism in 500 years." His second book was* Meditations with Meister Eckhart, *which is a simple "right brain" book that gathers many of Eckhart's most meaningful teachings, one per page. And most recently,* Meister Eckhart: A Mystic-Warrior for Our Times *pairs Eckhart with a different thinker in each chapter, whether Rabbi Abraham Heschel, Carl Jung, Pierre Teilhard de Chardin, Black Elk, Rumi, the Beguines, or Thich Nhat Hanh, and thereby draws out the deep and ecumenical wisdom of Eckhart.* (CB)

Via Positiva: "All Creatures Are Words of God" (Sermon 1)

Eckhart preaches: *God is a word which speaks itself. Wherever God is, there he speaks this Word; wherever he is not, there he does not speak. God is spoken and unspoken. The Father is a speaking action, and the Son is an active speech. What is in me goes out from me; if I am thinking it, then my word reveals it and yet remains inside me. It is in this way that the Father speaks the unspoken Son, and yet the Son remains in the Father. I have often said that God's exit is his entrance. As much as I am near God, to that extent God speaks himself in me. To the extent that all creatures who are gifted with reason go out from themselves in all that they do, to that same extent they go into themselves. With merely material creatures this is not the case; the more they do, the more they go out from themselves.* —PC 57

God said, "Let there be light" and there was light, we are told. God's Word gets things done. Thus Eckhart can say that the Father or Creator is a speaking action—who truly creates and does not merely cogitate about truth or about creating. So full of mystery and power in this creative Word who is God that we humans are left dumb and speechless by the beauty of creation. Creation is almost too holy for us, surely too holy for mere human words. "The entire created order is sacred," says Eckhart . . . . We cannot name God who "is higher than names or nature," and when we try to put a name on God, "then it is not God." God is bigger than we think, bigger than we speak. "God is the God beyond God." —PC 60

All creation is good and gift-giving. It is itself a blessing from God. Creatures—all of them—are divine blessings and a word from God. It is in their activities and in expressing their fullest potential that creatures echo God most loudly. Moreover, the most successful of all God's words, the word that is God's Son, is intimate to creatures and the continual act of creation. As Eckhart puts it, "The Father speaks the Son from his entire (creative) power, and he speaks him in all things." Elsewhere Eckhart says: "God pours out in the Son all creatures."   —PC 61

Another tension in creation is that between expressing God and failing to express God. "All creatures want to express God in all their works; let them all speak, coming as close as they can, they still cannot speak him. Whether they want to or not, whether it is pleasing or painful to them, they all want to speak God, and he still remains unspoken."

As much as creatures strive to reveal God, they are not in the long run up to that task, for "the brightness of the divine nature is ineffable. God is a word but an unexpressed word." The Word retains something of the divine silence, the divine mystery.
                                                                      —PC 62

God is constantly speaking only one thing. What is that one word? It is God and creation: "In this one utterance he speaks his Son and at the same time the Holy Spirit and all creatures." The word of God appears as things created here below and so we imagine that we hear *two distinct words—God and the creature*. But we need to improve our hearing. We are to hear just one; we are to hear creation and listen to the Creator in one act. For God and creation are one utterance. Creation is an expression of divinity, indeed a kind of divinity. . .   —PC 70

Via Negativa: How a Radical Letting Go Becomes a True Letting Be (Sermon 15)

"Blessedness opened its mouth of wisdom and spoke: 'Blessed are the poor in spirit, for theirs is the kingdom of heaven.' (Mt. 5:3). . . . This wisdom has declared that the poor are blessed. . . .

There is still another kind of poverty, an inner poverty, by which our Lord's word is to be understood when he says: 'Blessed are the poor in spirit.' He is a poor person who wills nothing and knows nothing and has nothing."   —PC 213

Eckhart invented words for letting go and letting be, *Abgeschiedenheit* and *Gelassenheit,* respectively. "If a person wants to become like God, insofar as a creature can have any likeness to God, then this can only happen through letting go." Indeed, we "sink eternally from letting go to letting go into God."

—PC 221

Letting be is a state of being open and sensitive. It means, says Eckhart, to be "receptive of all spirit." "Our Lord speaks very clearly*:* 'Blessed are the poor in spirit.' He who has nothing is poor. 'Poor in spirit' means that, as the eye is poor and bare of color and yet receptive of all colors, in the same way the person who is poor in spirit is receptive of all spirit, and the spirit of all spirits is God." Letting go leads to letting be and to developing an ever deeper sensitivity and openness to the spirit.

—PC 222–23

Compassion Is an Ocean (Sermon 31)

Eckhart hints that just as the best name for the unnamable God is Compassion, so too the finest name for the unnamable soul is Compassion. After all, the innermost part of the soul is the *imago Dei.* Where we create from our innermost being, we are always creating compassion.   —PC 444

For Eckhart, compassion is not only an ocean; it is a *fathomless* ocean; it is not only a sea, it is space itself. Eckhart is driven into cosmic language to call on his cosmic experience in an effort to picture compassion. A compassionate consciousness presumes a cosmic consciousness. "Compassion means that God sets the soul in the highest and purest place which it can occupy: in space, in the sea, in a fathomless ocean; and there God works compassion. Therefore the prophet says: 'Lord, have compassion on the people who are in you.'"   —PC 445

What are some consequences of this breakthrough in consciousness by which we are awakened to the fact of our swimming in a space and a sea of compassion? One consequence is the breakdown of all dualistic thinking. For we are not alone in this divine sea. All creatures have been born in the same holy fluid; we do not swim alone but in a common sea of oneness with others. This means that all beings are interdependent. "God's peace prompts fraternal service, so that one creature sustains the other. One is enriching the other; that is why *all creatures are interdependent.*" Creatures in this common sea serve one another and sustain one another. Eckhart's consciousness of interdependence is crucial to grasping what true compassion is about. Indeed, the late Thomas Merton defined compassion as a "keen awareness of the interdependence of all living beings which are all part of one another and all involved in one another."

Another consequence of our swimming together in a common sea of compassion is that all otherness is broken down. We truly see the oneness that is ours. As Angelus Silesius observed, drawing on Eckhart's theology, "there are no objects of compassion because there are no objects." To know that there are no objects but only interdependencies and shared energies—this is the consciousness behind true compassion. —PC 446–67

It is also the consciousness derived from today's physics, namely, that relation more than frozen atoms forms the basis of matter. Eckhart said as much seven centuries ago when he declared, "relation is the essence of everything that exists." —PC 198

Bathing in one sea of compassion, "I become all things, as he is, and I am one and the same being with him." When all otherness is broken through, then we may "be all in all, as God is all in all." Our oneness is a oneness in one another but also in God. This is why the two commandments that Jesus left us are really only one commandment—which is a reward, not an order. For the reward is the pleasure of swimming in a divine sea, and loving creature and Creator in one act of love. Dualisms cease. —PC 448

In this amazing sermon on compassion, Eckhart also challenges our understanding of *soul*. He declares that "a master who has spoken the best about the soul says that all human science can never fathom what the soul is in its ground. To know what the soul is, one needs supernatural knowledge. We do not know about what the powers of the soul do when they go out to do their work; we know a little about this, but not very much. What the soul is in its ground, no one knows. What one can know about it must be supernatural; it must be from grace. The soul is where God works compassion. Amen."   —PC 442

Eckhart is saying that until we know and do compassion, we do not have a soul yet. We are soulless. For Eckhart, compassion is not merely a moral norm. It is a consciousness, a way of seeing the world and responding to the world. It is a way of living out the truth of our inness with God and with one another. The word *in* plays a prominent role, for Eckhart develops his theology of compassion from his theology of inness or panentheism. Consider John's imagery of our panentheistic swimming in compassion: "Anyone who lives in love lives in God, and God lives in him." (1 Jn. 4:16)   —PC 443, 446

Justice, the Prophetic Side to Compassion

Eckhart links compassion and justice directly when he says, "compassion means justice." It is his emphasis on justice that drove him to develop sermons on how God is justice and justice must lie at the heart of our work; and how we need to drive the "merchant mentality" that consumer capitalism addicts us to from our souls and how we need to learn to work "among things but not in things" and how bread is given us "for others, on account of others and with others and especially the poor"; and "everyone is an aristocrat" or a "royal person" deserving of being treated with dignity; and how compassion is also about celebration, for "whatever happens to another, whether it be a joy or a sorrow, happens to me." This is also why Marxist philosopher Ernst Bloch points out that Eckhart was an important influence on Karl Marx.   —ME 235–37

Eckhart as Deep Ecumenist

Eckhart was an important influence on Carl Jung, who said he found "the key to the unconscious" in Eckhart. Eckhart's work is profoundly ecumenical—Japanese Zen teacher Dr. Suzuki urged Thomas Merton to read Eckhart, calling Eckhart "the one Zen thinker" of the West. In doing so, Merton was converted to being a prophetic Christian the last ten years of his life, writing in his final work, his *Asian Journal*, "Eckhart is my lifeboat." Ananda Coomeraswamy said reading Eckhart is like reading the Upanishads. I have brought these thinkers and also Thich Nhat Hanh, Rabbi Abraham Heschel, Pierre Teilhard de Chardin, Black Elk, Rumi, Hafiz, ibn Arabi, Adrienne Rich, Dorothee Soelle, Howard Thurman and others together with Eckhart in my book, *Meister Eckhart: A Mystic-Warrior for Our Times*. Eckhart is a deep ecumenist par excellence. Indeed, he gave credit for his concept of the "spark of the soul" to Muslim philosopher Avicenna at least thirteen different times in thirteen different sermons. He tapped so deeply into his own Christian soul that he came to that "underground river" (his term for God) that is the common river of universal wisdom.   — ME 1–220

Additional Rich Teachings from Meister Eckhart

On the Via Positiva

God becomes where any creature expresses God.

Isness is so noble. No creature is so tiny that it lacks isness. If a caterpillar falls from a tree, it climbs up a wall in order to preserve its isness. So noble is isness!

The moment I flowed out from the Creator, all creatures stood up and shouted: "Behold, here is God!" They were correct. . . . What is God? God is! . . . Isness is God.   — MME 12f.

Every creature is a word of God and a book about God.
                                                          —MME 14

God is at home. It is we who have gone out for a walk.
                                                          —MME 15

On the Via Negativa

When one has learned to let go and let be, then one is well disposed, and he or she is always in the right place, whether in society or in solitude. One who is rightly disposed has God with him/herself in actual fact in all places, just as much in the street and in the midst of many people as in church, or the desert, or a monastic cell.   —MME 63

As long as we perform our works in order to go to heaven, we are simply on the wrong track. Until we learn to work and to live without a why, we have not learned to work or to live or to love, or why. . . . The only way to live is like the rose which lives without a why.   —MME 61, 30

I pray God to rid me of God. . . . God's exit is her entrance.
—MME 50f.

One should love God mindlessly, by this I mean that your soul ought to be without mind or mental activities or images or representations. Bare your soul of all mind and stay there without mind.   —MME 46

On the Via Creativa

It is good for a person to receive God into himself or herself, and I call this receptivity *the work of a virgin.* But it is better when God becomes fruitful with a person. For becoming fruitful as a result of a gift is the only gratitude for the gift. I call such a person *a wife*, and in this sense the term *wife* is the noblest term we can give the soul. It is far nobler than *virgin.* Every day such a person bears fruit a hundred times or a thousand times or countless times, giving birth and become fruitful out of the most noble foundation of all.   —MME 77

This is the fullness of time—when the son of God is begotten in you."   —MME 84

Whatever I want to express in its truest meaning must emerge from within me and pass through an inner form. It cannot come from outside to the inside but must emerge from within.
—MME 87

On the Via Transformativa

Spirituality is not to be learned by flight from the world, by running away from things, or by turning solitary and going apart from the world. Rather, we must learn an inner solitude wherever or with whomsoever we may be. We must learn to penetrate things and find God there.

A person works in a stable. That person has Breakthrough. What does he/she do? She returns to work in the stable.

—MME 90f.

All virtue of the just and every work of the just is nothing other than the Son—who is the New Creation—being born from the Father. In the depths of our being, where justice and work are one, we work one work and a New Creation with God. . . . The just person is like God, for God is justice. Whoever resides in justice resides in God and is God. —MME 94f

For the just person, to act justly is to live; justice is her life; her being alive; her being to the very extent that she is just.

—MME 96

Whoever understands my teaching on justice, understands everything I have to say. —WG 112

The outward work will never be puny if the inward work is great. And the outward work can never be great or even good if the inward one is puny or of little worth. The inward work invariably includes in itself all expansiveness, all breadth, all length, all depth. Such a work receives and draws all its being from nowhere else except from and in the heart of God.

—MME 99

Those who follow compassion find life for themselves, justice for their neighbor, and glory for God. . . . Compassion means justice. . . . You may call God *love*, you may call God *goodness*, but the best name for God is *compassion*. —MME 103, 111

JULIAN OF NORWICH: THE RETURN OF THE DIVINE FEMININE

Julian of Norwich (1342–ca.1429) lived through the worst pandemic in European history. The bubonic plague, Thomas Berry proposes, practically killed creation spirituality in the West because it moved people from trusting creation and the God in creation to fearing creation. Julian, however, is a champion of the goodness and grace of nature—even while a pandemic raged around her. She is also the first woman to write a book in English (though it was not published for three hundred years). Mirabai Starr, translator of Julian's text, believes that Julian most probably lost her child and her husband in the pandemic. (MF)

Julian and the Pandemic

Julian is a stunning thinker, a profound theologian and mystic, a fully awake woman, and a remarkable guide with a mighty vision to share for twenty-first-century seekers. She is a special chaperone for those navigating a time of pandemic. Julian knew a thing or two about "sheltering in place," because she was an anchoress—that is, someone who, by definition, is literally walled up inside a small space for life. Julian also knew something about fostering a spirituality that can survive the trauma of a pandemic. While others all about her were freaking out about nature gone awry, Julian kept her spiritual and intellectual composure, staying grounded and true to her belief in the goodness of life, creation, and humanity and, in no uncertain terms, inviting others to do the same . . .

The plague first struck in Norwich in 1349, when Julian was only seven years old, but it kept returning in waves. By the 1370s, when Julian wrote her first book, the population of England was cut in half. So many people died that they were buried five deep in mass graves. All the street cleaners in London died of the plague, and two out of three clergy died—and probably the best and bravest since they were serving the sick and dying when they caught the deadly disease.

The bubonic plague was terrifying and ugly. . . . And not only was it highly contagious, but there was no Centers for Disease Control to inform populations of the source or how to avoid it, and certainly no hopes or promises of a vaccine. . . . Yes, this was the pandemic that stared Julian in the face her whole life long. She must have grown up with death and fear all around her. Yet she did not flinch . . .

Julian's visions or "showings" occurred in 1373, when she was thirty years of age. She edited and re-edited her book through her lifetime.

Her response to the pandemic is amazingly grounded in a love of life and gratitude. She is not in denial, however, about the deadly disease. It is from that experience of death all around her and meditating on the cruel crucifixion of Christ, that she interpreted as a communal, not just a personal event, that her visions arrived.

—JN xvii–xviii

Showings—Revelations of Divine Love

Julian offers us two titles for her book, one is *Showings* and the other is *Revelations of Divine Love*. Of course, neither title nullifies the other—the subject matter of these showings, revelations, and illuminations can be summarized as *divine love*—a love that Julian sees everywhere in creation and within the human soul. She insists that we must do inner work, including dying and letting go to come to grips with love all over again. Our outer worlds and our response to everyday events can conceal or distort our inner and deepest self, and so we must "dig and ditch" (Julian's words) to recover it . . .

Julian was so close to death that her friends called a priest to administer the last rites.

Instead of dying, however, she underwent a kind of death and with it a kind of resurrection like what Thomas Aquinas calls the "first resurrection"—that is, an experience of "waking up" in this lifetime. Some might call it enlightenment, others breakthrough, or *satori*.

—JN xxvi–xxvii

A Singular Theology

Julian chose not to live in a monastery as an adult but to become an anchoress, living more or less as a religious recluse in a cell attached to a church. . . . A singular characteristic of her writing is that she cites very few theologians or even biblical texts. Having learned to integrate her readings thoroughly into her own thinking and with years of contemplative study, she creates her own theology. She learns to trust her own experience, especially the revelations themselves, and she spends decades following her first book unpacking it for it is "full of secrets" and hold layers of meaning that it takes her years of deciphering to arrive at "the full teaching," which she comes to "understand over time."

—JN xxx–xxxi

All Spiritual Seekers Are the Cosmic Christ

Julian makes explicit on many occasions that she is speaking to a very broad audience—one that includes those of us who live 650 years later. "In God's sight, all humanity is one person, and all people are a single humanity." She sees Christ as an embodiment of humanity itself. "This is what I understood about Christ's human aspect: Christ himself embodies all humanity." If Christ offers liberation to any, he offers it to all. "His sweet incarnation and blessed passion will liberate us all, because he is our head and we all the parts of his body." For Julian, the traditional teaching of the church as the mystical body of Christ is extended to the entire human race. Moreover, "Christ represents the spiritual yearning in us all. Christ is all spiritual seekers, and all spiritual seekers are Christ." Here Julian is invoking the Cosmic Christ, who is found in all beings and in all human beings . . .

One must not fail to recognize what a powerful political stand Julian makes when she insists on her book being universal and for all. After all, one of the popular responses to the Black Death was to create scapegoats—namely, "heretics" and also Jews. Indeed, anti-semitism abounded during the pandemic as people looked for someone to blame. Many Jews fled England.

But there is not an ounce of anti-semitism or heresy attacks in any of Julian's books. She also utterly rejects the notion that personal sins were the cause of the pandemic (a mentality that found expression in the flagellation movements) . . . In fact, she prefers to say that our mistakes often lead to a greater good, and that sin is overrated. Instead of focusing on sin, she advises us to focus more on our better natures and the grace that is found there.

—JN xxxii–xxxiv

If the Church Had Chosen to Follow Julian

I might propose, after fifty years of researching, writing, and teaching the creation spirituality tradition, that if the church had chosen to follow Julian of Norwich and the lineage that she heralds, neither the Protestant Reformation nor the Catholic Counter-Reformation would have been necessary—not to mention the religious wars, imperial invasions, and decimations of indigenous people that followed. Nor would we be facing the devastating *matricide* toward Mother Earth that is happening today and that we have witnessed since the rise of industrialization.

—JN 39

The Divine Feminine and the Motherhood of God

The Black Death had a significant impact on motherhood and mothering in Julian's time. Barbara Tuchman, in her classic work on the fourteenth century, *A Distant Mirror*, reveals that "women appear rarely as mothers" in the art of Julian's time. Even the Virgin Mary is portrayed with the child Jesus always at a distance. No attempt was made to illustrate a close relationship between mother and child. Tuchman's explanation for this phenomenon is tied to the fact that the survival rate for children was very low in the time of the pandemic—one out of three. Mothers were, therefore, afraid to come too close to their children in order to spare themselves the agony of almost certain separation. Brendan Doyle poses the question: "Is Julian also trying to redeem the word 'mother?'" . . .

Julian's rich teachings about the motherhood of God include the following statements: "Just as God is truly our Father, so also is God truly our Mother." Delight and parenting go together in divinity: "God feels great delight to be our Father and God feels great delight to be our Mother."

What are the characteristics of a mother for Julian? "Compassion is a kind and gentle property that belongs to the Motherhood in tender grace." What is this tender compassion about? "Compassion protects, increases our sensitivity, gives life and heals." At the root of compassion lies love in action. "The ground of compassion is love and the working of compassion keeps us in love." Compassion, then, is love at work. It is an action. "Compassion is a sweet gracious working in love, mingled with abundant kindness; for compassion works at taking care of us and makes all things become good." Compassion is about putting kindness and caring into action. It is our work. "A mother's service is nearest, readiest and surest." Service is part of motherhood.

Often the test of compassion is not when things are going well, but when darkness descends and troubles occur. The dark night of the soul invites compassion and stretches our capacity for compassion—it becomes a school for compassion. Failure happens. As Julian puts it, "Compassion allows us to fail measurably and in as much as we fail, in so much we fall; and in so much as we fall, in so much we die; for we must die if we fail to see and feel God who is our life." Again . . . Julian addresses death and the many deaths we undergo in life, especially during a pandemic. Only after these dyings do we undergo that awakening we know as the "first resurrection" . . .

Julian acclaims the divine feminine and divine motherhood not only in God the Creator but also in Jesus and the Christ. Julian often speaks about the motherhood of Jesus and the motherly qualities of Jesus. In doing so, she underscores the importance of incorporating the divine feminine into our entire mindset, including our understanding of the Christ. For example, she assures us that Jesus "is our Mother, Brother and Liberator."

In the light of faith, she teaches, "our Mother, Christ, and our good Lord, the Holy Spirit, lead us in this passing life," And she tells us that "Jesus is our true Mother in whom we are endlessly carried and out of whom we will never come." He is "our Mother of Mercy" who "restores and redeems us."

Julian recognizes "three ways to look at" the motherhood of God: "the first is that she created our human nature. The second is that she took our human nature upon herself, which is where the motherhood of grace begins. And the third is motherhood in action." Clearly, she is bringing the divine feminine into the bosom of the Trinity with this teaching. For her the divine feminine is not a *supplement to* divinity but dwells and acts deeply *from within* the entire Godhead. Nature, grace, and action all come together, she says, for it is "All One Love" . . .   —JN 48–55

Goodness and Joy

Julian urges people to abandon ideas about a God who judges and punishes people—she says God has no wrath, and instead counsels people to dwell on goodness, joy, and awe . . .

"God had revealed his goodness with such abundance and plenitude," observes Julian. We live in a world abundant and overflowing with goodness—and "the first good thing is the goodness of nature." Here she tells us to get out of our own stuckness with the human condition and open our eyes and hearts to the abundant goodness found in nature . . .

Julian warns us that our "faulty reason" can often, and especially when times are rough, render us "too blind to comprehend the wondrous wisdom of God, too limited to grasp the power and goodness" of what is being revealed to us . . .

Julian identifies divinity with goodness itself when she declares that "God is all that is good. God has created all that is made. God loves all that he has created. And so anyone who, in loving God, loves all his fellow creatures loves all that is. All those who are on the spiritual path contain the whole of creation, and the Creator." Why is that? "God is the same thing as nature."

—JN 21–22

The Oneing of God and Us

Julian invented the word *oneing* in English, and even today, seven centuries after she lived, the word is rare for many of us English speakers. Maybe it is time to bring it back and alive again! . . .

Oneing is Julian's word for the mystical experience . . . "In our creation we were knit and oned to God. By this we are kept as luminous and noble as when we were created. By the force of this precious oneing we love, see, praise, thank and endlessly enjoy our Creator." Clearly, Julian identifies our oneing experiences here with our many experiences of the *Via Positiva* . . .

Julian testifies to a "true oneing between the divine and the human, forged in paradise," that makes it "impossible to separate them." When human nature was created, it was "rightfully oned with the creator, who is Essential Nature, uncreated—that is, God. This is why there is absolutely nothing separating the Divine soul from the Human Soul." It is love that does this, indeed "in endless love we are held and made whole. In endless love we are led and protected and will never be lost."

The "humanity of Adam, with all the wounding and weakness that attend the human condition" is everywhere visible. Divinity suffers also since "God shows us that his own Son and Adam are one and the same. We share the strength and goodness come from Christ and also the weakness and blindness that comes from Adam." Any guilt humans feel is lifted since "Jesus has taken upon himself all guilt. God therefore does not blame us." Christ became a human being "to save all human beings" and "return humanity to a state of grace." In fact, "there is nothing separating divinity from humanity." God sees us as other Christs because "God's love for humanity is so vast that he makes no distinction between the blessed Christ and the least soul among us."   —JN 59–62

Nondualism and the Joy of Trusting Our Sensuality

Julian combats patriarchy not only by insisting on the motherhood of God, but also by insisting on non-dualism of body and soul. "God is in our sensuality," she insists. Indeed, "God willed that we have a twofold nature: sensual and spiritual." And there exists a "beautiful oneing that was made by God between the body and the soul." God has forged a "glorious unity between the soul and the body."   —JN 77, 79–80

She teaches us to trust our bodies and our sensuality. Her very definition of faith is this: Faith means "trust that we are in God and God whom we do not see is in us." Faith is trust plus panentheism. "To behold God in all things is to live in complete joy." We are all "born into a birthright of never-ending joy." Trust is key to Julian. "Just as God loves and delights in us, it is his will that we love and delight in him, and fully trust in him, and all will be well."   —JN 71

Love, the Meaning of Her Work and of the Universe

Julian tells us that she was shown the "meaning" of her entire book:

> Love was your Lord's meaning.
> Who showed it to you? Love.
> What did you see? Love.
> Why was it shown? For Love.
>
> —JN 96

This message corresponds with her vision of a small ball she saw in her hand, the size of a hazelnut. She asked, "'What is this thing?' And I was answered: 'It is everything that is created.' I wondered how it could survive, since it seemed too little it could suddenly disintegrate into nothing. The answer came: 'It endures and ever will endure, because God loves it.' And so everything has being because of God's love." The Cosmic Christ was a very real experience for Julian.   —JN 40

THOMAS MERTON: CREATION MYSTIC, POET, PROPHET, AND LOVER OF MEISTER ECKHART

We have seen Fox's significant contribution in recovering the mystical tradition as a source of creation spirituality—particularly through the work of Eckhart, Hildegard, and Julian, but also his fresh discovery of the mystical themes in Thomas Aquinas, the great Dominican theologian. Fox has explored many others figures, too numerous to cover in this volume, including such contemporary mystics as Father Bede Griffiths, Howard Thurman, William Everson, Dorothee Soelle, Pierre Teilhard de Chardin, Thomas Berry, M. C. Richards, Mary Oliver, Clarissa Pinkola Estes, Sister Jose Hobday, Ernesto Cardenal, Nana Veary, Sister Dorothy Stang, and Bernard Amadei. Many of these are explored in Christian Mystics. *But his work on Thomas Merton deserves special attention here.*

Thomas Merton (1915–1968) was an influential Trappist monk, mystic, writer, poet, theologian, social activist, and scholar of comparative religion, particularly the connections between Christian mysticism and Zen Buddhism. In Fox's book, A Way to God: Thomas Merton's Journey, *he discusses Merton's rich development of each of the four paths of creation spirituality and the important role that Meister Eckhart played in the last ten "prophetic" years of his life. He also shows how Merton probably would have responded to the seven charges that Cardinal Ratzinger made against Fox's own teachings—teachings that he labeled "dangerous and deviant."*

Merton's influence on Fox was personal. In 1967, Fox wrote Merton where to study and pursue a doctorate in spirituality, and received a full-page letter in reply, urging him to go to the Institut Catholique in Paris. Fox credited that advice with leading him to the tradition of creation spirituality and thus for influencing all the work that followed. (CB)

Merton Encounters Meister Eckhart

Thomas Merton's intellectual and spiritual debt to Meister Eckhart was profound and long-lasting—as a student at Columbia University in 1938, Merton wrote about Eckhart in his master's thesis, and during his final journey to the East in 1968, Merton was invoking him. In 1966 Merton wrote: "Meister Eckhart may have limitations, but I am entranced with him nevertheless. I like the brevity, the incisiveness of his sermons, his way of piercing straight to the heart of the inner life, the awakened spark, the creative and redeeming Word, God born in us." Many of Eckhart's ideas—such as "ground of being," letting be and letting go, the Apophatic Divinity, the Godhead, the "unborn self," the "spark" of God—pop up regularly in Merton's work.

The greatest impact on Merton regarding Eckhart came about through Buddhist scholar Dr. D. T. Suzuki, with whom Merton had been in dialogue since about 1958, about the time of Pope Pius XII's death and the election of Pope John XXIII. In their dialogues Suzuki highlighted the importance of Eckhart. This dialogue became a life-changing experience for Merton, one that set him on a path of ecumenism between East and West and of prophetic action and consciousness that changed his spirituality forever. From that time until his final journey in East, Merton was indebted to Eckhart. Eckhart changed him from being the dualistic and sentimental Augustinian-tainted monk of the forties (as reflected in his autobiography) to being a prophetic Christian who, as it turned out, was the first religious figure in America to come out against the Vietnam War. This decision may have cost him his life. —WG 25–26

The Role of Spirituality in Art

Art was to Merton as water is to fish. He swam in it from the first, since both of his parents were artists. Having settled in southern France, the family no doubt enjoyed artistic acceptance as their daily bread, for it was in the air in France especially at the turn of the twentieth century. Why were his parents—his father was from New Zealand, and his mother from America—in Paris in the first place, except that both were artists and both felt at home there? Merton as a child drank this same nectar of artistic wonder and beauty, and might we say spirituality, that fed his parents, and he never forgot it. He wrote: "All that has been said . . . of Christian mysticism about 'dark contemplation' and 'the night of sense' must not be misinterpreted to mean that the normal culture of the senses, of artistic taste, of imagination, and of intelligence should be formally renounced by anyone interested in a life of meditation and prayer. On the contrary, such culture is presupposed. One cannot go beyond what one has not yet attained, and normally the realization that God is 'beyond images, symbols and ideas' dawns only on one who has previously made a good use of all these things." Merton practiced art as meditation as a photographer, poet, writer, musician and Zen painter. He also taught his novices to weave baskets.

—WG 83

The Prophetic Struggle with the World

"In the conflict between law and freedom God is on the side of freedom. That is a scandalous statement! But it is the New Testament! How are we going to affirm to the modern world the scandal of the New Testament? It is here that we confront the seriousness of our *prophetic* as distinct from our *contemplative* calling." These words from Thomas Merton frame well the biblical basis for the many positions he took on behalf of justice and freedom. He reminds us that we have both a contemplative and a prophetic calling. Merton was often controversial in his day, but he derived his passion for justice and the strength to ground his courage from the scriptures themselves. He was fully aware of the potential of our species to misuse its divine powers of creativity. Creativity does not stand alone cut off from values and priorities. We can use our creativity, after all, to build gas ovens to kill enemies more efficiently, or we can use our creativity to build community and to restore health and to heal. Creativity needs direction and parameters. Justice and compassion provide that testing ground for our creativity. Thus, the Via Creativa, along with the Via Positiva and Via Negativa, leads to the Via Transformativa.

There was never a prophet who was not also an artist—what I call a "social artist" or an artist at organizing and awakening the people. . .

Merton explicitly takes up the issue of prophecy and the poet, and he offers his own definition of prophecy: "To prophesy is not to predict, but to seize on reality in its moment of highest expectation and tension toward the new. This tension is discovered not by hypnotic elation but in the light of everyday existence." By stressing "everyday existence," Merton is teaching that prophecy is for all of us. Does his definition of prophecy correspond to Rabbi Heschel's, who says the primary work of the prophet is "to interfere"? I think it does. "Highest expectation and tension toward the new" is always a kind of interference, isn't it? It interferes with the status quo, and it interferes with despair. It is a road, therefore, to hope and possibility born of great expectations. —WG 107–11

Fundamentalist Religion, Empire, and Idolatry

Merton predicted that the marriage of empire and fundamentalist religion would produce "the greatest orgy of idolatry the world has ever known" and "idolatry is the greatest and fundamental sin." He also criticized Christianity, in an Easter sermon in 1967, of being "too often simply the cult of the dead body of Christ. . . . This is no joke. This is what actually happens to the Christian religion when it ceases to be a really living faith and becomes a mere legalistic and ritualistic formality." Christ becomes "a theological relic . . . a corpse-like figure of wax [that] can make you rich and happy by its powerful magic."
—WG 204–205

Technology: The Great Problem of the Day

Merton saw in technology "the great problem of the day. . . . The problem of getting technology back into the power of man so that it may be used for man's own good is by all odds the great problem of the day. And one of the things that is demanded is a real iconoclastic attack on the ambiguities and confusion surrounding the misuse of technology. . . . A naive optimism about technology is a source of great problems."

Merton felt machinery could replace the love of life that ought to lie at the heart of the spiritual journey: "Met a brother leading a young Holstein bull by the Bull's nose. Had this thought: 'thank God here is a living thing and not a machine, something big and warm and alive and unpredictable, with fears and angers and appetites.' And I was glad of all this and reassured by it because of the value that is in life itself. So the second thought won out over the first [that the bull could easily kill me]. I am willing to trust life more than machinery."   —WG 120–21

In response to space travel, Merton asked: "Even if humans can fly, so what? There are flying ants. Even if man flies all over the universe, he is still nothing but a flying ant until he recovers a human center and a human spirit in the depth of his own being.". . . Referring to the efforts to land the first person on the moon, Merton asked: "What can we gain by sailing to the moon if we are not able to cross the abyss that separates us from ourselves. This is the most important of all voyages of discovery, and without it all the rest are not only useless but disastrous."
                                                        —WG 121–22

Motherhood of God

Julian of Norwich developed the theme of the "Motherhood of God" more fully than any other theologian up to the late twentieth century—and Merton knew that. Merton not only approved of Julian's theology with gusto, he also developed his own teaching on the subject of the Motherhood of God. "God," he wrote, "is one's Father and Mother. As Father He stands as solitary might surrounded by darkness. As Mother His shining is diffused, embracing all His creatures with merciful tenderness and light. The diffuse shining of God is Hagia Sophia. We call her His 'glory.' In Sophia His power is experienced only as mercy and as love."

Elaborating on the Divine Feminine, Merton went on to suggest a Quaternity rather than just a Trinity in the Godhead with Sophia or Wisdom, which is feminine playing the fourth side. "I do not know where she is, in this Beginning. I do not speak of her as a Beginning, but as a manifestation."   —WG 158

The Cosmic Christ

The Cosmic Christ theology was important to Thomas Merton. On several occasions he declares that "we are other Christs." Echoing Eckhart, he writes in his journal: "Who am I? A Son of God . . . My true self is the self that is spoken by God—'Thou art My Son!' "Our responsibility (ability and obligation to respond). Tremendous happiness and clarity (in darkness) is my response: 'Abba, Father!'" God dwells in all things: "We do not see the Blinding One in black emptiness. He speaks to us gently in ten thousand things. . . . He shines not on them but from within them." This, too, is Cosmic Christ teaching, that the Christ is present in all beings and is more than present—is radiating light and shining forth. "Life is this simple: We live in a world that is absolutely transparent. The divine is shining through it all the time. This is not just a nice story or a fable—it is true."

—WG 232–33

He tells us of a mystical experience he underwent at Fourth and Walnut in downtown Louisville one afternoon. . . . Later, commenting on his mystical experience, he observed: "There is no way of telling people that they are all walking around shining like the sun." This is Cosmic Christ talk, Cosmic Christ intuition at its fullest.

—WG 62, 233

5

Spiritual Practices, the Cosmic Mass, and Creativity

PRAYER, ART AS MEDITATION, AND NEW PRACTICES AND RITUALS

The way we understand prayer is basic to the way we understand spirituality. Thus, my first book was on the meaning of prayer and was titled On Becoming a Musical, Mystical Bear: Spirituality American Style *after a powerful dream I received while writing it. In the dream, a musical, mystical, dancing bear appeared, and later I learned that the bear is the most ancient symbol for humanity/divinity in the Americas. To the indigenous peoples, the bear stands on two legs like a human but is powerful and full of healing powers like God—which is a fine image of a Christ figure.*

Shortly before the book was to appear, I found a couplet in T. S. Eliot that spoke deeply to me, and I was able to sneak it into the book at the last minute—"perhaps it is not too late and we must borrow every changing shape—dance, dance like a musical bear." It said what I was feeling—that things were getting very late in American culture and history and that creativity and imagination were our only hope. A more recent version of the book has gone by a more sober title, Prayer: A Radical Response to Life. *(MF)*

Prayer as a Radical Response to Life

Prayer in its primal and fundamental sense, I propose, means *a radical response to life*. I suggest that this description of the prayer-event will bear the burden of the best in former "definitions" and accounts of prayer at the same time that it carries the reality of prayer into the new spiritual age that is yawning before the awakening consciousness of humankind.

The English word *respond* derives from the old French verb, *respondre* (to answer), and the Latin verb *respondere* (to promise, to pledge, "to engage oneself"). A response is an answer with a promise to it: not the answer to the question "Will you go to the store for me?" but the answer to "Will you marry me?" The former calls for a reply; the latter for a response. The promise inherent in a response is a pledge of oneself, implying a certain degree of self-revelation based on shared trust and respect. I recall once asking another, "When were you happiest?" The first reply was: "that is a very personal question," but after a long pause for conjuring up response, the individual made the requisite act of trust and was ready to respond. The response marked a new stage, a deeper one of intimacy in our relationship, since clearly the response was both answer and promise.

Respond is not a *limiting* verb: it takes one beyond the ordinary connotations of the word "talk" (thus those who settle for prayer as "talking with God"); and beyond the more general word "communicate" (which, like "talk," suffers from an extreme anthropomorphism). Yet we all respond daily to the events and the mysteries that move us. One responds when one is moved, triggered in one's heart by the experience of mystery. One does not reply or talk or communicate when he hears for the first time of the death of a loved one: one responds, that is, even if nothing is heard verbally; an acknowledgement of the event is called forth from the depths of one's insides. Perhaps the language used is tears. Perhaps laughter. Or silence. Or a touch.

Our response is spontaneous (from the Latin *sponte*, of one's own will): it is free, it is mine. We respond *because we feel like it*—calculation and self-perpetuation are not a part of response; self-expression is. In this sense, to be childlike is to be responsive: open and free to express one's own self at the invitation of an event or a person.

A response is simple and directed to the simple; expressing oneself spontaneously is also expressing oneself simply. Our response to mystery in particular tends to be a response with conviction. A human Yes or No is the most simple and the most convincing response we can make during our lifetime. The simplicity implied in saying Yes or No is simple for its depth, for it comes from a place of honesty where one's very being and self-mystery senses its worth is at stake. It is the Yes and No that Luther uttered when he claimed: "Here I stand. I can do no other"; or that Christ spoke when interrogated about his kingship. It is not the consequences that dictate their response (as they so often do the reply) but the inner honesty. It is the No of Bonhoeffer to the Third Reich, the Yes of Mozart to his musical vocation, the Yes of Jesus to his messiahship. Mystery responds to mystery and the simple to the simple.

A responsible response is motivated from within, where one's certainty lies. Responsibility is the capacity to live up to one's response, to follow through on it. Response throws us into the future, a dark and unknown future, one that we believe can be somehow met. Ask the young couple saying Yes to one another in marriage vows, and interview the couple who have lived fifty years together to learn the risk and the consequences of responsible response. Response is an adventure; prayer is an adventure.
—PRR 49–51

The One to Whom We Respond

The one to whom we respond ultimately and pledge ourselves in promise is bigger than life with its mysteries and its problems. A mystery of mysteries, the One is everywhere life-giver. God is the lover of life above all else: its preserver; its enticer; its sharer. "To know God and to live are the same thing. God is life." (Tolstoy) The One is everywhere of Life, in it, with it; that is, God's presence is everywhere and always present. Providence is a life-breathing presence, and the process of prayer is the process of coming to realize this. God's presence is an immanence (intimacy) and a transcendence (calling us to expand outside of ourselves, such as stretching us to love our neighbor and struggle for justice).   —PRR 62

God has many names—Aquinas says every being can be a name for God. I bring 89 together in my book, *Naming the Unnameable: 89 Wonderful and Useful Names for God*. Life is one of them but so too are Love, Goodness, the One to whom we give our thanks, the Ground of being, the Cause of wonder, the Mind of the universe, Flow, Energy, the Self of the universe, Spirit, Consciousness, Joy, Light, Compassion, Justice, Beauty, Truth, Wisdom, the Goddess, Gaia, and much more. God is also the Great Mystery, Superessential Darkness, the Unknown One, Nothingness, Silence and more. We can offer a radical response of Yes and No in the presence of any or all of these names for the divine.   —NU xv–xx

The Meaning of "Radical"

The word *radical* means *root*. Prayer is a *deep* response to Life. Happily, our English language has superb expressions for the discernible directions of *radical* or *root*. The first direction is that of "becoming rooted in." Going deep into the ground. What is prayerful sinks so deep that it more profoundly upholds the daily: and attaches itself into the earth with strong and energetic roots. We become *rooted* into the pleasures and enjoyable places and persons and memories of the moments of our lives where we have learned to savor life and its mysteries.

The second direction is that of "uprooting." This is the war cry of that famous man of prayer of Jewish history, Jeremiah, who felt himself called to "root and to uproot," and is recalled in Jesus' words: "Any plant my heavenly Father has not planted will be pulled up by the roots" (Matt. 15:13).

A life-response of depth asserts itself in the tension between our desire to enjoy life and our drive to improve it and share it; in the struggle between allowing oneself to be changed and aiding the situations of others so that they might be changed; in the strife between receiving, seeing, listening, being, touching, dancing, singing, and expressing love by way of peace; and our giving, doing, acting, fighting, making, arguing, and expressing love through anger. The poles of the dialectic that we call *becoming rooted in* versus *uprooting* has classically been called that of mysticism versus prophecy (cf. Heiler). The reason that the process of life-response is a dialectic that remains in tension is that the roots of our uprooting are built right into those of our being rooted in. Our mysticism is our Yes to Life. Our prophecy is our No to forces hostile to Life. Both are prayer.   —PRR 73

A New Commandment: To Love Life

The understanding of prayer as a radical response to life suggests the following lesson: That a new commandment has been given to us: thou shalt love your life with all your strength and energy, growing daily in appreciation of the joys of life; and you shall allow and aid where possible your neighbor to love his/hers and do the same, using common norms of justice to determine life's priorities. Live to make life livable: fighting when necessary, learning by whatever means possible, having a good time when you feel like it, respecting life's mysteries in an active, not a passive, manner. In short, love life—and do whatever you want.
                                                                  —PRR 76

Prophets Respond by Creating

The prophet issues new life by his/her radical response to life: he/she creates. Creativity is related to reluctance because "creative power is mightier than its possessor." It is an authentic criterion for the prophet's word because "disease has never yet fostered creative work" (C. G. Jung). To be radical in one's social response to life is to be creative.   —PRR 110

Prayer Is Radical Socially

We have insisted that the prophetic response is a creative one. But creative of what? Above all of community, or the experience of life and its mysteries—death, evil, rebirth, nature, vocation, the other, love—with others. The first reason why radical prayer is a creation of community is that, as we have seen, prayer takes place at the level of the unconscious, where all persons share symbols and experiences in common. Prayer is then, by reason of its deep origin, radically social. —PRR 111

Meditation

There are many kinds of meditation or ways to train the mind that spiritual traditions the world over have developed. I distinguish them into two basic categories: the emptying kind and the filling kind. They are not at all exclusive one of the other. Quite the contrary, one serves the other. When one is very filled, for example, with the beauty of the ocean, one is often put into a state of silent appreciation. Filling turns to emptying. In contrast, when one fasts for a while or meditates by letting go of all images and distractions and goals, thereby emptying the mind, then the return to simple joys like eating a tomato or smiling with a friend take on all new levels of depth and delight.

The two kinds of meditation correspond to the two aspects of Divinity that we have discussed: form and formlessness.

We humans carry enough of the "image of God" in us that we, too, are form and formless; we have access to the God of form and Creation and the Godhead of nothingness. Meister Eckhart puts it this way: "In that respect in which the soul is an image of God and is, like God, nameless, there the soul knows no renewal but only eternity, like God." The Hindu teaching that the Eternal Godhead, Brahman, is known through human consciousness as Atman, is also saying what great things are before the human when we learn to perceive correctly.

That is why each of these meditation ways is appropriate and useful for us. At different times and episodes in one's life, we may need one more than the other. In general, I would say that Westerners today, so swamped in media-driven cultures of consumerism and affluence, and so distant from nature and her secrets and beauties, and so driven by busyness, will find themselves more and more drawn to the emptying kinds of meditation. Then we can return to creation itself with a clearer mind and calmer heart.

The goal of each kind of meditation is the same: to see reality as it is in all its clarity and radiance and truth. Jesus called it recognizing that the domain of God is among us. Thich Nhat Hanh describes it as developing our capacities for deep looking, listening, and awareness of the present state of things beginning with ourselves. In his own words: Meditation is "stopping, calming, and looking deeply. When we are mindful, touching deeply the present moment, we can see and listen deeply, and the fruits are always understanding, acceptance, love, and the desire to relieve suffering and bring joy."

Authentic meditation practice does not force one to withdraw from everyday existence but to stay there with new eyes and fuller heart and not to run away from things. It is about being fully present to what is. "The technique is to be in the present moment, to be aware that we are here and now, that the only moment to be alive is the present moment."

To arrive at the inner self where this God-birth really takes place, we need to let go of some of the soul's busyness. The soul is sometimes like a monkey cage, full of busy, busy monkeys. The soul gets to be very busy—it responds to everything about it not only during waking hours but in sleep as well. It wanders, it looks, it feels, it imagines, it helps, it remembers, it regrets, it rejoices, it longs. So much goes on in the soul that, at times, it needs slowing down, resting and repose, forgetting and emptying, letting go and just *being*, returning to its source. It needs a vacation. Recreation. Refreshment. Meditation is another word for that vacationing time, time-off for the soul.

When we meditate, we are changing our relationship to *space and time*. Meditation affects Creation and our perception of it. If Creation is so full of Divinity, a temple of the Divine, do we perceive it as such? We are talking about perception, clearing ours out and cleaning ours up. Says Eckhart: "Every angel is with his whole joy and his whole bliss inside me and God himself with his whole bliss. Yet I do not perceive this." Why don't we perceive it? What is in our way? Eckhart says that "everything of the past and everything of the future is present now in the depths of our soul"—but do we perceive this?

—ORMW 189–91

Some Fresh and Useful Spiritual Practices

1. Use my and Bishop Marc Andrus's *Stations of the Cosmic Christ* book and meditate on each of the 16 stations. Pray the Stations of the Cosmic Christ. Cards are available also.   —SSC 53–149

2. Chant Christian Mantras. For several years now I have been creating mantras from the Christian tradition and inviting people to chant them with me. The effects have often been profound. . . . A mantra is a device that is repeated over and over again. Think bumper sticker: Short, pithy sayings from Jesus or the Christ or the mystics. In this sense a rosary is a mantra, and a litany is one also, for repetition is at their core. . . . This practice is a powerful exercise for the right brain, which learns more from chanting and the rhythm it creates than from thinking about things.

    Mantras are very portable, accessible, approachable. They are a fitting way to exercise our mystical awareness, especially in this time when people are very busy protesting and need practices that are readily available, portable, and cheap.

    • The I Am sayings found in *Stations of the Cosmic Christ*. For example, "I Am the Vine," "I Am the Door," "I Am the Living Light," etc. Simply chant them over and over alone or with others and see what happens.
    • Words from Jesus' mouth, such as "The Kingdom of God is within you," and "The Queendom of God is among you," both of which are accurate translations.

Or: "Do it to the least and you do it to me." Or "Love
your enemy." There is no shortage of possibilities for
those who derive great benefit from the Scriptures.

- Short phrases from the mystics can be very powerful.
  For example, one might chant one of the following
  phrases from Meister Eckhart:

  "Is-ness is God."
  "Compassion is where peace and justice kiss."
  "God finds joy and rapture in us."

- From Julian of Norwich:

  "Goodness is God."
  "All will be well."
  "Jesus says: 'I am what you love.'"

- From Hildegard of Bingen:

  "Become a flowering orchard."
  "Mary, ground of all being."
  "Love was the first. She made everything."

- From Mechtild of Magdeburg:

  "Kneel at the feet of all creatures."
  "You God are the sun: I am your reflection."
  —SCC 189–90

3. Chant the "Ah" sound common to so many Divine Names.
   This is a practice in interfaith or Deep Ecumenism. Sit in
   a chair with feet on the floor so breath can move easily.
   Chant the sound "Ah" for several minutes. Then chant the
   following mantras, repeating each one several times, and
   emphasize the "Ah" sound in each:

   Aum
   Buddha
   Brahman
   Krishna

> Tara
> Gaia
> Shiva
> Shakti
> Kali
> Yahweh
> Adonai
> Sophia
> Hochmah
> Allah
> Tagashala
> Wakan Tanka
> Abba

To speak or chant the "Ah" sound is to open the fourth and fifth chakras. "Abba" was Jesus' favorite name for the Divine; it means "Father" or "Papa."   —SCC 193

4. Take the 89 contemporary names for God including names from science, the divine feminine, and the apophatic divinity in my book, *Naming the Unnameable, and* chant those names in mantra form. Or simply meditate on them separately. Or dance them; draw pictures of them; or put them into clay.   —NU xv–xx

5. Create your own stations of the cross appropriate to the crises of our time (Joanna Macy and I did this at Holy Week in Findhorn retreat center).   —MF

The Cosmic Mass (TCM)

I became an Episcopalian priest in order to work with young people to re-create Liturgy using postmodern art forms such as rave, DJ, VJ, rap, and more. To this day we have celebrated over 110 such masses in North America, including two at the World Parliament of Religions. After the WPR Toronto Mass, a forty-something woman said, "This was the most powerful religious experience of my life." The same was said by a Silicon Valley executive after a TCM at a Sounds True retreat. He pointed to his heart and said, "I've been a Catholic all my life and never understood the Mass until tonight." He gave us a two-year grant that allowed us to restart the TCM in the Bay Area and beyond. Following a TCM at a Soul and Spirit conference in a big hotel in San Francisco, three young men came up to me and said: "We have been attending raves every week for five years, and what we were looking for in rave we found here tonight: deep prayer, community, and something you don't get at a rave—a multi-generational celebration." One 84-year-old attending our Mass said, "I've been waiting 82 years for someone to invite me to connect my love of prayer with my love of dance. I took three buses to get here tonight so someone is going to have to take me home, and the buses won't be running when I am through dancing tonight."

In June 2014 we celebrated our first TCM in San Francisco's Grace Cathedral with about 800 people in attendance. The theme of the Mass was "Return of the Divine Feminine." The sound person said to us afterwards, "in my eight years of working in this cathedral, this event was without question the most energetic happening I have ever witnessed here."

—CNF 363–73, 7–16

Grieving Rituals and the Cosmic Mass

Integral to the Cosmic Mass is a grieving practice. People are in deep need of grieving rituals today. In 2012 I was invited by Sounds True of Boulder, Colorado, to lead a grieving ritual at their annual conference for 800 people of a great variety of traditions. Afterwards, one man said to me, "I have been seeing a psychiatrist for twenty years, and I am firing her on Monday. This is what I needed all along." Others told me their lives were changed by that one ceremony. At one of our cosmic masses, where we always include a grieving ceremony, a woman came up afterwards and reported that she was a "fierce atheist." Pointing to her heart, she said, "Something shifted in me today during that grieving ceremony, and by the time communion came along I was hungry for it. This evening has changed my life."

—CNF 370

Art as Meditation: The Way of the Prophets

Another kind of meditation centers on the experience of creativity and the focusing and gathering that follows from that discipline. This meditation takes us to the God of *form.* We call this *art as meditation.* Introvert and extrovert kinds of meditation are not exclusive. Creativity often begins with solitude and silence and emptying. And true emptying often leads to creativity. But the first kind strives to still the mind (by not striving); the second fills the mind by digging deep into the imagination and honoring the images that are there as gifts of the Holy Spirit. It gathers them up and then releases them into our work and into the world. —ORMW 189–91, 218

Art as meditation is the primary form of prayer in the creation spirituality tradition (and ritual is a practice of art as meditation as well, indeed it is a gathering of artists—which is all of us).

Psychologists Claudio Naranjo and Robert Ornstein, in their study *On the Psychology of Meditation,* contrast what they call introvert meditation with extrovert meditation—their "extrovert meditation" is what I call "art as meditation." It is meditation by giving birth, by creating, and they say it instills an "attitude of reverence toward all of existence." They also contrast it with introvert meditation in this important way: Art as meditation is "*the way of the prophets.*" The word *extrovert* does not mean "for extroverts" or "outer directed." It means flowing from the deepest and most creative center within us, the place where we give birth to our images. Says Meister Eckhart: "The truth does not come from outside in, but from inside out and passes through an inner form." —WP 224, 222

Art as meditation gets us in touch with our truth and provides a form. The book by potter, poet, and philosopher M. C. Richards called *Centering in Pottery, Poetry, and the Person,*

published in 1964, constitutes a veritable Bible of art as meditation. I wrote a Foreword to the 1989 edition, and she taught
wonderfully on our faculty for many years. She names elements
of art as meditation such as bodiliness and passion. "It is in our
bodies that redemption takes place. It is the physicality of the
crafts that pleases me: I learn through my hands and my eyes
and my skin what I could never learn through my brain." Art
as meditation cuts through the awesome and demonic dualism
of body versus soul that so much ascetic spirituality takes for
granted. Says Richards: "Incarnation: bodying forth. Is this not
our whole concern?"   —WP 227, 229

Art as meditation is an *incarnational* kind of meditation. Such
bodily participation leads to the body politic; that is why so
many prophets have been artists—did not Gandhi and MLK, Jr.
create social art by organizing non-violent marches and movements? Says Rabbi Heschel, "Asceticism was not the ideal of the
biblical man. The source of evil is not in passion in the throbbing
heart but rather in hardness of heart. . . . It is to the imagination and the passions that prophets speak, rather than aiming
at the cold approbation of the mind." Furthermore, there is joy
in creating art. Heschel: "What the prophet faces is not his own
faith. He faces God. To sense the living God is to sense infinite
goodness, infinite wisdom, infinite beauty. Such a sensation is a
sensation of joy."   —WP 231

Any educational program seeking to educate mystics to
become prophets has to teach the practices of art as meditation.
In art as meditation one enters into the artistic process *not* to
produce a work of art but to be with the process. . . . One can
experience deep spiritual experiences while working. This also
is art as meditation. There is no limit to the kind of art work.
It may be drumming or dancing, singing or painting, working
clay or sculpting wood, massaging or creating altars, chanting
or rapping—all these practices and more we have offered at our
schools of spirituality. I tell our students it really doesn't matter
which one you choose to take—the results can be the same in
anyone of them. Deep awakenings have occurred time and time

again by way of art as meditation experiences in our program
both for adults and inner city teenagers.   —CR 191–92

CREATIVITY

Potter, poet, and philosopher M. C. Richards warns us of the
power and omnipresence of creativity within us all: "We have to
realize that a creative being lives within ourselves, whether we
like it or not, and that we must get out of its way, for it will give
us no peace until we do."   —SNC 104

The working definition of a human being, according to
anthropologists today, is *a bi-ped who makes things*. They are
certain they have found one of our ancestors when they find a
two-legged one with artifacts nearby.

I propose that when all is said and done, *our true nature is
our creativity*. Psychologist Rollo May concurs when he says:
"The creative process must be explored not as the product of
sickness, but as representing the highest degree of emotional
health, as the expression of the normal people in the act of actu-
alizing themselves."

When the Bible declares that we are made in the image and
likeness of the Creator, it is affirming that creativity is at our
core just as it lies at the core of the Creator of all things. Not
only the Bible but other traditions also celebrate our nearness to
the creative powers of Divinity. The Sufi mystic Hafiz declares:

All the talents of God are within you.
How could this be otherwise
    When your soul
    Derived from His genes!

An ancient Mesoamerican poet tells us that God dwells in the
heart of the artist and the artist draws God out of his or her
heart when the artist is at work.

We are creators at our very core. Only creating can make us
happy, for in creating we tap into the deepest powers of self
and universe and the Divine Self. We become co-creators, that

is, we create *with* the other forces of society, universe, and the Godself when we commit to creativity. . . . We are makers and fabricators, we are free, we are active, we are interesting, we are interested and curious, we are part of the vast creative universe, we are energetic and alive, we are creators and co-creators.

Scholars of evolutionary history are telling us that today biological evolution is being overwhelmed by cultural evolution. The human species, which evolves by culture more than by slow-moving biological change, is overwhelming the planet. All the more reason to examine that element that makes human culture so amazingly rich and fast-moving: human creativity.

—CR 28–29

Our Creative Ancestors

Scientist Brian Swimme uses the following story to remind us of how ancient and how necessary for survival is our creativity. When our ancestors discovered fire back in the savannahs of Africa over 65,000 years ago, they set out on a great journey. When they arrived at the place we now call Eurasia, the ice age broke out. There they were, fresh from the heat of Africa, forced to live in caves for ten thousand years. Did they give up? Did they fall into masochism and say, "Woe is we!"? They got to work. They put their imaginations to work. They learned how to prepare hides, sew warm outfits, hunt animals for food and clothing, and how to tell tales around the campfire and entertain themselves. In short, this is where our creativity came to birth.

I draw two important lessons from this story. First is how strong our ancestors were. There are few adaptations that we are being asked to make today that are as profound as the adaptation from the heat of the African savannahs to the ice age. A second lesson I conclude is the realization of how *basic* our creativity is to our survival. Creativity and imagination are not frosting on a cake: They are integral to our sustainability. They are survival mechanisms. They are the essence of who we are. They constitute our deepest empowerment.   —CR 31

Our Creative Essence

Psychologist Otto Rank saw creativity as so basic to the essence of our humanness that he, in effect, substituted the human creative impulse or the drive for *production* for Freud's emphasis on sexuality and *reproduction* . . .

For Rank, at the heart of our dignity lies our power of creativity, where the human being "becomes at once creator and creature or actually moves from creature to creator, in the ideal case, creator of himself, his own personality." Our ultimate act of creativity is giving birth to who we are, and this individuality comes from a series of births corresponding to a continued result of births, rebirths, and a new birth, which reach from the birth of the child from the mother, beyond the birth of the individual from the mass, to the birth of creative work from the individual and finally to the birth of knowledge from the work. Thus our whole life long we are involved in creativity of the profoundest kind—unless we opt out of this responsibility. And this opting out corresponds, in Rank's view, to neurosis itself.

Rank observes that while the individual is at once creator and creature, in neurosis "the creative expression of will is a negative one, resting on the denial of the creator role." Rank learned that a lot of emotional problems are creatively brought about by the neurotic in a process he called a "gain through illness," which derives from a "philosophy of suffering." This pain "is self-willed, a sort of creation that can find expression only in this negative, destructive way." Since neurosis is a negative act of creativity, healing can happen through redirecting one's creative impulses to love of life rather than love of suffering, to creativity rather than control. The neurotic has failed to achieve normal development and corresponds to the failed artist (*artiste manqué*) . . .

It is because creativity is so central to our hearts and souls as human beings that Rank puts it at the same level as love itself as a sign of our health and well-being. Creativity and relationship, art and love, express our deepest beings, and what they share in common is empathy.   —CR 32–33

Creativity and the Demonic

Our powers for creativity can be used for blessing or for curse, for life or for death, for biophilia or for necrophilia. We do have choices. We can choose how to use our creativity and for what purposes. Another way of saying this is to say that our creativity is not only where the Divine and the human meet but also where the Divine and the demonic meet . . .

Evil happens not just in our misuse and misdirection of our creativity. It also happens because of what tradition calls "sins of omission," that is, because of our failure to utilize our creativity and stretch our imaginations to the fullest.   —CR 35–37

A Creative Universe

Creativity is not a human invention or a human power isolated from the other powers of the universe. Quite the opposite. First came the universe's power of creativity; only very recently did humans arrive on the scene with theirs. The modern view of the world did not endorse this notion of the omnipresence of creativity in the universe. The universe was considered to be dead, inert, and machinelike. But the ancient peoples, the premoderns, never saw it that way. Neither does today's science . . .

Today's science is also instructing us in the origins of creativity and finding that the whole universe is permeated with the power of change and birth. Physicist Brian Swimme summarizes the findings of science in this way: "If you let hydrogen gas alone for 13 billion years it will become giraffes, rose bushes and humans." This is another way of saying that *everything* has within itself the power of creativity, the power of giving birth, the power of surprising us (and presumably itself as well). One might say that hydrogen gas has the goddess busy creating within it.

— CR 39–40

The Creative Heart of God

All our spiritual traditions the world over agree that creativity flows through the human heart and flows from the Divine heart.
—CR 47

God as the Artist of Artists

"The Same Spirit who hovered over the waters at the beginning of creation hovers over the mind of the artist at work." (Thomas Aquinas)

Aquinas had a lot to say about God as artist—and by extension about us, born in God's image and likeness—as artists. Regarding the former, he used the term "artist" about God perhaps more than any other single name. For example, he declares that "God is an artist and the universe is God's work of art." And again, "all natural things are produced by divine art and can rightly be called God's work of art." And God is "the Artist of artists."

How does it feel to be called "God's work of art"? Compare it, for example, to being called a "sinner," a "wretch," a "worm," or an object of judgment and wrath by a punitive father God in the sky.   —SJ 65; TTA 53

Co-Creating with God

The work of the artist in all of us is to be in dialogue with our hearts, for God dwells therein. And the work of the artist is nothing less than to "put divinity into things" (Black Elk). That is to say, we are indeed co-creating when we create—we are not only co-creating *with* God and the powers of creation; we are actually co-creating God and the powers of creation! They happen through us—just as they happen to other species in the universe and through other expressions of time and space. Eckhart says: "There where God speaks the creatures, there God is." And "God becomes as creatures express God." How noble our creativity becomes! How sacred and holy. How full of responsibility.

But there is still more deep wisdom being taught here, namely, the *how* of our bringing the Divine forward in our creativity. This happens to the extent that "we converse with our own heart" (Black Elk). To be in touch with our hearts *is* to be in touch with the heart of the universe and the heart of the Divine Creator. Is this why the indigenous peoples around the world put so much faith in the drum as the basic instrument of prayer? Because the drumbeat bespeaks the beat of the heart—not just our human heart, but the heart of the universe, the heart of the Creator. To return to this heart is the purpose of all prayer and all meditation. When we return to this heart, the Divine creativity flows again.

The indigenous people of Africa understood this. Dancing to the beat of the drum releases both breath and spirit. It connects us to cosmic forces, which in turn energize us and bless us.

—CR 52–53

Imagination Is a Gift from God

In the Kabbalah, the medieval Jewish mystical work, we are instructed that "the fierce power of imagination is a gift from God." To call imagination a "fierce power" is to warn us that we are wrestling with wild forces when we enter the arena of creativity. A wrestling match not unlike Jacob struggling with an angel can be anticipated. Or David and Goliath. Did not David outwit Goliath? Was his victory not a victory of human imagination and spirit over mere brute strength? For Hildegard, heaven is a place filled with music.   —CR 58, IHM 157–62

Fundamentalist Imagination-Bashing

Fundamentalists who engage in imagination-bashing might take note of the following fact: the etymological origin for the word "hell" (real place where Satan dwells?) is *helan*, an old English word that means "to conceal" (in Latin, *celare*). In other words, hell is our place of concealment. Hell, then, is our refusal to create and our deadening the imagination of others. But if hell is concealment, then heaven must be creativity itself. Heaven would be the place of revelation, of unveiling, of telling the truth. Eckhart said: "The purpose of a word is to reveal." That is the purpose of all imagination. —CR 59–60

The Unimaginative Academy

It is not just religious fundamentalists who are scared of the fierce and wild power of imagination. Academic fundamentalists are also. I know a professor who received his doctoral degree from a very prestigious university on the West Coast. He did his doctorate in English literature on the sacred in D. H. Lawrence. He received two warnings from his doctoral committee: 1) You must not use the word "soul" in your dissertation, but, if you must, you have to put quotation marks around it. (I asked if D. H. Lawrence put quotation marks around the word "soul" in his work.) 2) You are forbidden to use the word "imagination" in the dissertation since it is a "romantic" concept.

—CR 60–61

Imagination Means "Soul"

Among the Celts, "imagination" means soul. Celtic scholar John O'Donohue points out that in the Celtic way of seeing the world, the "'soul' is the place where the imagination lives." The imagination operates at a threshold where light and dark, visible and invisible, possibility and fact come together. "The linear, controlling, external mind will never even glimpse" the gift that imagination is. The revelations of nature come to us by way of imagination—that is, what expands the soul. In a culture where anthropocentrism does not reign, imagination still does. For imagination needs the cosmos to feed on. It longs for relationships that stretch the soul. —CR 63

Patriarchy Seeks to Control

If we do not have a living imagination and are not busy feeding and nourishing imagination, then we simply lack soul. I feel sorry for fundamentalists of any kind who exclude powers of creativity and then wonder why fear and control addictions take over their life. All fascism wants to kill imagination and make control their God. That way lies cynicism as well. We have to learn to trust the universe and its creative powers. And to love them. The modern era's attempt to "master nature" (Descartes's term and Bacon's) is a pitiful, arrogant, demeaning, dead-end joke. Trust, not master. Dance with the rhythms of creativity, don't sit on the sidelines seeking to control it. Whether that compulsion to control comes from religious fundamentalism or academic fundamentalism, it leads to the same ennui for living and the same fixation on control. It also opens the door to cynicism and the desire to escape life by way of addictions, be they drugs, alcohol, shopping, TV, or more. It feeds patriarchy and pessimism for "pessimism comes from the repression of creativity" (Rank).   —CR 65

6

Combatting Evil:
Prophecy and Compassion

AWAKENING THE PROPHET

What Is a Prophet?

What does it mean to be a prophet? Who is a prophet? A prophet
is one who carries on the *Dabhar*, that is, the creative energy or
word of God, when it has been stymied or stifled by injustice or
laziness or too much belief in the immortality of what already
is. The prophet is passionate about justice-making and about
responding to injustice. There is an urgency to justice, as Rabbi
Heschel tells us. The prophet in each of us is our social conscience, our heartfelt concern about the loved ones of God who
suffer needlessly. "Prophetic inspiration," Heschel writes, "is for
the sake, for the benefit, of a third party. It is not a private affair
between prophet and God, its purpose is the illumination of the
people rather than the illumination of the prophet." The prophet
in us says, "NO! This is not the way the Creator wanted the
universe to respond to the blessing that creation is. We can—
we must—do things differently." Heschel says that "The major
activity of the prophet is *interference*."

To interfere with the way things are going, whether in terms
of denial of climate change by political leaders, militarism
among nations, sexism in churches, racism in education, or
dualism in self and society—the prophet criticizes and places
himself or herself in opposition and therefore in a position of

interfering with what is happening. Jeremiah talks of "tearing up and knocking down"—a Via Negativa that must precede the "building up and planting" that creative transformation is about. Biblical theologian Walter Brueggemann interprets this to mean that the prophet is sensitive to the *discontinuity* of history: how things need to break and be broken if New Creation is to emerge. The interference and therefore the discontinuity that are the prophet's concern are most evidently an interference in unjust situations and a break with the continuous injustice that is rained on, for example, women or artists, the earth or animals, Native Americans or people of color, or Third World peoples. The prophet does not hesitate to break with the recent past in order to regain an older past when the just harmony in order ruled the cosmos.

The prophet knows something about trusting anger, trusting one's moral outrage, trusting what is intolerable—and molding that anger and outrage into creative possibilities. When Eckhart says that "all deeds are accomplished in passion," he is underlining how important a blessing anger and outrage can be. The fall/redemption tradition has made far too much of anger as a sin. In fact, anger is often necessary to see one through the interference that must be accomplished. Anger, after all, is proportionate to one's love. Gandhi at one point called his work useful because it "struck the religious imagination of an angry people" . . . It is no wonder that Brueggemann sees the prophetic role as one of a "ministry of imagination." It is imagination that steers the sparks of anger in the direction of transformation and new creation. In this sense we need to realize that every prophet is an artist. And every true artist is a prophet.   —OB 260–61

The Prophet in Each of Us

Prophecy is about a return of blessing, our returning blessing for blessing. It presumes the kind of faith, that is trust, that we have named for each of the four paths. The prophet in us calls forth the excellence and beauty in each of us, it calls forth the best that we can give, the best that we can enjoy (Path I), the best that we can let go of (Path II), the best that we can create (Path III), the best that we can give to birthing the future by transforming the past (Path IV). Heschel says that the prophetic seed lies in the "recesses" of each person, so this means we are all called to be prophets. But what are these "recesses" where the prophetic lies? I believe that the four paths represent the recesses of each person: delight; stillness and grief; birthing and creativity; and transforming by way of justice-making and compassion. That is why the spiraling movement of the creation-centered journey necessarily leads to prophecy: because it is not a superficial journey but the deepest of all journeys. It is a journey from our recesses with others' recesses and beyond. It necessarily, then, feeds the prophet in each of us. —OB 262

Prophets Are Non-Elitists

The prophet is non-elitist in his or her empathy and understanding and in the means he or she chooses to arouse the people. The prophets present a street spirituality, one that the nonprofessional person can understand. That is why, as Brueggemann points out, the prophet must be an artist who calls forth symbols of justice and injustice that are universally recognizable. In this regard as in so many others, wisdom and prophecy are alike in the Jewish spiritual tradition. As one scholar puts it, "Wisdom acts like a prophet, walking through the streets and urging her doctrine on the people." —OB 263

Responding to Our Prophetic Vocation

The spiraling journey of creation-centered spirituality finds its fulfillment in persons responding to their prophetic vocations. The prophet falls in love with creation and especially with the little ones, the *anawim* (those without a voice), of creation (Path I); she then experiences the bottomless depths of suffering that beset the powerless and rob them of their beauty and dignity (Path II); from the nothingness experience she re-creates, working from the best that both left brain and right brain can offer (Path III); yearning for a New Creation, she launches her creativity in the direction of healing by way of compassion, celebration, and social justice (Path IV). In this manner she interferes with pessimism, cynicism, and despair, and channels moral outrage into a new creation.   —OB 264

The Oppressed (Anawim) Are a Source of Revelation

In reminding us of what the basics of living are about, the *anawim* return us to true humility, i.e., earth and earthiness. The *anawim* are an authentic source of revelation; they are our primary spiritual directors; they reveal where the kingdom/queendom of God is hidden. And they challenge all to metanoia, change of heart and lifestyle. Today, Mother Earth and her suffering creatures are calling us to eco-justice and new ways of living on the Earth. The prophetic response is one of generosity and creativity.   —OB 270

The prophet acts—as Aquinas puts it, the prophet "is moved not only to apprehend something, but also to speak or to do something."   —TTA 121

COMPASSION

We have seen in chapter 4 how Meister Eckhart develops a rich theology of Compassion, addressing both its mystical and its prophetic dimensions. Here we further explore the nature, power, and importance of compassion (MF)

Compassion as World Energy Source

Compassion is everywhere. Compassion is the world's richest energy source. Now that the world is a global village, we need compassion more than ever—not for altruism's sake, nor for philosophy's sake or theology's sake, but for survival's sake.
                                    —SNC xi

Compassion Is Not Pity but Celebration

Passion is not pity in the sense that our culture understands pity. It is not a feeling sorry for someone, nor is it a preoccupation with pain . . .

To reduce compassion to pity and to pitiful feelings is to exile compassion altogether from adult living. The word "pity" has evolved to mean something very different from compassion. What is the difference between pity and compassion? Pity connotes condescension, and this condescension, in turn, implies separateness. "I feel sorry for you because you are so different from me." Gestalt therapist Fritz Perls emphasizes that pity and compassion present shades of meaning that, "while subtle from the linguistic standpoint, are profoundly significant from the psychological." What are the differences? Pity "sometimes regards its object as not only suffering, but weak or inferior." There is less participation in the sufferings of another in pity than in compassion—compassion never considers an object as weak or inferior. Compassion, one might say, works for a strength born of awareness of shared weakness, and not from someone else's weakness. And from the awareness of the mutuality of us all. Thus to put down another as in pity is to put down one's self. "Most of what passes muster as pity is actually disguised gloating," warns Perls. . . .

The surest way of discerning whether one has pity towards or compassion with another is to answer this question: Do you celebrate with the same person or these same people? Max Scheler, in his study on *The Nature of Sympathy,* takes for granted not only the fact that true "fellow-feeling" or compassion includes joy but also the fact that joy and celebration constitute the better half of the whole that compassion is about.   —SNC 2–3

Compassion Is Not Sentiment

In the late Middle Ages a sentimental piety was developed that sidetracked the true meaning of compassion, and instead of

celebrating and relieving one another's pain together, the people "drew up a minute inventory of the torments inflicted on Christ; they enumerated the steps that he made on the *Via Dolorosa*, the bruises of his body and the drops of his blood" (Rapp). One can explore how much of this masochistic and sentimental energy of pity is still present in pieties and hymns, in sermons and in petrified languages of Christian churches, Protestant and Catholic.
—SNC 5

God Is Compassionate

The very name *Yahweh* designates God as Compassion, and God is called "The Compassionate One." God is full of compassion (Ps. 103.11), promises this compassion toward people (Dt. 30.3) and delivers on this promise (Dt. 13.17). "His compassion fails not, being new every morning," sings one psalm (Lam. 3.22). Time and again God demonstrates compassion (II Kings 13.23; 2 Chron. 36.15), and the divine love is extended especially to the poor, the widow, the orphan, and the stranger. God is called the "Father of Compassion," and according to Midrash, creation was born of the divine compassion toward creatures.

To say that God is compassionate is to say that God suffers at the sufferings of others. God suffers. God is in pain. Human compassion then becomes the relief of the pain of God as well as the relief of human pain.   —SNC 19

Wheel of Compassion

We have seen that compassion without joy and celebration, without action and public justice-making, without ideas and ideals, without passion and caring, without a consciousness or a way of living, without cosmic and divine awareness and interaction, is not compassion at all. It is a co-optation of compassion. It is a demonic substitute for compassion. It is death-dealing, not lifegiving. All these elements of compassion are themselves interconnected, and to fail in one of these is to threaten compassion altogether for each energy depends on the others, much like spokes on a wheel.   —SNC 34

Climbing Jacob's Ladder

A major cause for compassion's having played so much smaller
a role in Christian spirituality than it did in Jesus' teaching and
spirituality is that Jacob's ladder has played so powerful a role.
There is no theme in all of male-dominated mystical teaching in
Western Christianity that is more recurrent than that of climbing
Jacob's ladder. One theologian put it this way: "The theme of the
ladder is constant, indeed capital, in the spiritual life and in the
history of spirituality." He should have said "in *my* understanding of the spiritual life and in the history of *Western* spirituality."
In the *Dictionnaire de Spiritualité*, an encyclopedia of numerous
volumes dedicated to Western spirituality, the entry under "spiritual ladder" comprises twenty-four full columns and includes
an apology from the author for the treatment being only partial.
—SNC 37

Where did Christian mystics get this "up" oriented motif in
their vision of the spiritual journey? It is derived from hellenis-
tic and not biblical sources. It is, for example, the dynamic of
Plato's way of conceiving of our experiences of reality, and the
upward journey is also a journey into abstractions, as Thorleif
Boman points out. "Plato starts from the individual concrete
thing, always thinking more generally, more abstractly, and more
mentally, and *mounting ever higher* until he sees the prototypes
of all appearances, the Ideas." . . . There can be no question that
this drive upwards in the name of spirituality is a drive away
from body, earth, matter, mother, the sensual.

It is also uber masculine and phallic to be always striving to
be climbing up and away from mother earth and matter.

In contrast, for the Jewish mind, which considered hearing to
be the most important sense and music the paradigm of reality,
a spiritual person grows ever more sensitive to those *around*
one. God is not spatially up but in one's midst. "And I will know
that I am the Lord their God, who brought them forth out of
the land of Egypt that I might dwell among them" (Ex. 29.45f.).
Amongness, not upness, is the dynamic of the spiritual journey.
The journey of the Four Paths is best pictured as a spiral that

celebrates an open-ended circle with a direction and an in and out dynamic that brings together both the feminine and the masculine.   —SNC 41

Dancing Sarah's Circle

I believe that a far richer and more scripturally grounded symbol for our spirituality is that of dancing Sarah's circle. "Dancing Sarah's Circle," people ask, "where is that in the Scriptures?" Let us look at what the Scriptures tell us of Sarah. Sarah was ninety years old and Abraham was one hundred when she heard from a visitor that she would bear a child . . . Sarah named her first and only son "Yitzchak" (Isaac), which derives from the root word "to laugh," because "God has given me cause to laugh [because she bore a child in old age]; all those who hear of it will laugh with me" (Gen 21:6-8).

A spirituality of Dancing Sarah's circle is one of laughter and joy. Sarah was able to be surprised, filled with unexpected wonder, and to laugh. This already sharply distinguishes her symbol from that of male interpretations of Jacob's dream, since as you may have observed, there is little laughter and joy among those who climb ladders. Ladder-climbing is ever so serious. Egos are so much involved. A second insight from Sarah's story is that the cause of her laughter is pregnancy. She is a symbol of birthing, creating, and fruitfulness—her laughter stemmed from the fact that God's imagination for creativity is so much greater than the human imagination. She laughed because human wisdom said pregnancy was impossible; but divine wisdom said nothing is impossible. Sarah, then, like Mary, the mother of Jesus, was to turn the tables on the strict and serious knowledge that people presume they possess about exactly when and where the boundaries to birth are to be found.   —SNC 44–45

Climbing Jacob's Ladder versus Dancing Sarah's Circle

Sarah then is a symbol of laughter and creativity. One might say, of Shalom (Peace, Wholeness). But the contrasts between

Dancing Sarah's Circle and Climbing Jacob's Ladder are even more telling than that. They can be diagramed as follows:

Climbing Jacob's Ladder	*Dancing Sarah's Circle*
up/down	in/out
climbing	dancing, celebrating
Sisyphian	satisfying
competition	shared ecstasies
restrictive, elitist: survival of the fittest	welcoming, non-elitist: survival of all
hierarchical	democratic
violent, distant	eye to eye, strong and gentle
sky-oriented, fleeing mother, matter	earth-oriented, grounding
ruthlessly independent	interdependent
envy and judgement-oriented	non-judgmental
abstract, distant-making	nurturing and sensual
linear, ladder-like	curved, circle-like
theistic (subject/objects)	panentheistic (rounded)
love of neighbor is separate from love of what is at the top	love of neighbor *is* love of God

—SNC 45

A Compassionate Future

As long as the West remains dependent on the ladder symbol, there will be more violence, more sadism and masochism in the name of all of our numerous gods—and the exile of compassion will continue. Phallicism, the worship of up-ness, remains America's dominant religion. The great locker room in the sky urges men on and dictates how "their women" will be treated. But heaven is not so distant, not so up. It is, as Jesus tried and tried and tried to teach, "in our midst." The "kingdom/queendom of God is among you." It is where people can learn to love as

brothers and sisters, eye-to-eye, dancing Sarah's circle and relieving one another's pain. It is wherever compassion is practiced.
When theologian Edward Schillebeeckx speaks of transcendence
as "no longer being up but the future," he is correct. Now, however, we can begin to name that future. It is Sarah's Circle. Transcendence is Sarah's circle, and Sarah's circle is transcendence.
Therein lies salvation for a global village and the holy people
who inhabit it—which is all of us.   —SNC 65

Compassion and Competition

Compassion suffers miserably at the hands of competition, for
compassion seeks our common likenesses—which in fact are joy
and tragedy—and not our differences. Yet it is competition's task
to make us different—winners and losers, ins and outs. In doing
so competition often demands violent and destructive energies
which are not those of compassion which flow one into another.
Competition isolates, separates and estranges. (Modest competition can be a source of excellence, however.) Compassion
unites, makes one, and embraces. Since thankfulness is lacking
in all sick competition, then too is all potential for celebration
or Eucharist, which is merely the theological name for thanking.
Here, more than in revised rituals or liturgical scholarship oriented at lost periods of ecclesial history, may lie the richest soil
for turning over and planting a revitalized worshiping community. If we can move from competition to compassion, we will
have moved from dull and moralistic and ungrateful and legalistic worship (or is it worsh*up*?) to celebrate thanking.   —SNC 72

Compassion versus Compulsion

Psychologist William Eckhardt, in his ground-breaking book
entitled *Compassion: Toward a Science of Value*, suggests that
competition, "far from being a function of nature . . . is a function of compulsion" (100). He feels that the opposite energy
to compassion is properly named compulsion, and that it is in
instructing ourselves and others in compulsion that we drive

out any hope for compassion and that we introduce the gods of competition . . .

This temptation to compulsion is one more reason why contemplation and solitude are so important an ingredient for compassion. We need to learn to let go even of our good intentions, our good works and attitudes, and this kind of letting go is learned in solitude and cosmic contemplation. It has been my experience that behind these compulsions there generally lurks a fear of nature and a fear of things. —SNC 74–75

Compassion as Salvation

The Biblical sign of salvation is not control (whether self-control, control of others, or being controlled)—it is celebration. Thus *celebration* is a proper word for transcendence in Biblical thinking, just as compassion is, for the celebration is one of the two basic energies of compassion. Compassion is heaven come to earth, as Eckhart put it: "To rejoice at another person's joy is like being in heaven." And "whatever happens to another, whether it be joy or sorrow, happens to me." —SNC 89

Solitude and Celebration

Solitude is closely related to celebration because, like celebration, it is a form of forgetting for a while. Very often we want to leave our memories behind in solitude or purify them by means of solitude. —SNC 94

Forgiveness Frees Us to Be Compassionate

We cannot forget that forgiveness, like freedom and releasement, is a political as well as a psychological act. We forgive systems that coerce and control us by replacing them with structures that release us for compassion. —SNC 102

Resurrection

The symbol of the empty tomb of Christ is an important challenge to "when cross and ladder reigned supreme." "Resurrection" does not mean rising up, since if Jesus had risen up in the cave, he would have bumped his head. It means exiting, going out, leaving death and its shrouds behind. It is an empty tomb into which persons entered and from which one left. Being empty and having been emptied, it is not a closed circle but an open circle.   —SNC 113

SENSUALITY AND THE PROPHETS

Passion, Imagination, and the Prophets

Rabbi Heschel tells us that the prophets were not ascetics. Rather, they were earthy people. "Asceticism was not the ideal of the biblical man. The source of evil is not in passion, in the throbbing heart, but rather in hardness of heart, in callousness and insensitivity . . . We are stirred by their (the prophets') passion and enlivened imagination. . . . It is to the imagination and the passions that the prophets speak rather than aiming at the cold approbation of the mind."   —WS 198

Sensual Spirituality

The surest way to change people and hopefully their institutions is by way of pleasure. Not by words but by appealing to interests of persons, which is to say, by appealing to what they consider their fullest pleasure to be. A student of mine decided to do an experiment. He went to a coffee shop in the bus station in Chicago and ordered a bowl of popcorn. Then he meditated on each individual kernel of popcorn and slowly, slowly chewed it. It took him several hours to eat this one bowl. During his experiment at least eight individuals came up to him and asked: "Where did you ever learn to enjoy your food so much?"

Does this story not demonstrate that people are looking for greater pleasure? That people are attracted by pleasure? That people are also united by pleasure? Perhaps there has been a dearth of nonviolent social change in the West because there has been too little consciousness of pleasure and the political force that it is and can be. Pleasure obviously has a deep social meaning—otherwise advertisers, the manipulators of social symbols, would not be so bent on forcing *their* definition of pleasure (pleasure as consumerism) upon us. The biblical tradition sings of pleasure for the many, not for the few. The pleasure of all or of none. To find true pleasure, all of us need to let go of certain ways of pleasure-seeking. This is one meaning of living a "simple lifestyle," namely the redefining of what authentic pleasure is and where it can be found. The problem is that today even sensuality has been reduced to a consumer item. Thomas Merton foresaw this when he wrote one day that it was raining outside and that he was going to walk bareheaded in the rain "because before long they will be selling you the rain."

Mysticism is not in itself ethics, though in all authentic instances mysticism leads to ethics, and indeed a living ethic leads to mysticism. Some persons get confused when hearing of a "sensual" or a "pleasurable" spirituality and feel this is synonymous with moral anarchy, at least at a personal level. The question often arises: How about personal ethics or ethics between individuals? Are there norms in this regard when it comes to our sensual pleasures? A norm that emerges from the biblical tradition is that for a person or people to pursue pleasure at the expense of others is morally wrong. The proper name for this kind of pleasure-seeking is sadism, and we engage in it whenever we fail to question the roots of our pleasures. For example, tearing down tropical rain forests in Brazil for the "pleasure" of McDonald's hamburgers borders on the sadistic. There is a profound connection between pleasure and justice—who defines pleasure for us? W. H. Auden warned: "As a rule, it was the pleasure haters who became unjust."   —WWW 26–27

Ecstasy

An ecstatic experience is one of forgetting oneself and of being turned on in a full and deep way. Our ecstasy is our getting outside ourselves (the word comes from two Greek words meaning "to stand outside of"); our forgetting ourselves—if only for a second, a minute, an hour, a day . . . or a lifetime. Ecstasy is our getting high. For this very reason, because ecstasy is a forgetting, it is also memorable. Ecstasy is a memorable experience of forgetting oneself, of getting outside of oneself. Our ecstatic experiences, then, are the memorable experiences of our lives.

—WWW 43–44

Natural and Tactical Ecstasies

In discussing our experience of ecstasy, I distinguish between natural and tactical kinds of ecstasy. Natural ecstasies include nature, friendship, sexuality, arts and craftsmanship, sports, thinking, travel and visiting, involuntary deprivations, celebration, work. Among tactical ecstasies are the following: chant, processions, rituals, fasting, abstinence, drugs, drink, celibacy, yoga, Zen exercises, formal meditations, retreats, biofeedback, and more.

The most fundamental contrast between natural and tactical ecstasies is that a natural ecstasy is an end in itself, while a tactical ecstasy, as the name implies, is only a means. How simple and basic is this rule, yet how frequently violated! By calling natural ecstasy an end in itself, we mean that God is directly experienced in these actions. In tactical ecstasy a person is rendered vulnerable for a God-experience, but the tactic itself is no guarantee of God's presence—it is a preparation for an event but not the event itself. The natural comes first because first, a spiritual person receives. The tactical is second because it is man-made, a strategy devised by humans and our religious cultures. The personal experience of creation needs to proceed cultural experience, and when this basic rule is violated, an act of repression risks being canonized a sacred act. The tactical, then, presumes the natural and should build on it. Tactical divorced from natural ecstasy is an invitation to danger. For example, celibacy without first knowing the sexual; or fasting without first knowing the joys of eating; or drugs without friendships or highs from nature.

There are also significant differences among tactical ecstasies themselves—namely, the difference between an external stimulus (as in the case of drugs or drink, for example) whereby a person receives aid from outside his body and personality, and an internal asceticism (as, for example, in fasting or celibacy or Zen meditation). While risks abound in each of these ways, at least those that are internal are not as severe or as potentially upsetting to the operation and chemistry of a person as outside stimuli can be. Nor are the internal tactical trips as habit-forming or as hard to break away from once the ecstasy from this strategy is achieved. Both kinds require a guide or a group to encourage and support when the trip gets dark or lonely.

—WWW 63–64

Natural Pleasures

Nor should we be deterred from the pleasures of natural ecstasies because we fear what the hedonist within us might do and what lengths he or she might go to. This fear breeds more rules, more limits, more fear. Instead, we need to keep our heads about us and realize that the Creator has implanted certain limits within all natural ecstasies. A setting sun sets; a vision from a mountaintop ceases; lovers do not stay in bed forever; a symphony has an ending. I have an aunt who loves opera and cries each time she leaves one, saying, "Why did it have to end?" Life itself has its ending and its limits, as do all the joys within life. We do not have to play patrolman or God and project our puny limits onto the Creator's beauties.

The hedonist fears we harbor are invariably manufactured fantasies. As such, they tell us more about the repression within ourselves than about the way to experience the beauties of life. If we were to live our fantasies more and manufacture them less, we would become realists overnight. And far less fearful. And much more loving of life. And willing to allow others to enjoy the pleasures of living.

The road back to sanity, to everyday experience of God by natural ecstasy, will not be an easy one. But is there any other route?   —WWW 67

Cherish the Body

"We ought to cherish the body [and] celebrate the wonderful communion of body and soul," says Thomas Aquinas. His whole life long, from his early *Commentary on the Sentences* written at about twenty-eight years of age to his midlife work *De Veritate* and to his final work, *Summa Theologiae,* Aquinas waged a fierce battle to rebut dualism of body and soul, spirit and matter. Throughout his life he never altered his position on this critical and highly debated issue. In so doing, he took on the entire ascetic tradition of the fourth-century church fathers and church councils that, as Rosemary Ruether points out, "tended to equate the dualism of soul or mind over body with the dualism of male over female," which results in "a fearful view of sex and fanatical misogyny toward women." Consider what boldness this took on Aquinas's part—challenging the entire patristic inheritance on so basic a topic as dualism and misogyny! This battle still wages today, of course, because fundamentalism and patriarchy are philosophies that are built on dualism, while a feminist consciousness opts for nondualism. It was on this issue that Aquinas welcomed Aristotle as a liberator from Platonism's antipathy toward matter.   —TTA 57

Aquinas says, "The soul is more like God when united to the body than when separated from it." He draws practical conclusions from this position saying, "We ought to cherish the body. Our body's substance is not from an evil principle as the Manicheans imagine, but from God. And therefore we ought to cherish the body by the friendship of love, by which we love God." Here we hear Eckhart's words, "the soul loves the body." Matter is not responsible for evil, insists Aquinas, our bad choices are, and they do "not come to the soul from the body, but to the body from the soul." It is a law of nature that we should care for our body, and it is for this reason that "the sensitive appetite and passion are the subject and seat of the virtues."　　—TTA 61–62

EVIL

My book on evil, *Sins of the Spirit, Blessings of the Flesh: Transforming Evil in Soul and Society*, first came out the very week that the horrible murders at the Columbine High School occurred in 1999. In it I attempt to create a new language and new setting for speaking of evil. The setting was the "blessings of the flesh," including universe flesh, earth flesh, human flesh, and the seven chakras. Cheap religion has been scapegoating flesh for long enough. We need to put evil in the context of cosmology. The book owes its title to Aquinas who said, "sins of the spirit are more grievous than sins of the flesh, for sins of the flesh take you toward God while sins of the spirit take you away from God." How would history have been different if religion had taught that truth?

Evil is far bigger and more powerful that we give it credit for: "Sin" talk invariably trivializes what evil is. By restarting the conversation of Evil with 1) blessing of the flesh and 2) comparing the seven chakras of the East with the seven capital sins of the West, we had a fresh methodology and perspective to talk about evil.

In the Foreword to the new edition of my study on evil, Deepak Chopra predicts that evil will be the number one spiritual problem of the twenty-first century.　　—CNF 396–97; SS xiii

Evil Evolves

In my opinion we do need to talk about sin today, but not in the same way we talked about it in the past. Evil evolves, as culture evolves. Our capacity for destruction and alienation, self-hatred and social resentment, luxurious living among gross injustice, evolves. We must talk about sin again because not to do so perpetuates our problems, just as any kind of denial invariably creates more complex problems.　　—SS 7

Evil as Chaos

The biblical tradition treats sin as a *cosmological event*. The Jewish scholar Jon D. Levinson, in *Creation and the Persistence of Evil*, tells us that in apocalyptic literature, Israel's struggle is against "cosmic forces of the utmost malignancy. Their evil reaches everywhere, even into the human heart, and their defeat requires nothing less than a cosmic transformation, a new cosmogony—a new creation." Chaos happens when evil happens; it constitutes the undoing of creation.   —SS 11

Bored by Sin

Our culture is frankly bored with the word *sin,* and one reason is that we are bored with everything. We are a species made for cosmology, yet our culture has rendered us passive couch potatoes and shopping and entertainment addicts. In short, we have been cut off from the big universe, and consequently we are bored, boring, and violent. We have even managed to render sin boring!   —SS 11

The Body Doesn't Sin

Sin, most believers have been taught, means sins of the flesh. But the body does not sin, as Aquinas observed—it is the soul that sins. And the soul's most grievous sins are less sins of the flesh than sins of the spirit. These spiritual sins get us in our deepest trouble with self, relatives, spouses, earth creatures, and future generations—in other words, with all our relations, and with all flesh.   —TTA 145–48

Death Is Real

Death is real and will not be trivialized. Death's reality is what makes flesh so real as well—real, though short-lived. Flesh is so vulnerable. Humanity has to recover the sacredness and blessing that flesh is before it is too late. The ecological crisis is a *flesh crisis*. It is about our home (*eikos* in Greek) being invaded, being toxic and unhealthy for our flesh and future generations not only of human beings but of all of creation.   —SS 56

No Dualism

There is no dualism between flesh and spirit. Spirit breathes through flesh, and flesh receives its existence from spirit. We call all this breathing *life*, and the mystic Thomas Aquinas said, "God is life, per se life." And spirit is "the élan or vitality in all matter." Is this different from Einstein saying $E = mc^2$?   —SS 59

Awesome, Sacred Flesh

Instead of the "fear of flesh" that guilt and patriarchal regrets instill in us, a new cosmology can teach us *the awe of flesh* and with that the *sacredness of flesh*. Awe is what Thomas Aquinas called "chaste fear"—a fear that leads to reverence and gratitude, rather than a servile fear that renders us afraid and masochistic in the presence of bullies. A pleasure is built into what is awesome. Pleasures contain beauty, and beauty is goodness. The needs of the flesh are pleasurable and good. We eat to stay alive and preserve our health but also because food is good and delicious.   —SS 40

Flesh Redeems

Our new creation story teaches us that all flesh has a 13.8-billion-year history. Only if we know that history can flesh become a *redemptive force*. When we know it, we become *grateful* and *reverent* toward our bodies, food, flowers, forests, soil, other animals, birds, fishes, and other human beings. Gratitude and reverence heal. They redeem. They cure us of diseases of the soul and mind and heart and body.

Flesh redeems because it awakens awe and wonder and delight. Awe is redemptive, returning us to our origins—every baby is easily awestruck. This is the positive side to vulnerability—to be struck by awe, spellbound. Mystics promise that we can return to the state of vulnerability and awe, to the "unborn self," as Meister Eckhart put it. And we can be free there. We can start over there.

This "return" is redemptive. It heals us from sin—our own, our cultures, our enemies' sins against us. Salvation is a return.
—SS 40–41

Evolutionary Understanding

I propose that it is this evolutionary understanding of sin that has been missing in the Theodicy dilemma (the question: How can a good God allow so much evil?). We need to remember—as process theologians and creation mystics remind us—that God's awareness of sin also evolves. "God becomes as creatures express God," says Eckhart. Does Satan become as humans express him? Did Hitler teach God something—even *regret* at sharing so much divine power of creativity with an animal capable of so much treachery?   —SS 155

Creative Evil

Evil abounds when humanity's capacity for creativity is the greatest. Consider how the Hitler regime "progressed" from killing victims in the back of trucks using carbon monoxide exhaust fumes to the far more efficient methods of elimination through gas showers and crematoria.   —SS 155–56

Acedia: Ennui and Couch-Potato-Itis

Acedia was defined by Thomas Aquinas as the "lack of energy to begin new things." It is a kind of ennui, depression, cynicism, sadness, boredom, listlessness, couch-potato-itis, being passive, apathy, psychic exhaustion, having no energy. An ancient text from the monk Evagrius calls it the "noonday demon" that is "the most oppressive of all demons." The desert monks considered it the most dangerous of the demons, for it tempted a monk to flee from his vocation back to the comforts of "the world."
—SS 167–68

I believe that acedia is the most dominant sin of our culture today. Couch-potato-itis is a conspiracy (conscious or unconscious) of an economic system that is geared to rendering consumerism a daily addiction. Our economic system creates a kind of spiritual enslavement. Just recently a mature African-American pastor in a city church told me how sad she is at seeing how little energy the young people have. "They are so tired. I am much more energetic than they are!" she exclaimed. Another adult I met recently said: "This generation of young people seems to wake up tired. Why is that?" Where has all the energy gone? That is the question of acedia. —SS 168

Adam and Eve

A strong argument can be made that the primal story of our first parents' sin is about acedia. Why do I say this? First, because the very word *disobedience* means, etymologically, "failure to listen." (*Obedire* in Latin means "to listen.") A failure to listen is clearly an imbalance of the first chakra, whose task it is to take in the sounds of the universe. The first chakra critique of true disobedience—failure to listen—lays open the sick and sinful kinds of obedience that have been very evident through history. In the modern era, I propose, *obedience has proven to be a far more serious sin than disobedience.* Consider, for example, the obedience of the mass murderers under Hitler—"I was just following orders," they declared. Yes, they were following orders and obeying. But they were not listening to the cries of their victims or to teachings of justice and compassion that society and religion are supposed to pay heed to. Such sinful disobedience is the opposite of listening. — SS 177–78

Arrogance

Arrogance is a better word than pride for naming misdirected love in the first chakra. The word "arrogance" comes from the Latin word *agro,* which means "to appropriate to oneself something to which one has no claim." Racism and sexism (one sex

superior to another), colonialism and heterosexism, adultism
(the older superior to the younger), and ageism (one age superior
to another) are all species of arrogance and are all connected to
the first chakra. So too is speciesism whereby humans think they
are more important than all other creatures. It is this unhealthy
pride or *arrogance* (what Eastern spirituality calls "ego") that is
the problem.   —SS 179

Racism

The arrogance that comes when humans isolate themselves by
nationality or religion or race or class or sex or sexual orientation is evident everywhere in our world. Racism would be one
example of this son or daughter of acedia.   —SS 179

Addiction

Is it not true that most addictions are offensive to the flesh? We
might even say that they are sins against the flesh. Alcoholism,
drug addiction, watching too much TV, excessive eating—these
are all exercises in failing to love the flesh. Tradition has called
lust and gluttony "sins of the flesh," but I would call them *sins
against the flesh*. If we lived in a society that truly honored and
celebrated the flesh, we would have fewer addictions.   —SS 219

Dualism

Dualism is about imbalance. It is one-sided, not two-or-more
sided . . . Dualism also separates, keeps people apart. It is not
about love-making in any form. Refusing to give birth, it is bar-
ren—it repeats what is, but it does not bring something new into
the universe. Addicts as addicts are not generative; they repeat
old, familiar routines. Little new is born of that repetitive process; little is given birth to.   —SS 224

Victimhood

If we do not give our anger the appropriate and creative outlet it
needs, we fall into victimization. We come to define ourselves as

victims and then fulfill the self-defeating prophecy by acting like victims. A victim is one who is already served up as dead. A victim is not living. One who chooses victimhood is choosing not to live fully. When we are out of touch with our anger, we often give up. Our anger allows us to live fully even under the most trying of circumstances. It puts living before languishing, victory before victimhood, and empowerment before disempowerment.

—SS 237

Self-Pity

In my experience men are especially prone to self-pity. The reason is that authentic compassion is a motherly thing—if men do not realize the mother in themselves (in Hebrew the word for *compassion* is the same as the word for *womb*), then they are condemned to looking outside for the mother. And that quest is fated to disappoint.

—SS 251

Authentic Empowerment

Ironically, the cure for self-pity is authentic empowerment, which for men means recovering the true power of compassion. A patriarchal mind-set actually prevents men from curing themselves of self-pity, but they need to rediscover their maternal powers of nourishment. Only opening up to the possibility of their psychic bisexuality allows men to be "real men," that is, full human beings, capable of offering compassion to themselves and others, capable of mothering themselves and others. The cure lies in men finding the mother *inside them.* (Similarly, the cure for bitterness in women is to find a father-principle, a way of expressing anger and strong passion, inside themselves.) Maybe behind Jesus' powerful statement that "unless you leave father and mother you are not worthy of me" lies the idea that adults have to learn to father and mother themselves if they are to grow into the kind of compassion that Jesus represents.

—SS 252

Envy

Envy is in some ways more powerful than hatred, for it feeds hatred and gives birth to it and is more subtle. Hatred tends to be more out in the open; it is as if people are more ashamed of their envy than of their hatred, so they keep it inside, where it rankles and rots, decays and putrefies, all the time seeping bile into the imagination, which works it over and over until it gives birth to shadowy beings that come into existence by way of projections. Traditionally these beings have been called *demons*.

—SS 319

From Evil to the Sacred

We often talk about "good vs. evil," but I think a more accurate understanding would be "the sacred vs. evil." Bad is the opposite of good. But evil is bigger than bad and bigger than sin. "Fear is the door in the heart that lets evil spirits in," Lakota teacher Buck Ghosthorse taught me one day. Sin is the door in each chakra that lets evil spirits in. When our seven chakras awaken, we are ready to wrestle with the energy of what we call in the West *the seven capital sins*.

Like St. Paul, who said our battle is against "powers and principalities," that is to say spirit beings, we need to be alert to the spiritual power of evil. Racism, sexism, injustice, do not disappear and die. They come back every generation. They are spiritual therefore. Recovering a sense of the sacred empowers us to do something about evil.   —SS xxxvii

7

Youth, Education, and Work

YOUTH, ELDERING, AND VOCATION

In addition to working with young people to develop the Cosmic Mass, Fox has worked with rapper Professor Pitt and with Ted Richards (now president of the Chicago Wisdom Project) in developing the YELLAWE [Youth and Elder Learning Laboratory for Ancestral Wisdom Education] project for inner-city high school students. The educational philosophy for that project is laid out in his book, The A.W.E. Project: Reinventing Education, Reinventing the Human. *He also collaborated with Adam Bucko of the Reciprocity Foundation, who works with young adults living on the streets of New York. Together they wrote* Occupy Spirituality: A Radical Vision for a New Generation *and in the process interviewed many young adults in North America about their quest for and experience of spirituality. Fox's work with the Order of the Sacred Earth will be discussed in chapter 8.* (CB)

YELLAWE

I commit myself to working with young people who recognize the power of this revolution in education, who want to educate the next generation, and who carry the skills of postmodern language that can have an impact as "edutainment." One of these people, Professor Pitt, a 31-year-old African American rapper, video maker, and martial arts practitioner, has put the themes of this book, including the 10 Cs to rap and video. The 10 Cs

177

are: cosmology or creation (including ecology); contemplation; creativity; chaos; compassion; courage or magnanimity; critical consciousness and judgment; community; ceremony and cele- bration; character and chakra development. Working together, we launched an alternative educational model not by challeng- ing public schools head on, but by offering courses after school hours. That way, educators need not feel personally threatened. We follow the advice of Buckminster Fuller, who proposed that those who want to bring about social change should do so not by frontal attack, but by offering better models. Fuller said, "You never change things by fighting the existing reality. To change something, build a new model that makes the existing model obsolete."

We called this project YELLAWE, which stands for Youth and Elders' Learning Laboratory of Ancestral Wisdom Education.

—AWE 150–51

Vocation

Adam Bucko: I often use the phrase "being in vocation," because following my calling feels more like being in the field, where I'm an expression of something that is arising in me. It's more like "I'm either in this field or I'm not." And being in this field in my vocation requires a constant practice of receptivity, so the call, the inner arising, can be sensed and consented to.

Matthew Fox: That's a wonderful way of putting it, being "in vocation" and working "from" that place. I think [the poet] Bill Everson would say your vocation discovers you; it carries you along. It's like a big wave. It's like love, which until it is awakened in you, you don't know what it is. The British scientist Rupert Sheldrake talks today about how the word *field* may be today's parlance for the word *soul*, which has lost so much of its meaning of late. Your talk about vocation being "in this field" resonates well with his insight.

I think it is also important to acknowledge, as you say, that vocation is not a fixed thing. It is always evolving. *Vocation* is a verb. When I look at my life and my vocation, originally I thought my vocation was to be a Dominican priest and preacher in the Catholic Church. And then, in trying to be that, the whole thing exploded, and what can I say? I was exploded out of the Catholic Church, but I'm still responding to the same call, it's still the same vocation, it's still the same wave that I'm on. I am doing it in a much larger field, however, then the narrow boundaries of contemporary Catholicism allow. —OS 97–98

Vocation as Via Creativa

Fox: In many respects I would classify vocation as the Via Creativa; it is a creative call that we respond to creatively and generously and, as you say, it is always evolving and often surprising us by the directions it takes us. I love what Joseph Campbell says: "None of us lives the life we had intended." That has certainly been my experience—I thought I was going to be a Dominican preacher until death. I am still a preacher (mostly a lecturer), and I surely draw on my Dominican tradition daily (and great spirits from that tradition), but I have moved out of the literal mold, or as I said above, I've been exploded out of it. Evolution happens.
—OS 99

The Future Is Calling

Bucko: Going back to the question of vocation, if vocation is a call, who's doing the calling?

Fox: Certainly—and we can all agree on this, whether we are atheists, theists, panentheists—the future is doing the calling. The unborn children, our great-great-grandchildren, are doing the calling. A mere seventy-five years from now they're going to be saying, "What did you do, Daddy, when the Earth was collapsing and when militarism was where you were putting so much of your money, and when empires were still the mode of the day, and when religions were at each other's throats and Christianity was collapsing? What did you do? How did you interfere and say no?" So I think we could all agree that the call is from the future.

Now, the call is also—and Bill Everson would emphasize this–from the collective, from the species. He calls it a *race*, but I think *species* has a little more palatable tone. But it's not just our species, it's the other species that are calling today too, and I think more and more people are waking up to this. Of course, the traditional language for all this calling is that God is doing the calling.   —OS 108

Only One Vocation

Fox: There is really only one vocation: that's to be mystic-prophets, to be lovers and defenders of what we cherish. What form it takes, how it is incarnated in history and culture, of course, will vary. However, we really do all have a common vocation. If we could begin to think like that, whether we're Muslim or Jewish or Native American or Buddhist or Hindu or Christian or atheist, it would create an incredible bedrock of commonality for service to community.

You know, I've always been struck by the word *community* itself. It's really based on the words *cum munio*, "to do work together." Maybe it really means to do vocation together—to gather our vocations. Again, that's what worship should be. Worship should be the gathering together of the wonder and joy and pain and suffering we encounter while attempting to live out our common—though unique—vocations.   —OS 110

Mentoring

Fox: All kinds of studies have shown that young people who find mentors have their lives transformed. I experienced that also when I found Père Chenu in Paris. And I found him because I contacted an author—the monk Thomas Merton—and asked him for advice about where to study spirituality; since he told me to go to Paris, I thank him for bringing me to Chenu, who became my mentor and named the creation spirituality tradition for me.

Having Chenu as my mentor gave me courage. First of all, his life gave me courage, because he was silenced by the pope for twelve years, forbidden to write; he worked with the worker-priest movement and Marxists; he contributed substantively to Vatican II; and he helped launch Liberation Theology. This guy did so much, but he kept his humor, he kept his love of life, and he was not bitter or anything like that, right up to the end. At the end he was asked, "Aren't you depressed by what's happening in the Church today?" And he said, "Oh, if you're going to have omelets, you've got to break the eggs." He said that Vatican II was prophetic, so it's already obsolete anyway. He said now is the time, when everything's in chaos, this is when the Holy Spirit loves to go to work. He said now is the time for theology to really happen. He was about ninety-two years old when he said those things. So he maintained his youthfulness and his love—not an ounce of cynicism in him. And the way he treated young students taught me a lot—no sadomasochistic one-up-man-ship games, which are so common in academia.

Bucko: That's beautiful. The beautiful thing about mentorship is that an authentic mentor always shares his or her life, love, and wisdom with the student, which means that it's very integrated and all-encompassing. The experience affects all domains of life. One of my mentors, who is a rabbi, once said to me that in his particular lineage, a rabbi is never a guru. He said you move in with the rabbi, you become part of his family, just to make sure that you can see all the problems of the household. And, to me that's really what mentorship is about.   —OS 167–68

Eldering and Evolution

Fox: What scientists have now found is this: that the Neanderthals lived to be only about thirty years old, whereas our ancestors lived longer—this means that *Homo sapiens* had grandparents and elders, and the Neanderthals did not. This is what seems to have saved our species! That we had the wisdom of the elders. This is very important information, and both elders and young people should reflect deeply on it. It also helps to explain the great esteem for elders among ancient peoples and among indigenous peoples today. They remember how vital the contribution of the elders was to their very survival in the past. And, of course, good communication among generations. All that is part of the history of our species, and we are foolish if we block out the wisdom of any one generation. We are in this together. Let us learn from one another and learn mutually.

—OS 170–71

Refirement, Not Retirement

The intergenerational wisdom I speak of cannot happen if all generations of men, from youngest to oldest, don't meet together. . . . I believe we must retire the word *retirement*. I think a better word is *refirement*. Once the need to put bread on the table for our families fired us up. Now we ask: "Where is the fire in my belly now?" We can still contribute in special, important, and unique ways, but they will be different ways.   —HSM 200–201

EDUCATION

A Need for Wisdom Schools

We might say that our era is in need of wisdom schools, as opposed to the knowledge factories that have characterized education during the industrial era. It is difficult to underestimate how many jobs and how much new energy could be generated by making this shift alone. A wisdom school would honor the heart and body, the right brain of awe and wonder and intuition, as much as it would the analytic, rational, or left brain. It would therefore honor the artist by inviting her to teach not just art but life—to teach images that are within all of us. By eliciting images through art as meditation, a wisdom school would pay attention to people's pain, grief, and anger as well as their desires and dreams. When people can express the truths that are in them, they are truly learning . . .

Education, from the Latin word *educere*, means "to lead out." It is the way that our species leads the best out of our children and adults alike. Unlike other species, we are not programmed by our DNA; we have to be mentored and challenged; we have to undergo practice and exercise to lead our wisdom out. And our compassion. And our skills are in bringing both to the practical order. But it is increasingly clear that models of education we have established during the industrial era are not adequate for a postindustrial era. If it is to once again live up to its task of leading wisdom and compassion out of our species, education will need some basic and deep remodeling. In other words, it needs some *work*.

—RW 170

Education for Work

The first task in remodeling education is to understand it as education *for work* and not merely *for jobs*. If we are to educate our young to enter a postindustrial workplace (because the definitions of work offered up in the industrial era are no longer adequate for our time), then we need to borrow from more ancient—that is preindustrial—forms of education. David Purpel, professor of education at the University of North Carolina, asks the basic question: What are we working hard to make happen in education? He feels we have trivialized education through "the evasion or neglect of larger, more critical topics and the stress put on technical rather than on social, political, and moral issues." He is critiquing the so-called value-free mentality of the modern era and daring to bring the "prophetic tradition" (his words) into the debate about education, along with commitment to "compassion, creativity and justice." Purpel is himself accomplishing a prophetic task within his profession, urging it to move from a machine model to a greener one. He feels we lack a mythos or overarching belief system in our education efforts.

—RW 171

The Power of Storytelling

One lesson we can learn from preindustrial peoples is the power of storytelling. I am struck by how important storytelling is among tribal people; it forms the basis of their educational systems. The Celtic peoples, for example, insisted that *only the poets could be teachers*. Why? I think it is because knowledge that is not passed through the heart is dangerous: it may lack wisdom; it may be a power trip; it may squelch life in the learners. What if *our* educational system were to insist that teachers be poets and storytellers and artists? What transformations would follow!

Education on a mass scale *is* the new work. Our minds never know too much. Our minds want to be stretched to experience the infinite, another word for which is *Spirit*. The mind yearns for Spirit; it yearns to be always new, to be young, to be learning, to be alive. Minds—all minds—have a right and desire to be stretched, to know wisdom itself, whether they are seven-year-old or seventy-seven-year-old minds. A Native American friend of mine tells me that he is often invited into public schools to speak about Native American ways and wisdom. But he is forewarned that he must not use the word *spirit* because that would violate the separation of church and state. "But I'm an Indian," he tells me. "I can't speak about life without speaking of Great Spirit and the other spirits of creation." I asked him how he handles it. He says, "I use the terms *spirit* and *Great Spirit,* and when my talk is finished, I leave the classroom quickly and never return to the same school twice."   —RW 171–72

Institute in Culture and Creation Spirituality

Several models of wisdom schools already exist to point the way toward refashioning education. There are Waldorf schools, based on the teachings of Rudolf Steiner; Montessori schools; and the Institute in Culture and Creation Spirituality (ICCS) that I first launched in 1977 at Mundelein College. In all of these models the need for cosmology is recognized—the need for some form of meditation that allows us to internalize cosmology. Since I know our model the best, I will reflect on it in relation to needed reforms in our education system.

The key to education at ICCS was threefold. First, we taught the new creation story from science. This story tells of the wonder of our bodies, our food, our planet, our cousin creatures. It must be told again and again by scientists as well as artists, who are our mystics. It affects us all.

Second, we teach art as meditation, for art is the language of mysticism. In art as meditation, we unearth and honor the latent images in all persons. In art as meditation, persons become empowered from within; they learn to resist images coming exclusively from the outside. They pay attention to their inner work, since one cannot lie to inner images, whether they be images of wonder and awe, on the one hand, or images of grief, sorrow, and rage, on the other. All images need space in which to breathe. That is the work of art as meditation: to let our images breathe, to give them life, to bring them out so that community can help us interpret and critique them and so that the images can in turn give life to the community.

Of course, art as meditation includes the body: there is no art without the body. And so education at ICCS honors the body by including it in our learning process. Consider the sweat lodge, for example, where Lakota teacher Buck Ghosthorse led sweats for faculty, administration, and students for the three years he taught with us at Holy Names College. In a sweat lodge the body is teacher, and the body is tested. Circle dances, drumming, massage, clay, movement, sculpture, are additional ways we can learn from and with the body.

Third, we teach left-brain knowledge about the spiritual heritages of West and East as well as skills for implementing compassion in our society. Compassion can be understood as living out the cosmic law of interdependence. It is celebration because we find ourselves in a gratuitous universe; unconditional love has brought us here. Justice making and other types of healing are forms of compassion because we all live in human societies that yearn for healing from many kinds of injustice. *Compassion is the goal of education in the ICCS model.* It is the starting point not only because the mystics teach compassion ("whatever God does, the first outburst is always compassion," Meister Eckhart observes), but also because scientists teach this same truth today whenever they teach about the habits of interdependence in the universe. Consider that our universe can best be imaged as an organism; an organism is an interdependent entity. If the foot hurts, the whole body hurts. That is the truth of the universe story as we are learning it today.   —RW 173–74

Educating for Awe

Awe leads to something more than mere knowledge. It leads to wisdom itself. "Awe is the beginning of wisdom," declares Rabbi Heschel. Awe is far more interesting than information. Awe opens the door in our souls, in our hearts and minds. Awe is bigger than we are—like the sacred is bigger than we are—and so it pulls us out of ourselves, it touches on transcendence. It elicits memorable experiences. Awe awakens reverence, respect, and gratitude. How important is gratitude? . . .

There has been very little room for awe in the classrooms of the modern age. The result is that many youth try to escape education at the earliest possible moment. Education becomes a trial and a burden rather than an occasion for expansion and wonder. Education loses its joy. It becomes less than human. It is a job, not work. The success we had with our YELLAWE program for inner city teenagers derived from the fact that our students made movies—the work of creativity excited them so much that 100% said they wanted to stay in school. There is great satisfaction and reward in creating things. To insure that their creativity when making movies or poetry or rap was grounded, we required that they incorporate a few of the "10 C's" in their creative projects. Our creativity contributes to the awe of our world.

Healthy education will put awe first. When humans care about awe, great things can happen. The mind opens up, and the heart, and, one might say, the soul. Expansion occurs. Wonder returns. The child is kept alive and eager throughout his or her life. Learning becomes a daily event. Books are not put on bookshelves, and television does not take over one's psyche.

Indeed, our minds are made for awe. They respond altogether spontaneously to awe. They remember awe. Even on our

deathbeds—especially on our deathbeds—do we remember awe
. . .?

When awe is killed or neglected, we are capable of anything.
Hope dies, and despair takes over. We lose interest in preserving either our own goodness or anyone else's goodness. We
grow indifferent and callous, responding only to the noise of
the marketplace and the enticements of commercial numbers.
We become prey to an infinite number of options to buy things.
We fall out of the real universe and into a man-made perverse
universe, a cosmos of consumerism, an ever-expanding shopping mall that goes on to infinity. We shop until we drop. And
another life is wasted. Love is missed. Regret reigns. Fear takes
over. Flight from death rules the day. "Forfeit your sense of awe,"
warns Rabbi Heschel, "and the universe becomes a marketplace
for you." Without awe, only power and materialism count.

—AWE, 51–52, 55

Educating about Evil

Education has to confront evil and study it. We need to remember evil and learn from it, to teach about evil, our capacities for
it and ways beyond it. Evil is itself awesome in its scope and cru-
elty. Evil is not "out there" somewhere. It is potentially within all
our institutions and professions as well as each of us. Any one
of us can be a receptor for evil and an instrument for evil. . . .

We need to study oppression and greed, racism and violence,
hoarding and what makes a cold, uncaring heart, if we are to
learn anything about liberation or generosity or non-violence or
sharing or compassion. It is often wise to first study the opposite
of what we want to learn. We appreciate something more when
we arrive where we want to go, for we have tasted its opposite.
Furthermore, evil is often what we have been most exposed to; it
is our neighbor; it is near at hand and familiar. Why not look it
in the eye, and thereby let it lead us to the other side? How will
we arrive at the other side without first looking evil in the eye,
considering all its dimensions and appeals and powers.

—AWE 55–56

Learning from Our Ancestors

Now we will break down the word *A.W.E.* First comes the letter A. A stands for ancestors. An authentic education today must honor the ancestors.

The ancestors are listening and watching, listening to what is going on and what is not going on. Watching our education and our miseducation; what we are teaching our young and what we are failing to teach them; our choices that are life-giving or biophiliac, and our choices that are death-dealing and necrophiliac. The ancestors are with us hoping to guide us, encourage us, give us direction and support. They know we need help, that we are ignorant. And they know how dangerous we have become, with so much knowledge and so little wisdom. . . .

In the modern era, driven as it was by the myth that we were constantly making progress just because we were gathering more and more knowledge, we were taught to always look forward, to look ahead, to dream ahead of better and better times. We were taught, verbally and non-verbally, to ignore the past, to ridicule the premodern peoples, to hold the medieval world in disdain (confusing the Middle Ages with the "Dark Ages"), to believe that the Native American, African, Pacific Island peoples that Europeans "discovered" (i.e., ran into) in the late 15th century were in every way and every respect inferior to the great Western and white race, religion, and "civilization."

The Western word that comes closest to that of *ancestor* is probably *tradition*. (I prefer the term ancestor because it is more personal.) Fierce wars have been waged over traditions all around the globe. . . .

One of the tasks of elders is to pass on traditions, to pass on stories and the teachings of the ancestors, and to make wise decisions about which stories are most needed at certain points in time. For elders to emerge to do their important task, they themselves must know the traditions, know the ancestors. It is scary when you encounter in our day some of the silly and dangerous notions that people, who claim to know the ancestors, propound when they in fact have not done their inner work or their intellectual work and do not know their own ancestral heritage. This is true of politicians who do not know the constitution of the United States, as well as of people who call themselves Christians but do not know their tradition in any of its diversity and richness. . . .

Honoring and respecting those who have gone before does not come easily to the modern mindset. But to a postmodern consciousness, our ancestral awareness can be a kind of salvation. One reason for this is that, in many respects, our ancestors represent the shadow side, the neglected or repressed side of our own selves. True self-knowledge includes awareness of our hidden and neglected side. It is not that we pine to, or even could if we wanted to, return to the past and live there.

We are postmodern. All of us, even indigenous peoples. We have passed through a time as a species that cannot be undone. We cannot turn back; it is too late for that. And besides, not everything we learned in the modern era was negative by any means. What we *can* do is reconnect our lost selves, those parts of ourselves that were cut off or forgotten or buried by the heavy agendas of the modern period. We do this by paying attention to our ancestors and how they lived on this earth, how they educated their young and themselves, the important questions they set for their young and the pedagogy by which they did so.
—AWE 61, 63–66

The Cosmos as Ancestor

But our ancestors are not just the two-legged ones. Now that today's science is helping us to relearn the ancient principle of interconnectivity, we are continually made aware that we humans and all our human ancestors owe our existence to rocks and waters, to forests and soil, to oxygen and carbon, to sun and moon, to tides and photosynthesis, to the solar system itself and to the supernovas and the galaxies and the atoms and the original fireball. All are kin. All are of the same stuff, the same kind, all are connected. And all are our ancestors. —AWE 67

The 10 Cs to Balance the 3 Rs

Certain educators and politicians like to talk about "returning to the basics" in education, meaning the 3 Rs of "Reading, 'Riting, and 'Rithmetic." Technology and computers and social media provide a new set of "basics" for today's educators it seems. I believe we have to update our naming of the basics with what I call the 10 Cs of education: cosmology or creation (including ecology); contemplation; creativity; chaos; compassion; courage or magnanimity; critical consciousness and judgment; community; ceremony and celebration; character and chakra development. These 10 Cs will ensure that we educate the whole human being and not just a small corner of one's brain (a corner of the left hemisphere). Albert Einstein said that he "abhorred" American education because it honored the "gift" of rationality that we have all been given; but it ignored the "gift" of intuition from which we derive our values. He warned us not to overvalue the rational because values are not found there but in the intuition. Yet we live in a society, he felt, that has shut itself down to intuition (and with it creativity). The 10 Cs bring intuition alive and with it values we can discuss, debate, and hopefully agree on. The language is consciously nonreligious so that these values can be discussed as part of an educational curriculum in a public school system.

Our experience is that debating them, discussing the 10 Cs, and playing with them created a lively learning experience that excited young people's work and imagination long after leaving the classroom.   —AWE 103–104

WORK

Following a talk I gave at a conference in a university in Australia, a young man rose and asked this question: "Does creation spirituality have a program for social change?" An excellent question, to which I replied, "I think if we could reinvent education, worship, and work, we would have a nonviolent revolution

that could save the planet as we know it." In previous sections
we have considered issues of education and worship (or ritual).
Working to reinvent both has been central to my vocation. Here,
we consider our worlds of work. Of course, all three areas are
richly interconnected. (MF)

Changing How We Define Work

It is time to change the way we define work, compensate work,
create work, let go of work, and learn to infuse it with play
and ritual. A paradigm shift requires a shift in the way we think
about, talk about, and undergo work. We are undergoing today
a crisis in our relationship to work and the challenge put to
our species today to reinvent it. We must learn to speak of the
difference between a job and work. We may be forced to take a
job serving food at a fast food place for $7.25 an hour in order
to pay our bills, but work is something else. Work comes from
inside out; work is the expression of our soul, our inner being. It
is unique to the individual; it is creative. Work is an expression
of the Spirit at work in the world through us. Work is that which
puts us in touch with others at the level of service in the community. Work is why we are on earth.

Work is not just about getting paid. Indeed, much work in
our culture is not paid at all, for example, raising children, cook-
ing meals at home, organizing community activities, singing in
a choir, repairing one's home, cleaning up one's neighborhood,
listening to a neighbor or friend who has undergone a trauma,
tending a garden, planting trees, or creating rituals that heal and
celebrate.

The very word *job* fits the Newtonian parts mentality. In the
Garment District of New York City, the term *job work* used to
mean "piece work," and the now obsolete word *jobbe* meant
"piece." In a mechanical view of the universe, a job is all one can
hope for. Job denotes a discrete task, and one that is not very
joyful. In contrast, work is about a role we play in the unfolding
drama of the universe.   —SS 5–6

Prophetic Work

Sometimes our work gets us into trouble. That's okay. In fact, I seriously question the spiritual and ethical life of anyone whose work has never gotten him or her into trouble—if no issues of conscience have ever emerged or no clash of values has been experienced with the ongoing guardians of the status quo. After all, it was Jesus' work that got him into trouble. Christians who claim to follow in his footsteps ought to sentimentalize his crucifixion less and emulate his message more—that there are values worth dying for and that often the struggle between values will be found in one's work world. Today every profession requires prophets. If the planet is to flourish again, the paradigm shift will put new demands on business people, medical people, artists, economists, clergy, politicians, parents and children, blue collar workers and white collar workers alike. No industry, no office job, no church, no institution, no union will be exempt from a deep critique of its impact for generations to come on children and the environment. The prophet, by definition, "interferes," and one significant place for our interference is where we work and earn a living.

All work worthy of being called spiritual and worthy of being called human is in some way prophetic work. It contributes to the growth of justice and compassion in the world; it contributes to social transformation. Such work is, in a real sense, God's work. By it we become cocreators with God.   —RW 13

Inner and Outer Work

There are essentially two kinds of work: inner and outer. The inner work refers to that large world within our souls or selves; the outer is what we give birth to or interact with outside ourselves. The industrial revolution was essentially an outer revolution. Its engines and machines were cold and lifeless external objects. The philosophy of that period taught us to relate to things as we would to machines—objectively. Much was gained by this new objective relationship. Work became more efficient;

a machine can do far more work than could a horse-drawn plow with a person behind it.

But much was lost also. Prior to the industrial revolution, work was more relational. To be successful as a farmer one had to relate well to one's farm animals; humans and animals were interdependent. One could not survive or thrive on subject-object relationships.

The myth of work in the industrial era fed on this outer directedness. The myth holds to this day. For example, if an automobile factory closes in Detroit (or, more likely, moves to Taiwan or to Mexico), the immediate response is, "We're devastated. We have lost our jobs." *But we no longer have to internalize the industrial era myth that work is primarily about factories and industry.* Indeed, by paying attention to the question, "What are the work needs of our time?" we can actually launch new ways of doing work, being workers, creating jobs that serve the common good. The heart of the matter lies in paying attention to the work that the industrial model practically ignores: our inner work. As economist E.F. Schumacher put it in the epilogue to his classic book *Small Is Beautiful*: "Everywhere people ask: 'What can I actually do?' The answer is as simple as it is disconcerting: We can, each of us, work to put our own house in order." Putting our own house in order will prove the key to reinventing work for the human species. And not only individuals have inner houses but communities and organizations and all our professions do too. They all have an inner house to put in order.

The human species has always worked; long before the industrial revolution, there was plenty of work for humans. For the sake of the future, we must dismantle the war industry and redirect our economy towards sound and life-sustaining enterprises. If the government were to truly support this effort, losing one's job would not seem like the end of the world, for there is so much *new* work that needs doing. When people lament the loss of the competitive edge in the car industry, for example, another question arises: The loss of dominance in certain industries might be a blessing in disguise, freeing us up for more pressing work in our time, for work to keep Earth healthy.

Mystics East and West have lots to say about our work. Meister Eckhart says, "The outward work can never be small if the inward one is great, and the outward work can never be great or good if the inward is small or of little worth. Inward work always includes in itself all size, all breadth and all length." And the Bhagavad Gita warns us that "All actions take place in time by the interweaving of the forces of Nature; but the person lost in selfish delusion thinks that he himself is the actor."

What a powerful reminder that we are part of a much larger work that is going on—the work of the Earth, the work of the cosmos. Our work is not insignificant but contributes to a much larger whole. Hildegard of Bingen taught that our work makes the cosmic wheel go around. It follows that we should take pride in our work and find joy there. A consensus about this exists among spiritual traditions of the world. Says Thomas Aquinas, "God works at the heart of all activity . . . through good works one puts forth the image of the heavenly person in themselves. . . . Always rejoice in the good work that you do." The *Tao Te Ching* says: "In work, do what you enjoy."   —RW 58, 91

Studs Terkel, in his classic book on *Working*, says this: "This book is about a search, too, for daily meaning as well as daily bread, for recognition as well as cash, for astonishment rather than torpor; in short, for a sort of life rather than a Monday through Friday sort of dying." Kay Stipkin, one of the many workers he interviewed in his book, said simply: "Work is an integral part of being alive. Your work is your identity. It tells you who you are. . . . There's such joy in doing work well."
                                                            —RW 91

What might this new work be? I am convinced that it is *work on the human being itself.* We might call this "inner work." We have lost our sense of an inner life; we have become so alienated from ourselves by work or the lack of it in the industrial era that abuse of alcohol or drugs or some other addiction is often the nearest thing we have to an inner life. Addiction is a larger industry in America today than automobile production. The effort to combat addiction is also a rapidly expanding industry. But we cannot combat it without the tools of spirituality aiding our efforts to heal the inner child and to release the authentic adult. Scientist Peter Russell has written that we need a project to explore human consciousness today comparable to the Manhattan Project of fifty years ago. Just as we set about to discover the core of energy in the universe at that time—and managed to explode the atom—so today we need to explore the core of human energy. The models he suggests for exploring consciousness are Teresa of Avila and Francis of Assisi, who showed us by their lives and teachings that there *is* a mystic inside every one of us.

Why is this work on ourselves so pressing? Because we are the problem; we are the ones who are destroying our own habitat and that of other species by our blindness, greed, envy, violence, and rapaciousness. These *spiritual sins* are destroying the planet and creating despair in the young.

The new era in work, the postmodern and post-industrial era, will be the era of doing our inner work. And from there, good work will happen to save the planet.

We need a massive investment of talent and discipline in our inner lives. When we do this, we will find some solutions for the overwhelming issues of matricide and killing of our Mother Earth, of violence and self-destruction, of internalized oppression and external acts of oppression, of the sexism, racism, homophobia, and fear that overwhelm our species and that are played out from generation to generation in acts of abuse—physical, emotional, sexual, and religious. All the sources of injustice are not to be found in systems alone. Within our psyches lie clues to our resistance to justice and our constant denial of injustice all around us.

Once one has a spiritual center from which to work, no work (provided it is good work) is alienating; no work is just a job. A person who sweeps floors can, by knowing the meaning of his or her tasks and appreciating its contribution to the cosmic community's history, sweep floors as an act of sacred work. But if one's work is useful and not harmful, it can always be holy work and part of one's meditative discipline—provided one is aware. This is not a new idea but a very ancient one. In its healthy periods, the monastic tradition taught it, as did the Shaker movement at its zenith. We praise God by our work. And this in turn gives our work grace and purpose. As farmer Wendell Berry points out, all work contains drudgery; the issue is whether it holds meaning or not. If we do our work from our center, from our source, it will always hold meaning.

In bringing together outer and inner work we are contributing to a cosmology, a making whole, a putting of order into our lives and that of our species. Hildegard of Bingen, Thomas Aquinas, and Meister Eckhart all state that the soul is not in the body, but the body is in the soul. This implies that our inner work is not an *inward* work but a *deep* work. Work emerges from our innermost depths and radiates out to wherever our soul extends contributing to the fuller community. Here psyche and cosmos are one. Here the dualism between us and the cosmos is erased. Here is where the healing of the deep wounds we received during the modern era begins. As cosmologists Brian Swimme and Thomas Berry put it, "In the modern period, we are without a comprehensive story of the universe. . . . Thus we have at the present time a distorted mode of human presence upon the Earth." When that distorted mode of human presence is healed, work itself will be healed. Healing that distorted mode of presence will itself constitute good work and connect us again to the Great Work that the universe is asking of us, work that includes saving the planet as we know it from our own self-destructive tendencies.   —RW 20–23

All people doing good work in the world are priests in the archetypal sense of the word, that is to say, *midwives of grace.* That is what workers do—we midwife grace. We also educe grace from one another's work, encouraging it and building it up. Work itself becomes a sacrament in these circumstances.

This is not just a theory or a speculative idea. This concept of workers as priests or midwives of grace became the foundation of our doctor of ministry program at the University of Creation Spirituality for its nine rich years of existence. People of all professions joined because they felt the need and the call to ground their work in an alive spirituality. We attracted psychologists and social workers, artists and activists, engineers, business people, clergy, educators, politicians, workers of many kinds because all were hungry for deepening their spiritual roots—an opportunity that was denied them in great part in their professional academic training. Knowledge factories are ill suited to train mystics and prophets. One engineer on entering the program confessed that he was "burned out" from academia and engineering after twenty-seven years of teaching and did not know what was next for him. Two weeks into our program, he came to me and said: "I've got my soul back" and returned to his university and started Engineers Without Borders, which now has over 18,000 members doing very good work in Haiti, the Amazon, Africa, and Afghanistan providing solar-generated irrigation systems and so many other miracles (wonders) that the world needs. He told me recently, "It was all due to the time at UCS."   —CNF 343

8

Social, Political, and Ecological Activism

SOCIAL AND POLITICAL ACTIVISM

Behind a successful social movement, there is very often a spiritual grounding. This was true of the civil rights movement, the labor movement, and Gandhi's Satyagraha movement. It may prove to be pivotal in the ecological and social movements of our time also. Creation spirituality lends itself to such values and actions, linking people up with other like-minded activists. In Occupy Spirituality, *Adam Bucko and I discuss six features of a new activist spirituality, of which two are ecumenical, interspiritual, and posttraditional as well as contemplative and experienced-based. I relate these also to the four paths of creation spirituality.* (MF)

Fox: The four paths are conceptual, but they're thoroughly grounded in experience, and they return to experience. The backbone of the creation spirituality tradition is its naming of the spiritual journey in the four paths. The four paths address the question, where will God—where will the experience of the Divine—be found in our life? Creation spirituality responds: The Divine will be found in our experiences of the Via Positiva, Negativa, Creativa, and Transformativa.

Each of the paths is valuable in itself. But also, any one of the paths done on its own could be seductive. For example, the fourth path, being an activist: I remember one of my students said to me when I first met her, "I am a cause junkie." One can become a cause junkie—one can make one's whole life social activism and leave no room for the soul, no room for the mystical juice that, first of all, is the very goal of social justice. The goal of social justice is that the whole community can live life fully. It's about celebration of life. If you've left that out of your path because you're so married to being a warrior twenty-four hours a day, seven days a week, then first of all you're going to run out of steam and juice, but also you're not going to taste what it is you're really trying to bring about, which is the flow of justice that allows the flow of life to move on.

So there is a danger that any one of these paths can be an end in itself. That's one of the great values of the four paths: to remind us that we move in and out, in and out. That's how they feed one another, and that's literally how one stays young, because one is staying spiritually alive.   —OS 20–23, 25

Bucko: For our first few meetings with homeless youth, we focus on two questions: "What breaks your heart?" and "What makes you truly alive?" We spend about one week on each question.

Fox: Your two questions sound like you are applying important questions about the role of the Via Negativa and the Via Positiva respectively in each of their lives.

Bucko: The goal is not to answer these questions. The goal is to be present to them with all that we are. In a way we are following the poet Rilke's advice when he counseled the young artist "be patient toward all that is unsolved in your heart and try to love the questions themselves. Perhaps you will then gradually, without noticing it, live along into the answer."

—OS 93–94

Includes Psychology, the Body, and Creativity

Bucko: A third point in this new spirituality is that practice goes beyond traditional contemplative exercises. People still practice meditation and contemplative prayer, but this new spirituality understands that the journey needs to include good psychology and shadow work, as well as integration of the body through things like yoga, sacred sexuality, and deep human relationships. This includes conscious romantic relationships as a path into life and into spirituality. Basically, this new spirituality expands the focus of transformation from just one dimension of our being—the soul—to all aspects of our being.

Fox: Yes, and included too, I think, would be the role of creativity as a path, as a spiritual discipline, as a yoga—what I've called and practiced through forty-some years of teaching spirituality, "art as meditation." So that focusing through clay, through dance, through painting, through music, and so forth—that too is meditation, and that too incorporates the body. All art is bodily. And that can be missed. Of course, for many people, it also includes athletics, sport–running or climbing or walking or hiking. These should not be denigrated as inferior, so long as you bring your heart and your focus to it. Or even exercising, working out—if it is just about beefing your body up, well, that's one thing. But if it's also about centering and about focusing, there's definitely a spiritual dimension to it.   —OS 26–27

Action Rooted in Vocation

Bucko: Point number four is related to what you were saying—that this new spirituality says that spirituality that does not include action is no spirituality at all. But it's not just about action—it's about action that comes from one's deepest calling. This spirituality does not accept the reality of living a divided life, such as complete withdrawal or a separate career divided from one's soul and its deepest aspirations. Those dualities of the past no longer apply here. For young people today, the sense of vocation and the sense of a calling become the very doorways into spirit. So this new spirituality also realizes that the new world can be created only if people incarnate their unique gifts and callings in the world and employ them in the service of compassion and justice.

Fox: As I reflect on the topic of vocation, I remember the distinction I make in my book, *The Reinvention of Work*, in

which I point out the difference between a *job* and *work*. A job is
something we do to pay our bills. Work is the reason we are here
on Earth. It is a call; it is our purpose; it is how we give back.
Today I find lots of young people who are willing to sacrifice an
overcommitment to job in order to devote themselves more to
their work. This entails living a simpler lifestyle, of course, and
often living in community. Vocation rises to importance in such
a value system. —OS 28–29

Joy, Sensuality, and Celebration

Bucko: This takes us to point number five, which is that this
new spirituality includes joy, sensuality, celebration, and heartful
aliveness.

Fox: Fun!

Bucko: Fun, absolutely. This new spirituality celebrates life
through meaningful connections, works of art, music, and all
things that essentially help to grow the soul.

Fox: Exactly. And again, to invoke a concept, you are speaking of the Via Positiva—that there is a joy of life, a celebration
of life that permeates and that really holds all the crises and all
the breakdowns and all the chaos and all the vicissitudes that life
also offers. But that fun is itself a value is something that many,
many spiritualities have not taught over the centuries.   — OS 30

Democratic

Bucko: The sixth point is that this new spirituality is more democratic. As a result, the role of the teacher changes from a traditional tell-you-what-to-do teacher to a spiritual friend. The role
of the teacher is to point students back to their own experience
and to name their experience for them so that they can start
paying attention to the movement of the spirit within. Discern-
ment becomes a big part of this new democratic and dialogical
way of being. Elders are not so much recognized for their titles,
resumes, or fame, but rather their ability to relate to the younger
generation from their lived experience.

This new spirituality is much more about taking off the masks of pretense and cultivating genuine heart connections that inspire growth in both elders and youth, rather than in keeping with tradition or respecting authority. . . .

Fox: Yes, I think it's taking seriously the advancement of the Enlightenment consciousness that fought so hard for democracy—so the American Revolution and its great thinkers, the French Revolution, and so forth. The whole idea that we're not eternally bound to hierarchy, to monarchy in any of its forms, to dictatorships—even benign ones—that we're not just in vertical relationships, we're in horizontal relationships also, and we are individuals. That is, I think, one of the major accomplishments of the modern-era enlightenment consciousness: the dignity of the individual. That spirit works through democratic and horizontal directions and through circles, not just down from ladders.

So a spiritual democracy incorporates the wisdom of the Thomas Jeffersons of the world, if you will, that this is not just a secular, political shift of power. It is a spiritual insight, and it's not unrelated to the teachings of Jesus and the Cosmic Christ and Buddha and the Buddha Nature, and so forth. The Iroquois were already practicing democracy centuries before the Europeans landed here.

The notion is that Spirit works through democracy, through shared distribution of power, through debate and disagreement and compromise, and to every citizen having an insight about what life is about. So again, it's about moving from the vertical idea to horizontal.

Now this does not mean that you're without leadership. But it means that, first of all, leadership can evolve, and no one is meant to be a king for life, and we have to elicit leadership from one another. And it's not an ego trip; therefore, it's not a power trip. Leadership is, again, a mode of service, as Jesus tried to teach. So it's not as if we're without a leader, but that ultimately the leader is responsible to the group itself, and the group is responsible for itself. You're not surrendering power to some kind of individual . . .   —OS 31–32

Based in Community and Serving Humanity and Life

Fox: I think that point number seven is that this spirituality is meant to be lived in communities. And, I think that you and I would agree that hints and echoes of what we're talking about have already emerged in base communities in Latin America—which, interestingly, we're so badly treated by the Vatican, by hierarchical powers, almost to the point of wiping them out. And yet their resilience is such that today they are simply divorcing themselves from organized religion, from the church as such, from the institutional church, and continuing their practice of democratic spirituality and democratic leadership—in other words, the church of the people.

Bucko: And serving not the church, but humanity, which is also life.

Fox: Exactly—serving life and humanity, and letting the church go in its own direction as it travels down the path of death.   —OS 33–34

Solidarity with Liberation Theology Movement

During my year of silence, I visited Latin America to see the base communities and liberation theology in action. Afterwards, I wrote the book *Creation Spirituality: Liberating Gifts for the Peoples of the Earth*. The book is my thank-you to my brothers and sisters in the soul and my expression of solidarity with them. I begin with a story from a Costa Rican I met on my "sabbatical" who urged me to write about the liberation of North Americans, for, he said, "we in the south have gone about as far as we can go in liberating ourselves. We are stuck until you northerners start doing your own liberation."   —CNF 218

GENDER: THE DIVINE FEMININE AND THE SACRED MASCULINE

A revolution in our time and a needed one is the work of women's rights and the return of the Divine Feminine or goddess.

*In addition, there is needed a development of a more healthy
and sacred masculine. Without such movements, we will remain
stuck in patriarchal mindsets that are pessimistic, violent, and
unjust.* (MF)

Embracing Feminism

The Sacred Heart sisters I got to know at Barat College were
intelligent, fun, and committed to their work, which was to
educate women of all ages. There were Sister Martha Curry
of the English department, Sister Sophie Cooney, the brilliant
and well-traveled head of the humanities department, and many
others I counted among my friends on and off campus. At this
time (the 1970s) many middle-aged women were beginning to
return to school. We began the year with three students major-
ing in our department of religious studies, and by the time I left
four years later, there were twenty-nine. We did many creative
things, including sponsoring a mass in Latin complete with Gre-
gorian chant sung by students of my medieval class. I enjoyed
teaching interdisciplinary courses with other departments,
including sociology of religion and literature and spirituality,
where I was introduced to Adrienne Rich's poetry. Rich has been
a tremendous gift to me ever since. I employed Albert Einstein
as reading material for my basic course on religion in America,
for I was moved by his conscience and his sensitivity to mystery
and mysticism. I also used Norman O. Brown's *Love's Body*
and *Life Against Death* and Sam Keen's work on Dionysian
vs. Apollonian thinking. Being the only full-time teacher in the
department, I taught subjects ranging from the Scriptures to the
mystics, from liberation theology to psychology and religion. It
was great fun teaching these women. They were eager to learn
and just getting their wings, thanks to the emerging feminist
movement.

Feminist Catholic Theologian Rosemary Ruether agreed
to teach a course with us, and I invited Mary Daly to speak
at a school-sponsored symposium. I had been deeply affected

reading Mary Daly's *Beyond God the Father*; I felt here was a theology doing more or less what I was trying to do: leaving behind symbols, names, and metaphors that were not working for us. In my enthusiasm, I telephoned her at Boston College where she was teaching, introduced myself, and thanked her for her book. I told her that her book "made Karl Marx look like a wimp." There was a long pause and she said, "Thank you very much." Later, when she came to campus and I met her, I realized I had said the right thing in praising her over Marx. I remember her Irish wit and dancing eyes over dinner, but I also remember the commotion she caused when, at question-and-answer time following her presentation, she refused to let men ask any questions; it was time for men to listen to women for a change, she explained. Half the Barat faculty walked out at that point. Her visit raised the roof at Barat, and for months afterward people were still talking about it.

Of course, the biggest single gift granted me at Barat College was a deepening of feminist awareness. Sitting day after day and hearing women's stories in class and out of class was an eye-opener. It was not unlike visiting a third-world country for the first time. One's own privileges came into focus. I remember telling a friend one day that, based just on stories I had listened to at college, the statistics we had been given in America about rape were all off. It was my experience that one out of three women had stories of rape to tell.

Middle-aged women would come in and tell me stories of how they had to fight with their husbands (who had MBAs and were running things in the city of Chicago) just to return to college and finish their BAs. One woman had to move out of her house. I felt a solidarity with their struggle. Together we read women philosophers and theologians, and I was able to enter into the awakening of many of these women. I remember one day a young woman, who was fulfilling a class requirement by leading the group, came in with red tea. We sat around drinking it as she expounded on what it was like going through her

menstrual period. It was as if I was making up for those years
of training in the order and in Paris without women instructors,
and I was being given a crash course in women's studies.
                                                                    —CNF 109–10

Feminists Are Prophets

There can be no question that the creation tradition is the
feminist tradition in the West. Feminism of its very nature is
prophetic during a patriarchal period of history. Accordingly,
feminists have been treated very often the same way as prophets
were treated by those in power with power. Many persons on
the Family Tree of Creation Spirituality are women or worked
closely with women, such as Francis of Assisi and Meister Eckhart who worked with the Beguines.

When I read feminist thinkers and poets like Adrienne Rich,
Susan Griffin, Rosemary Ruether, Starhawk, Carol Christ, and
Beverly Harrison, I find all the themes of creation-centered spirituality. In their works, all four paths of the spirituality journey
are named and celebrated. I am a spiritual theologian, and there
is simply no doubt in my mind or heart that feminism today is
bringing back the creation tradition. The *anawim*—the poor, the
suffering, the marginalized, the disenfranchised, the oppressed—
are being heard from at last. One hopes it is not too late. And
one hopes that the dominant powers in religion and society and
in the hearts and minds of persons everywhere will let go of
their arrogance enough to listen to this recovery of wisdom in
our midst. One hopes that all peoples will welcome the prophets
among us. And today in no small measure these prophets are
feminists.   —OB 271–72

God Is the Black Madonna

The Black Madonna, commemorated in shrines in Sicily, Russia,
Poland, Czechoslovakia, France, Spain, Switzerland, Germany,
Turkey, derived from the African goddess Isis, whose name
means "throne." The great 12th-century renaissance was in great
part inspired by a return of the Goddess and included the birth

of a new and exciting architecture. This, the Gothic revolution, as Henry Adams convincingly argued in his classic work, *Mount Saint Michel and Chartres*, was a direct assault on the Romanesque and singularly masculine consciousness of the dark ages. The very word *cathedra* means *throne*—a Cathedral is where the goddess sits ruling over the city with love and justice, celebration and compassion. In many medieval gothic cathedrals there sits a Black Madonna mirrored after the goddess Isis.

The Black Madonna stood for many things including, according to China Garland, "life, life with all its teeming diversity of peoples, our different colors, our fullness." She also represented grief, celebration, the cosmos, people of color, and much more.

—NU 92–93

God Is Mother

The ancient *Vedas* of India call God "motherliest," and fourteenth-century English mystic Julian of Norwich developed the Motherhood of God profoundly (*as we saw in chapter 4*). She writes: "God feels great delight to be our Mother . . . The deep Wisdom of the Trinity is our Mother. In her we are all enclosed." Indeed, God is "our true mother in whom we are endlessly carried and out of whom we will never come." Again, "God is the true Father and Mother of Nature," and "Christ is our mother." Hildegard of Bingen celebrates God as Mother and as circle embracing all things. —HBST 111–26

Ramakrishna teaches this about the Divine Mother: "Whatever we see or think about is the manifestation of the Mother, of the primordial energy, the Primal Consciousness . . . The Primordial Power is 'ever at play.'" He advises us to "Pray to the Divine Mother with a longing heart. Her vision dries up all craving . . . and completely destroys all attachment." The *Tao Te Ching* calls the Tao the "Great Mother of the Universe." —NU 73

God Is the Goddess

God is also known as the Goddess. The Divine Feminine is an important name for the Deity that often gets forgotten when

Patriarchy rules unchecked. Marija Gimbutas, a very accomplished anthropologist who spent her life finding and uncovering myriad artifacts and relics from the goddess times, has this to say about the Goddess: "The Goddess and all her manifestations was a symbol of the unity of all life in nature. Her power was in water and stone, in tomb and cave, in animals and birds, snakes and fish, hills, trees, and flowers. Hence the holistic and mythopoeic perception of the sacredness and mystery of all there is on Earth."

The Goddess has many names. While we are free to apply every name we have given to "God" to the "Goddess," some unique names have been forged for the goddess as well such as Tara, Kuan Yin, Isis, Kali, Mary, Shekhinah.   —NU 87

God Is Tara

The name "Tara" is a Tibetan name that means both "Star" and "Tear." Mahayana Buddhism worships the Divine Mother as Tara, who is said to have been born out of one of the tears of the Buddha of Compassion that fell to the earth. She who saves and restores was born from that tear. She offers liberation and illumination in our everyday life. Enlightenment is available to all. She is addressed in a Tibetan litany as "Our mother: great compassion! Our mother: a thousand hands, a thousand eyes! Our mother: Cooling like water! Our mother: ripening like fire! Our mother: spreading like wind! Our mother: pervading like space!"   — NU 88

God Is Kuan Yin

In China, Kuan Yin is considered the Bodhisattva of Compassion who listens and responds to the cries of all beings. Like Mary and Artemis, she is a virgin Goddess who "protects women, offers them a religious life as an alternative to marriage, and grants children to those who want them." She is omnipresent for "in the lands of the universe there is no place where she does not manifest herself," and her wondrous compassion "pours spiritual rain like nectar" everywhere while "quenching the flames of distress."   —NU 89

Recovering the Sacred Masculine: The Blue Man

Both Swami Muktananda in the twentieth century and Hilde-gard of Bingen in the twelfth century honor the archetype of the Blue Man. (MF)

The Blue Man represents our expanding consciousness, and this is critical today for our survival as a species. And our consciousness *is expanding* today—scientific discovery is expanding our consciousness, so that we understand how interconnected and interdependent humans are to each other and to the Earth and to the cosmos. Global warming expands our consciousness and can yank us out of our petty anthropocentrism. Even the HIV epidemic, coronavirus, nuclear proliferation, and the obscene gaps in wealth worldwide can expand our consciousness. They are all "wake-up calls," invitations to deepen our awareness and seek justice and healing.

When science tells us that the human species originated in Africa, and all peoples originally migrated from there, we are invited to embrace the Blue Man, to expand our consciousness, and understand the complete *relativity* of our racial and ethnic and religious differences. As we learn about our planet's uniqueness in the universe, and about its fragility and suffering—all this can expand our consciousness and open our hearts to the *compassionate action* that Hildegard wrote about. For her, the Man in Sapphire Blue represents consciousness put to the service of compassion.

The Blue Man can be found everywhere we turn and whenever we seek to learn and expand our minds—whether we look at sexuality, diversity, economic justice, war, or the deep ecumenism and wisdom found among all religious traditions. All learning nourishes and feeds our consciousness and expands it. Are we up to it? Are we embodying the Blue Man in each of us?

—HSM 160

The Earth Father

The Earth Father, the authentic father with a fatherly heart, incorporates *all* the metaphors and archetypes found in *The*

Hidden Spirituality of Men. An authentic father passes on by example and story the amazing news of cosmology and how the sky lives—that Father Sky is for real. An authentic father is also a Green Man—grounding our consciousness and literally being a caretaker for Mother Earth, working to make sure her creatures, soil, water, air, and forests are healthy. A fatherly heart goes out of its way to foster mutual communication within a family and a community, a communication that flows both ways, listening and speaking, teaching and learning. A father speaks not one language, but new languages—reaching across cultures and generations and respecting new ways of speaking and communicating with his children and grandchildren.

An authentic fatherly heart is open to the deep and ancient stories of our hunter-gatherer ancestors: he provides for the survival of the tribe, and he fosters an energetic curiosity of and passionate engagement with the natural world. The Earth Father understands reciprocity. He teaches his sons and daughters how to "hunt" in the world and how to trust their own hunter-gatherer instincts when they are on their own. The fatherly heart also celebrates and models the spiritual warrior; he is comfortable expressing both joy and grief, and knows and assists in rituals that can hold these emotions in the home and community. In this way, children grow up emotionally whole and aware, safe and expressive. A father does his inner work and has gone into grief and loss, into initiations of many kinds, and does not hide this from his children.

A healthy father is not silent about sexuality, its power and its dangers, but discusses it openly and models healthy and responsible sexual expression. A healthy father takes delight in showing his children what a healthy life entails: how to eat healthy, cook for themselves, grow food, exercise properly, and honor the body in all its wonder and amazement.

Finally, a healthy father instructs by example and word how to foster an expansive consciousness and how to respond to life creatively, artistically, compassionately. Creative compassion is a primal value that is critical at this time in history. The Blue Man will not be kept under wraps.

The Earth Father, having incorporated all eight archetypes, is the healthy father, one with a fatherly heart. He exemplifies a healthy, integrated masculinity, and of course, in the real world this process is never complete. We never reach a static place in which our work is done. Then, eventually, as we grow into our eldership, our masculine archetypal role shifts again. We learn how to enter "refirement," rather than "retirement," and model that for our children and grandchildren.   —HSM 180–81

Eagerness for the Sacred Masculine

The very first response to my men's book was from a woman who wrote to me, "I have over 200 books on the goddess in my personal library and not a single book on the sacred masculine. And I have two sons! Until I read your book, I had not understood how much men have suffered under patriarchy also." Just as healthy men welcome the return of the divine feminine, so too healthy women welcome the healthy masculine in themselves and others. A second response to the book came from a Native American who told me, "I have been working with men in prison for twelve years. It is very difficult to get men in prison to look at themselves—they are always projecting onto others. Yours is the first book I have come across that got men to look inside *and find the nobility inside.*" I love that phrase—the nobility inside. Isn't that what we mean by "original blessing"?   —CNF 419

If we are here to accomplish something that's good, beautiful, and just, one thing is certain: it can't be accomplished if yin and yang, feminine and masculine, are out of balance. It can't be brought about by exterior force or "power over" dynamics. It can only come together in a balance of the Divine Feminine and the Sacred Masculine. We have to integrate these energies in our own person, then in all of our institutions from religion to education, economics, agriculture, the media, and politics. This is why Hildegard is back.   —HBST 128

ECOLOGY, ECO-JUSTICE, ORDER OF THE SACRED EARTH

Creation spirituality is, of course, by its very name, about the sacredness of the universe and nature, about the divine presence within nature. Our experience of the divine in nature is therefore about loving and preserving the goodness of the earth. (MF)

Thomas Berry on Creation Spirituality

Eco-prophet Thomas Berry reflects on creation spirituality this way: "Matthew Fox speaks of his teaching as *creation spirituality*, it seems to me, because he feels the need to understand the deep experience of the human soul within the sacred dimension of the universe itself. . . . That Matt has consistently used the word *creation* in identifying his work indicates the cosmic orientation of his thinking. By the term *creation spirituality* he turns the Western mind away from its exclusive redemption fixation to the more primordial experience available for the Western soul in the universe itself. . . . As Saint Thomas indicates consistently throughout his writings, the objective of the divine in creating is the grandeur of the entire universe community:

> The divine presence is primarily in the comprehensive community of existence. Any communication made to a component of the universe is ultimately for the sake of the universe just as the artist selects the color and form of a painting in relation to the composition of the whole. As Thomas tells us, 'The whole universe together participates in and manifests the divine more than any single being whatsoever.' He tells us also that the Order of the Universe is the ultimate and noblest perfection in things." (cited in Mary Ford Grabowsky, ed., *The Unfolding of a Prophet: Matthew Fox at Sixty*, 71, 68, MFG)

Green Man

The Green Man archetype is decidedly *not* about mastering nature. Rather, the Green Man is about *relating to nature*, about finding the essence of nature within our own nature—indeed, he is about our generating nature, especially from our fifth chakras, where our words represent the combined wisdom of our hearts and heads (the fourth and sixth chakras, respectively). The Green Man is about wisdom holding sway over mere knowledge. In Native American traditions, plants are considered the wisest of all living creatures. They have been here the longest, and by inventing photosynthesis, they learned how to eat the sun. By doing so, they make life possible for animals, and as a consequence, humans. Plants could live without us, but we could not live without them; we are indebted to them. The Green Man reminds us of that.

The Green Man is an ancient pagan symbol of our relationship to the plant kingdom. Men become tree-like, and the Green Man sports plants and leaves and boughs growing from his mouth or his beard or his hair. Green Man festivals are celebrated even to this day on village greens in England. Christianity adopted the Green Man in a special way in the twelfth century in France, England, and Germany in particular, and he is found in many cathedrals dating from that and later periods around Europe.

In the Green Man we have an archetype of our relationship to *both* the cosmos and the Earth—to Father Sky and Mother Earth. Plants connect sky and earth.

Fred Hageneder, in his book *The Spirit of Trees*, points out that "trees are the most successful life forms on Earth" and the most dominant since they first appeared over three hundred million years ago. Communities of trees "are fundamental to weather and climate, for a beneficial water cycle; for the development of minerals; for balancing the electrical charges between the ionosphere and the Earth's surface; and for the maintenance of the Earth's magnetic field as a whole."

What makes up a tree? The body of a tree is mostly filled with sunlight. "Light courses through its structure, navigating vital processes and maintaining the balance and health of the whole organism. . . . The tree produces a continuous light show from its very cells."

Trees are like "cosmic antenna," and radiation from supernovas—the gigantic explosions marking the death of a star—
has been shown to influence tree growth. Scientists studying
an 807-year-old juniper tree in Tajikistan found that the trees
annual rings showed a definite slowing down of tree growth
with each known date of three supernovas. Thus we can say,
"Every star that dies in our galaxy is perceived by trees."

When humans left the woods for the open savannahs and discovered fire, "fire became the driving force in the development of
the human species . . . and it was always trees which supported
the human need for fuel."

Sacred groves are a universal phenomenon. For "almost
everyone in the world the beginnings of social and religious life
took place under trees."

Because many of the boughs, leaves, and trees emerging from
the Green Man emerge from his mouth, we know we are looking
at an archetype about our fifth chakra. The fifth chakra, located
in our throats, is essentially a birth canal. This is particularly
true for men; the fifth chakra is a birth canal. Our throats are
meant to give birth to our heart and head wisdom (from the
fourth and sixth chakras), and the Green Man reminds us that
the color of the fourth or heart chakra is green! The Green Man
has found his voice—have we? The Green Man puts compassion
and generativity first, and this generativity, this birth canal, primarily gives birth to green compassion.   —HSM 19–21

Silence and Introspection

Interestingly, the archetype of the Green Man also respects
silence and introspection, which are common traits among farmers and indigenous peoples, those who remain close to the land.
In some depictions, the Green Man appears cross-eyed, which is
surely meant to symbolize looking inward.   —HSM 22

The Green Man and the Black Madonna: A Sacred Marriage

The Green Man honors our relationship to other Earth creatures
and the plant world in particular. The Green Man is a spiritual

warrior standing up for and defending Mother Earth and her creatures. He is in touch with his heart chakra, the greening power of compassion, since the color of the heart chakra is green. And he represents holy sexuality, our renewed powers of generativity in all their diverse and manifold manifestations.

Does the Green Man return alone? Does he find a mate? Does a feminine companion also emerge who might make a good marriage, a bonding of equals, friends for life? I propose that the return of the Black Madonna represents such a partner, such a consort. Why?

The first reason is historical. The last time the Black Madonna emerged in force in Western culture was at the very time that the Green Man arrived—twelfth century, the "only renaissance that worked in the West" (according to Chenu), when the goddess emerged and society reinvented itself. As we have seen, the Black Madonna is found all over Europe, and she is Tara in China and Kali in India and Our Lady of Guadalupe in Mexico (sometimes called the "brown Madonna"). The Celts knew her as "Hag," or the *cailleach*, the dark feminine who exercises "tough mother love that challenges its children to stop acting in destructive ways. . . . It is the energy that will bring death to those dreams and fantasies that are not for the highest good."

In her study *Dark Goddess,* Lucia Birnbaum describes how the African goddess Isis "prevailed through the force of love, pity, compassion, and her personal concern for sorrows." She was associated with healing; she was a "compassionate mother" and represented not only the earth but also water, which "held a sacred quality: holy water, holy rivers, and holy sea." A mistress of medicine, she also signifies nonviolent transformation. The brother of Isis was Ma'at, and together Isis and Ma'at epitomized justice and order in nature and society. For all these reasons, the Black Goddess seems right for our times. —HSM 231–32

The Order of the Sacred Earth: A Dream

One night, while teaching in Boulder, Colorado, I was awakened at four in the morning with a message and "mandate." The words were these: "Do it." Do what? Start a new spiritual (not religious) order that is beholden to no religious headquarters. I believe St. Francis had this in mind originally. This order would be all embracing—people from all religions or none, from all lifestyles and professions, would agree to join. The binding vow would be one: *I vow to be the best mystic (i.e., lover) and best prophet (or warrior) on behalf of Mother Earth that I can be.* Much of the community aspect would be through online friendships and communication, though in-person gatherings would be encouraged also. It would not be an institution, but a network.

Vows can be very useful devices for focusing and deepening one's commitment. And maybe such an order would serve as a half-way house between "church" and no community at all. Many people, exasperated by institutional religion, are leaving the structure but still keen on community after all. I shared my dream with Skylar Wilson, a young friend of mine who also had a dream of his own parallel to mine, and together we wrote a book along with his then-girlfriend Jen Listug (now married to each other) entitled *Order of the Sacred Earth.* We launched the Order of the Sacred Earth on winter Solstice, 2019, and about 80 people took the vows together. Some were Jewish, others Christian of various stripes, some were indigenous, Muslim, Buddhist, and at least one atheist who said to me, "I have been eager to find a community that shared my values. Yours sounds spot on." A twenty-six-year-old woman said, "My generation is so distracted by social media and the rest. We need a focus and a vow like this and community committed to it may be just what we need."   —CNF 359

Who Is Welcome to the Order?

- Everyone who cares deeply about the fate of the earth and wants to contribute to her healing and survival.
- Everyone therefore who cares about the next generations of humans *and* other creatures whether four-legged or winged ones, finned ones or slithering ones, whether tree

people or water people or forests and soil and air and therefore healthy food and bodies and minds and spirits. . . .   —OSE 7–8

Mystic Warriors Are Needed

The next level of human evolution requires an explosion of mystic warriors feeling a common call to defend Mother Earth. It is not important from what tradition one derives but rather how fully, courageously, and generously one is living out one's life as a mystic-warrior on behalf of Mother Earth. It needs to steer contemplatives into action and activists into contemplation so that a deeper activism emerges.

The awe that the sacred arouses is the basis of this mysticism or love affair with Mother Earth. The world needs contemplative activists and active contemplatives—mystic-warriors therefore—people committed to *interfere* (the primary work of the prophet) with the ongoing destruction of Mother Earth.

—OSE 28

9

Church and Beyond

FROM RELIGION TO SPIRITUALITY?

As we have seen, many people today are abandoning institutional religion for spirituality and for new forms of community. This is especially true of the young (though not exclusively so). When I was a young Dominican student, I approached my superiors and told them: "My generation is going to be more interested in spirituality than religion." I do not think I have been proven wrong.

The question need not be either/or, however. Hopefully, one can still find authentic spiritual experience within pockets of religion, and spirituality might wake religions up. (MF)

Spirituality or Religion?

Adam Bucko: Seventy-five percent of Americans between the ages of eighteen and twenty-nine now consider themselves "spiritual but not religious."

Looking at this from a perspective of young people that I work with, I think that young people are very much interested in spirituality, but they find it outside of organized religion. They tend to adopt spiritual practices from various traditions, have interspiritual mentors, and thus create a post-religious and interspiritual framework for their spiritual lives. Even young people who are still connected to a specific tradition usually have a different relationship with that tradition than their parents did.

Fox: I have a friend who's Buddhist, from Thailand, and two summers ago he did the pilgrimage to Santiago de Compostela on foot. I think it's about a four-hundred-kilometer walk; he got halfway, and his feet were bleeding so badly he had to quit. But then the following summer he went back and started where he had left off and finished the pilgrimage. As far as he knew, he was the only Buddhist he met on the entire journey. He's in his young thirties. I think it's very interesting that this Buddhist was happy and willing to make this sacrificial pilgrimage.

I asked him what he learned, and he said, "Well, I learned that God is in everyone and everything—but, of course, I knew that already." But again, to me, this just underscores what you just said, that this generation is not the least bit hesitant to mix practices and traditions. And that's a pretty new phenomenon.

Bucko: I think that is because they are sensing that the God they want to experience is a God of Life and not a God of Religion. It's about deepening their experience of life.   —OS 21–22

Today many people, especially young adults, are surmising that the times are too dire and the demands too great to be journeying with all the paraphernalia of religions that has accumulated during the past eras. We need to travel with "backpacks, not basilicas" on our backs. We also need to take the treasures from the burning buildings that were our religious institutions of the past.

We have all heard the story of how Nero fiddled while Rome burned, but today the Earth itself is burning and many are still fiddling—not just climate change deniers but even those supposedly in the know and paying attention to what scientists are telling us about the waters rising, the snows melting, the disappearance of countless species of animals, birds, fishes, trees, and forests. We can easily be so swept away in our anthropocentric work, media distractions, social media, and daily obligations that we lose sight of the burning going on around us. We fiddle while the Earth burns. Academia fiddles, economists fiddle, politicians fiddle, media fiddles (and titillates), religion fiddles as it argues over doctrines, dogmas, buildings, rules, legalities, accounting, power games, ordinations, men, women, sex, gays, other religions, and more.

At this critical time in human and planetary history, what Buddhist scholar and activist Joanna Macy calls "The Great Turning," the world does not need a new religion or even a recycling of our old religions. It does not need a new church either. Maybe what it needs is a new Order, that is to say, a community and movement of people from varied backgrounds of belief systems (or non-belief systems) who share a sacred vow to preserve Mother Earth and to become the best lovers (mystics) and defenders (warriors) they can be on behalf of Mother Earth. A postdenominational Order and a post-religious Order. Therefore, a *Spiritual Order*.   —OSE 3–4

On Coming Out of an Enforced Year of Silence

My first public speech in America on coming out of my enforced fourteen months of silence by the Vatican was in Chicago at a Call to Action Conference. About two thousand people had gathered in February, 1990. Call to Action is a group of Catholics committed to change within their church. There was a palpable electricity in the air. Before I was introduced, they played one of my favorite pieces, from Bernstein's Mass: "Go and lock up your bold men and hold men in tow/you can stifle all adventure for a century or so/smother hope before it's risen, watch it wizen like a gourd,/but you cannot imprison the word of the Lord." Sister Teresita Weind, an African American sister who was a real leader in the Chicago church, introduced me in the most moving fashion: she invited all participants to join her in a hymn of liberation from her own people. "Oh, freedom! Oh, freedom! Oh, freedom over me! An' befo' I'd be a slave, I'll be buried in my grave. An' go home to my Lord an' be free."

It was the most powerful introduction I have ever experienced. When it came my turn to speak, my opening lines caused quite a sensation. I said simply, "As I was saying fourteen months ago . . . when I was so rudely interrupted . . ." These words had come to me in a dream—in fact the dream had awakened me at the time. I had thought it might bring a laugh—but in fact it brought two long-lasting and sustained laughs, the first after the first phrase, the second after the second. The cheers went on for a long time. I don't know if anyone remembers my talk, but the opening lines stole the day. —CNF 228-29

On Becoming an Episcopalian Priest

On the night before the press conference in which the Episcopal bishop of California, Williams Swing, and I were to announce my switch to the Episcopal Church and my reasons for it, I had a dream that seemed significant. The operative line in it was clear and lucid. It was from the gospel: "Shake the dust from your feet." This was Jesus's advice when he spoke about entering a house and wishing "peace upon it" and not getting peace in return. This pretty much summarized my struggle with the Roman Catholic Church at this time in history. By going public with the Episcopal bishop, I was indeed shaking dust from my feet. Now the work could go on—not outside the tradition or church community, but very much within it. Yet in a more modest corner of that tradition. —CNF 277

Pounding Theses at Luther's Church in Wittenberg: A Dream

When I heard of Pope Benedict's "election" in Spring, 2005, I was preparing to go to Germany to give some talks at a healing center near Frankfurt on Pentecost, which is a national holiday in Germany. I was concerned since Pentecost traditionally celebrates the "birth of the church," and knowing Cardinal Ratzinger as I did from twelve years of dealing with him, there was little birthday-like celebrating that I could envision on the horizon for the church. I thought seriously of cancelling my engagement, but I also felt that would be unfair to the group that had invited me and promoted and organized the event. What to do?

When I went to bed that night, I asked for a dream, and a dream came. I was reminded of how a certain Martin Luther was also disturbed by papal corruption and had responded by

posting ninety-five theses on the local church door and of how
Ratzinger was a countryman of Luther. I woke up at about 3
a.m., sat in a rocking chair with a pad of paper, and started to
sketch out theses. I said to myself, "Maybe I have twenty-five or
so within me." By the time the sun came up three hours later, I
had before me ninety-five theses. And I was exhausted! I went
back to bed, woke up a few hours later, looked over the theses
and said, "Yes, I can live with these."

Thus I did indeed keep my commitment at the Healing Center, but afterward I continued on to the church at Wittenberg to
pound my theses at the same doors where Luther had done so
500 years previously.   —CNF 377

Shortly afterwards, I wrote the book, A New Reformation.
(MF)

Two Christianities: Time for a Divorce?

For the new Reformation to take place, the West must acknowledge what is now obvious for all to see: there are two Christi-
anities in our midst. One worships a Punitive Father and leads
with the doctrine of Original Sin. It is anthropocentric and patriarchal in nature, links readily to fascist powers of control, and
demonizes women, the earth, other species, science, and homosexuals. It builds on fear and supports empire building.

The other Christianity recognizes the Original Blessing from
which all beings derive. It recognizes awe, rather than sin and
guilt, as the starting point of true religion. It thus marvels at
today's scientific findings about the wonders of the 13.8-bil-
lion-year journey of the universe that has brought our being into
existence and the wonders of our special home, the earth. It prefers trust over fear and an understanding of a divinity who is
source of all things, as much mother as father, as much female
as male. An emerging "woman church" does not exclude men,
and tries to consider the whole earth as a holy temple. Because it
honors creation, it does not denigrate what creation has accomplished, which includes the 8 percent of the human population
that is gay or lesbian and those 464+ other species with gay and

lesbian populations. It considers evil to be a choice that we make as humans—one that separates us from our common good—and that we can unmake.

For some time, Christian churches, both Protestant and Catholic, have been trying to coexist within these two traditions. But with world developments being what they are—with the marriage of fundamentalist ideology and religious forces and the ignoring of issues of climate change and poverty and economic justice—it is time to separate these two versions of Christianity.

It is very difficult to imagine the historical Jesus, who took on the Roman Empire of his day, being at all pleased with the cheerleaders of the American empire rallying in his name. St. Paul also took on the Roman Empire—indeed the phrase he applied to Jesus, "son of God," was borrowed not so much from Jewish theology as from the Empire's theology, which taught that Augustus was the son of God.

In fact, as a rabbi taught me, "Everyone who is living out God's wisdom deserves to be called a son or daughter of God." We can hope that this includes all of us, along with Jesus, who lived so generous a life of wisdom.

Spirituality as the basis of a New Reformation, a new renaissance—indeed, a rebirth of humanity—is once again possible, with a vision that is earth-honoring and oriented toward ecologic, economic, gender, racial, social, and political justice. A New Reformation will seek mightily to balance female with male elements and to honor in every way the Mother-Father God of divine wisdom. It will consider the morality of keeping the earth beautiful and healthy to be at least as important as the morality of keeping human relationships beautiful and healthy.

This new humanity will have a vision of compassion that will render sustainable our lives and our planet, for what is just *is* sustainable. What is unjust, however, is unsustainable; it falls apart and leads to war, resentment, and violence. A new spiritual vision will focus not on religion, but spirituality, and in doing so will no longer serve empires and their aspirations, for empires legitimize their violence in the name of religion. A New

Reformation will acknowledge the wisdom that emanates from all the world's spiritual traditions, with an authentically humble understanding that no one culture and no one way is the path to the Source. Interfaith movements and deep ecumenism will be necessary ingredients of a spirituality for the twenty-first century.

The split between the two existing versions of Christianity is not disappearing; on the contrary, it is widening. The issue of homosexuality is splitting the Anglican, Roman Catholic, Lutheran, Presbyterian, and Methodist churches. Some churches such as the United Church of Christ, Unity Church, United Church of Canada, Quakers, and Unitarian Universalism have left this behind them. They are already part of the divine wisdom tradition and deserve to be joined by those of us from the more "catholic" traditions, which spend far too much energy and time on trying to reform or conform to structures that are old, obsolete, and museum-like. This has led to the committing of numerous sins of omission, which, as Thomas Aquinas points out, are *always* sins against justice.

In turning our backs on these traditions, we leave them not because we dislike the people within them. On the contrary, at this dangerous time we leave them in order to live more fully the future to which they once called us. We leave them in order to carry on their best values, which are being tarnished by fear, tiredness, institutional rot, prejudice masquerading as tradition, and just plain necrophilia.

We leave behind the museum-like Christianity as we would a burning building—seizing what is most valuable and letting go of the rest. We take what is best from the old ways and leave behind what is unnecessarily burdensome, such as Saint Augustine's teachings about sex, which lead to opposition to birth control and condom use even in an age of AIDS and population explosion as well as to vilification of gays and lesbians.

What is the origin of the certainty that fundamentalists exhibit?

I think it comes from several sources: a fear of chaos, fear of the feminine, and a fear that displaces trust and compassion.

Above all, it comes from the wound inflicted by the Punitive Father. All fundamentalists have father wounds. Not just our personal experience but our very culture leaves us with father wounds. We are told, for example, that the universe, the home of Father Sky, is a junkyard of inert machine parts—the basic story emanating from Newton's view of the universe, which dominated for many generations in the modern era and which deeply wounds the masculine soul in particular. This is so because men retreat into themselves; men must be able to project their greatness into the vast universe. When the cosmos is no longer considered vast, their greatness gets appropriated locally, through violence and war, hatred and power trips—and these characterize not only the fundamentalist impulse but also its political projection onto fascism in its many forms.   —NR 19–25

Ninety-Five Theses or Articles of Faith for a Renewed Christianity

Like Martin Luther before me, I present here ninety-five theses. These have been drawn from my sixty-five years of living and practicing religion and spirituality. I trust I am not alone in recognizing these truths. For me they represent a return to our origins, to the spirit and teachings of Jesus and his prophetic ancestors, and to the Christ unleashed by Jesus' presence and teachings.

These theses are an invitation to discussion and debate. They are about not just a Reformation, but a *transformation*. Can Christianity transform itself for a new millennium and the generations to come? Can it take from its past only what is wise and move into a new age with a renewed commitment to sustainability for the earth and justice for the earth's people, human and more than human? Below are a few of the these:

1. God is both Mother and Father.
2. At this time in history, God is more Mother than Father because the feminine is most missing and it is important to bring back gender balance.

3. God is always new, always young, and always "in the beginning." . . .

8. All are called to be prophets, which is to interfere with injustice.

9. *Wisdom* is love of life. (See the Book of Wisdom, "This is wisdom: to love life," and Christ in John's Gospel: "I have come that you may have life and have it in abundance.")

10. God loves all of creation, and science can help us more deeply penetrate and appreciate the mysteries and wisdom of God in creation. Science is no enemy of true religion.

11. Religion is not necessary, but spirituality is.

—NR 60–61, 64–65

Some Similarities between Creation Spirituality and Liberation Theology

Liberation Theology and Creation-Centered Spirituality share much in common. Both movements seek to understand Christian love within the Jewish, biblical context of justice—there can be no love without justice. Or as Meister Eckhart puts it, "love will never be anywhere except where equality and unity are. There can be no love where people do not find equality or are not busy making equality." The goal of the entire spiritual effort in Creation-Centered Spirituality is compassion, and "compassion means justice" (Eckhart) and celebration. Both Liberation Theology and Creation-Centered Spirituality consider that a consciousness of faith needs to include a social, political, economic awareness that is critical and that offers workable and creative alternatives.

Both Liberation Theology and Creation-Centered Spirituality celebrate *orthopraxis*—the question of *how* we live our lives as an essential test of what we *say* we believe in. Belief is not a weapon for covering up truth or pain or injustice but is the opposite: our way of living out truth, justice, and compassion (the effort to relieve pain) in our work, our citizenship, and our lifestyles. Both Liberation Theology and Creation-Centered

Spirituality insist on a working dialectic and mutuality between theory and practice. Ideas are too valuable to remain in the head alone, and experience is too basic to be relegated to being a shadow of ideas. Rather, the richest ideas come from practice, and practice in turn needs to critique ideas. —WP 156

In addition, both Liberation Theology and Creation-Centered Spirituality emerge from the experience and wisdom of the *anawim*—"the forgotten ones." Liberation Theology has been born of centuries of colonialism and exploitation of the peoples of Latin America by the dominant powers of Europe and North American governments and giant corporations in alliance with military forces from without and within the countries at hand. Creation-Centered Spirituality comes to Christianity from the tens of thousands of years of experience of *anawim* peoples— namely women, native peoples, peasants, artists, and people of color. —WP 157

Some Differences between Creation Spirituality and Liberation Theology

First is the fact that Liberation Theology owes more to the German Enlightenment than does Creation-Centered Spirituality. Karl Marx, a genius and prophet born of the Enlightenment, offered much that is still useful today in terms of critique of social justice and class struggle in particular, but the patriarchal Enlightenment leaves much out—for example, artists, workers who are not industrial workers, non-two-legged ones, the cosmos and creation, music, celebration, childlikeness, art, women. Creation-Centered Spirituality is far more ancient than Liberation Theology and owes more to native peoples of the Americas and Africa and Asia than it does to the European Enlightenment.
—WP 157

Liberation Theology tends to be patriarchal. Creation-Centered Spirituality is explicitly feminist, which means that it not only names the oppression of women in a patriarchal society but of men as well. . . .

Creation-Centered Spirituality insists on psychic justice as well as structural justice. The structural justice of the human psyche must itself be critiqued and transformed. What does this mean? It means that mysticism—what philosopher Joseph Pieper defines as "affirmation of the Whole" and what Rabbi Heschel defines as "radical amazement"—must be included as part of any valid social change . . .

Creation-Centered Spirituality seems very appropriate for First World cultures because there is an immense spiritual deprivation among the people. Why else is there such a hunger for drugs that keeps the drug cartels south of the border in business? When this spiritual poverty is released, much energy will be unleashed—including the vigor to address poverty and racism and inequities in systems of policing and courts, education, and finance.   —WP 156–62

10

Deep Ecumenism, Interfaith

DEEP ECUMENISM

Deep ecumenism is a movement that can unleash the wisdom of *all* world religions—Hinduism and Buddhism, Islam and Judaism, Taoism and Shintoism, Christianity in all its forms, and native religions and goddess religions throughout the world. This unleashing of wisdom holds the last hope for the survival of the planet we call home. For there is no such thing as a Lutheran sun and a Taoist Moon, a Jewish ocean, and a Roman Catholic forest. When humanity learns this, we will have learned a way out of our anthropocentric dilemma that is boring our young, killing our souls, trivializing our worship, and exterminating the planet.

Cosmology is three things: the scientific story of how we got here, mystical experience, and art. The scientific story is today being heard and believed globally. East Indians and Africans, Russians and Latin Americans, Europeans and North Americans, Chinese and Australians are beginning to hear the same story—that this planet was not an accident, that we have been "loved from before the beginning" in the original fireball itself, that the universe wanted us and awaited us eagerly. We have a responsibility to give back the cherished blessing of our lives with grace and gratitude. We must return blessing for blessing. Generativity and creativity have been built into the universe from the start.

Like science, art too is transcultural. Music, dance, drama, ritual—all the arts—have long held the power to connect, the

229

power to make whole what was separate, the power to move the human heart to wholeness instead of piecemealness. With today's instant communications and social media, much can happen that holds promise for a global artistic awakening, one that hopefully incarnates the new, global, and therefore radically ecumenical cosmology into our psyches, dreams, and bodies, and even our bodies politic. A global awakening *is* possible— and necessary to save the planet as we know it. The emergence of folk arts and personal arts that will put people to good work, which will bind together communities at the neighborhood level, and which will revitalize our lifestyles is equally a part of the hope that a new cosmology brings to a suffering planet. . . .

A living cosmology cannot happen from science and art alone. Mysticism too must be integral to this awakening, basic to this global renaissance. Mysticism represents the depth of religious traditions the world over—but it has barely ever *been tried on an ecumenical level*. I cannot emphasize this fact enough. We have no inkling what power would ensue for creativity, for employment, for peace making, for exciting the young to deep adventures once again (other than that dated adventure called war), were mysticism to be unleashed on a globe scale. Because it has never been tried, we cannot predict the consequences.

Why have we never tried it? Because the West has been so thoroughly out of touch with its own mystical heritage. How could the West dialogue on mysticism with the East when it did not know its own mystical roots? What can Christianity say to native peoples whose mystical traditions are so rich when Christians don't know their own mystical experience? After all, the great encounters between Christianity and native peoples and between Christianity and the Eastern religions *have occurred only in the past few centuries, i.e., during that exact point in the West when Newton and the Enlightenment extinguished the Cosmic Christ*. And, with the bubonic plague in the fourteenth century, creation spirituality was effectively extinguished due to fear of nature and trauma at the plague. The result was that redemption became the singular occupation and veritable meaning of religion. The point cannot be emphasized too much: We have never attempted a rapprochement between the Cosmic Christ in Christianity and the Cosmic Christ in the universe and the Cosmic Christ in other religions (the Buddha nature in Buddhism, for example, or the Image of God tradition in Judaism).

—CCC 228–29

The Universality of Experience

Religions are integral to Creation because they are themselves created, set up by humans in relationship to their stories of the Divine. In addition, religions provide us with a perspective, a lens through which we see Creation and interpret it. Therefore, it seems appropriate to consider Deep Ecumenism even before we delve into the deep mysteries of Creation itself.

I am writing these words at the ocean in Northern California, where the waves are churning and inspired, full of energy and rushing where they will. Spirit is like that—full of energy and free to choose its own path.

My thoughts turn to the subject of our various religions. None of them is mother of the ocean; rather, the ocean is mother of them. All religions are so recent in relation to the lifetime of the sea and to most other creatures—including humanity itself. What religions did our ancestors practice for the two million years that preceded the forms we now recognize as "world religions"? How humble our religions ought to be before all creatures. As Mechtild of Magdeburg said, "the truly wise person kneels at the feet of all creatures."

Deep Ecumenism should be *deep;* it ought to demand of human religions that they imitate the depths of the sea (*la mer*) in its capacity to maintain mystery and energy, being mother (*la mère*) to all beings. Varying with the course of seasons and the topography of land and water alike, ecumenism ought to be big, accepting, magnanimous, forgiving.

Our souls are meant to imitate the sea also. That is our origin. Our very lifeblood imitates the saltwater of the ocean. But culture so often shrinks our souls that they fit a consumer mold or some other tribal size.

I am not alone in calling for religions themselves to practice the humility they so often preach to individual adherents. All the mystics—the truly deep ecumenists—speak as I do. Hear them out. Consider how well we are doing.   —ORMW 15–16

Universality in Indian Mysticism

The Indian mystic Kabir sings:

Neither a Hindu
Nor a Muslim am I!
A mere ensemble
Of five elements is
This body,
Where the spirit
Plays its drama
Of joy and suffering!

Kabir is telling us how the cosmic gift of his body supersedes the claims of organized religion to his allegiance. The spirit plays within that body; it plays games of joy and games of suffering. Life is a drama where one moves beyond mere religious allegiances. Divinity cannot be locked up.

The god of Hindus resides in a temple;
The god of Muslims resides in a mosque.
Who resides there
Where there are no temples
Nor mosques?

We are reminded of Jesus saying, "Do not look here nor there. The kingdom of God is among you." True religion is not about institutions, be they mosques, temples, or objects of any kind. It is about relationship. It is about intersubjectivity and not objects and the objectifying of objects that we so often fall into. Creation brings us all together. As Kabir put it, "Once you experience his presence in all beings, all debate comes to naught!"
—ORMW 17

Universality in Islam

Islam, too, is ecumenical in its core, according to Seyyed Hossein. "Islam considers the acceptance of anterior prophets as a necessary article of faith (iman) in Islam itself and asserts quite vigorously the universality of revelation. No other sacred text speaks as much and as openly of the universality of religion as the Quran. Islam, the last of the religions of the present humanity, here joins with Hinduism, the first and most primordial of existing religions, in envisaging religion and its universal manifestation throughout the cycles of human history."

Following are some passages from the Holy Quran apropos of Deep Ecumenism. "Surely, of the Believers, the Jews, the Christians and the Sabians, those who truly believe in Allah and the Last Day and act righteously, shall have their reward with their Lord and no fear shall come upon them nor shall they grieve." Respect for Moses and the Hebrew Bible as well as for Jesus and Mary is offered. "Indeed we gave Moses the book and caused a number of Messengers to follow after him; and to Jesus Son of Mary, we gave manifest signs and strengthened him with the Spirit of Holiness." Again, "We gave Jesus Son of Mary clear proofs and strengthened him with the Spirit of holiness . . . We make no distinction between any of his Messengers."

—ORMW 19

The Sufi tradition sees all mystical traditions as one. Rumi says:

> All religions,
> all this singing,
> is one song.
> The differences are just
> illusion and vanity.
> The Sun's light looks a little different
> on this wall than it does on that wall. . .
> but it's still one light.

Rumi grounds the likeness found in every mystical tradition to the depth of the experience of the Divine one touches in a particular tradition. Love is the key.

> For those in love,
>
> Muslim, Christian, and Jew do not exist . . .
> Why listen to those who see it another way?—
> If they're not in love
> Their eyes do not exist.

Thirteenth-century Sufi Hafiz also addresses Deep Ecumenism when he writes:

> I have learned so much from God
> that I can no longer call myself
> a Christian, a Hindu, a Muslim, a Buddhist, a Jew
> —ORMW 20

Unversality in Buddhism

From the Buddhist tradition, Thich Nhat Hanh speaks of the centrality of going deep if we are to do ecumenism. "Through the practice of deep looking and deep listening, we become free, able to see the beauty and values in our own and others' tradition." Yet, to get to the point of seeing the beauty and value in others' traditions, one must look and listen *deeply* into one's own. One must practice some path along the journey that leads to depth. One must enter the well of mystical experience.

To meet another is to meet oneself and one's own tradition, Thich Nhat Hanh insists. "When you touch someone who authentically represents a tradition, you not only touch his or her tradition, you also touch your own." The implication is that every tradition accomplishes like things in the soul of individuals—so alike are the things accomplished that we become *mirrors* to one another: We can see ourselves in one another. What we see emphasized by Thich Nhat Hanh is found in all mystical traditions: experience is key. The sixteenth-century Indian saint-poet Dadu once wrote:

> All men of wisdom have one religion;
> They all have one caste:
> They all behold the face of the One!

It has been said that Buddhism teaches that kindness and love are the universal religion. —ORMW 22

Universality in the African-American Tradition

From the African-American tradition we listen to the voice of a great mystic and prophet, Howard Thurman, who was the spiritual mentor to Dr. Martin Luther King, Jr. Howard Thurman saw what we are calling Deep Ecumenism as the central call of his vocation when he wrote: "A strange necessity has been laid upon me to devote my life to the central concern that transcends the walls that divide and would achieve in literal fact what is experienced as literal truth: human life is one and all men are members one of another. And this insight is spiritual and it is the hard core of religious experience." He too, like Thich Nhat Hanh, Kabir, and the Dalai Lama, is calling us to experience that of which we speak. Thurman develops his Deep Ecumenism even more explicitly in another place when he writes: "It is my belief that in the Presence of God there is neither male nor female, white nor black, Gentile nor Jew, Protestant nor Catholic, Hindu, Buddhist, nor Muslim, but a human spirit stripped to the literal substance of itself before God."

Thurman had an experience of Deep Ecumenism vs. theology when he visited India in the 1930s. He dialogued with a Hindu, Thurman speaking as a Christian, for half a day and with little result. Then they shifted gears, putting the discussion at the level of experience instead of concepts. Says Thurman: "We were thus released to communicate with each other as sharers of what each in his own way had discovered of his experience of God. We were no longer under the necessity to define anything but were free to be to each other what was most fundamental to each." —ORMW 23

Universality in Judaism

The Jewish mystical work of the Middle Ages, the Kabbalah, says: "The only genuine proof of this wisdom is experience itself." If our faith has not given us experiences to share, then we ought to spend more time with it or find another. Just as our times call for Deep Ecumenism, so Deep Ecumenism calls for 1) experience and 2) the sharing of experience. At the level of experience we are all one, and we encounter the One Divinity, however he/she be named. But experience also leads to Deep Ecumenism, for when one encounters the beloved, one wants to share that encounter and one is curious about the encounters others behold. Am I alone in this experience? Have others before me undergone such wonders? Will others after me? What about my community—do they, can they, share in the same glory and revelation? Many questions are aroused by love experiences.

—ORMW 25

Universality in Christianity

Consider these words from Thomas Aquinas in the thirteenth century:

> Every truth without exception—and whoever utters it—is
>   from
> the Holy Spirit.
> The old pagan virtues were from God.
> Revelation has been made to many pagans.

Imagine how different history would read if the European explorers and exploiters of the fifteenth and sixteenth centuries had approached the shores of Turtle Island and Africa and the Pacific Islands with this theology instead of proposing that indigenous people have no souls and treating them as such through slavery and conscription and cultural annihilation.   —ORMW 24

Christian and Buddhist Goals

When I look at goals, in terms of my lineage, two words rise to the surface: one is *compassion*, and one is *generosity*.

For me, compassion very much comes out of mysticism because it comes out of our awareness . . . of interdependence. Once we recognize how truly interdependent we are, compassion just happens. It flows. It's absolutely natural. Eckhart put it this way: "What happens to another, whether it be a joy or a sorrow, happens to me." That's compassion. It is our common joy and our common sorrow. And it's also an effort to relieve the sorrow to the extent we can, to relieve suffering to the extent that we can, the work of relieving ignorance or relieving physical pain through healing and education and medicine and so forth. That, of course, is the Jewish tradition, from Isaiah, of what we call the works of mercy . . .

So I think there's a wonderful coming together, then, of what the East would call "non-action and action," and what the West, I think, would call "being in action." Meister Eckhart says, "We should worry less about what we do and more about who we are, because if our being is just, we will be just. If our being is joyful, we will be joyful." This reintegration of being and action and doing, if you will, is part of the accomplishment of a mystical lineage and of our own practice . . .

For me, *generosity* has become a very important word lately. It's an amazing word in English when you look it up etymologically. I end my book, *Sins of the Spirit, Blessings of the Flesh,* with an essay on *generosity*, the word. It's amazing. From this word we get *genesis, generativity*—it's from the Greek. Generosity includes creativity; you can't be generous without being creative. Indeed, creativity is a giving away of our gifts. It's like the Native American give-away. That's generosity. But it's more than that. Also in the word is the word *genus*—and *lineage* and *kin*-ship, from which we got the word *kind. Kindness* is related to the word *kin,* and *kin* is related to the word for genus and kind, what we come from. Our species is a kind. Our families are a kind and kin. Kindness is related to the word *kin.* So all of this is also from our talk about the mammal brain, about our capacity for compassion, for kinship . . .

When I read Buddhist literature, it's interesting how smoothly generosity and compassion glide together in the writings. And I think that's as it should be, because when you come down to this bottom question, "Who are human beings?" I think all the great teachers, the Buddhas, and the Lao Tzus, and the Isaiahs, and the Jesuses, and the Dorothy Days, and all have been trying to remind us that we are generous in our roots. The ocean is a very generous source from which we come, and we are capable of compassion. I think that as a species we need to continually not just be reminded of this but be led to this. Part of the struggle we're up against today is that the forces that dominate our awareness—like the media for example, and the powers behind them—their bottom line is anything but generosity and compassion. The world in which we find ourselves, the human-made world, is not conducive to bringing the best out of us. It's conducive to the reptilian brain, not to the mammal brain.

Part of our awareness is to cushion ourselves, buffer ourselves from this energy of greed, which is the opposite of compassion and generosity, and fear, which is the opposite of sharing. Fear, literally, tightens us up. In fact, Aquinas warns that "fear is such a powerful emotion for human beings that when fear takes over the soul, all compassion goes out the door." So fear and compassion are incompatible. The compulsion for security and the presence of fear kill compassion.

The implications of putting these practices of compassion and generosity into action are huge for our own souls, our own hearts, but our own culture, too. This is going to be a clash, and yet I think that this is what the next level of evolution of our species is all about. Either we learn what our teachers, East and West, have been telling us—that we're compassionate beings and we're generous beings—either we learn this and practice it, or we're probably finished as an experiment on this planet.

—LR 51–54

Aboriginal Religion and the Dreamtime

The beauty that is the Dreamtime is everywhere. The question is: do we have the eyes to see it and the ears to hear it?

I feel it is pure nostalgia to think that only people in the wilderness, in the bush, can experience Dreamtime. It is part of our nature and our histories.

On the other hand, the fact that there is so much wilderness in Australia and that the Australian Aborigines have lived so long and spent so much spirit in this land does invite people here to a special experience of the wilderness Dreamtime as well. And there is a challenge to bring the two together: how does the outback relate to the urban?

What we need is *biculturalism*. By this I mean that we need to live both in Dreamtime and in clock time. I am really convinced that we have to find this balance in our civilization. We are so unbalanced. You cannot be a mystic twenty-four hours a day. You would blow all your tubes! You need the dialectic, the dance, the balance . . .

Let me begin by pointing out the connections between our biblical heritage, mysticism, and the Dreamtime. We have learned that there is no word for time in the Australian Aboriginal language. Everything is always *now*. This is exactly how Meister Eckhart talks. "God," says he "is always in the beginning, making things new!" And he adds, "If you can return to the beginning, you will always be new, always be young, always be in touch with God." This is why our scriptures begin with 'In the beginning . . .' —both Genesis and John's Gospel. And all four Gospels begin with the creation story, as I have demonstrated in my book, *The Coming of the Cosmic Christ*. The Cosmic Christ is celebrated in the first chapters of each of the Synoptic Gospels, just as he is in the first chapter of John's Gospel.

Another phrase that Eckhart uses is *living in the Eternal now*. What we find in the Australian Aboriginal understanding of time is a one hundred percent pure mystical consciousness. We white people will never get it until we sink into our own mystical experience. That explains the clash between white and indigenous cultures.

We have to listen with our hearts, not just our heads, as Eckhart says, "God is creating the entire universe, fully and totally, in this present *now*."

"This is the Dreamtime," Eddie Kneebone says, *"now."* Eddie would undoubtedly feel that Meister Eckhart is an Australian Aboriginal too!

All the stories of original creation are Dreamtime. It is all *now.* This view is, of course, scientifically correct. All 13.8 billion years of history are behind us. They don't exist anymore. The original fireball is gone. The supernova explosion that gave birth to the elements of our body is gone. But it is present in today's sunshine, in today's photosynthesis, in *our* bodies and minds. And in the sky where it travels millions of years to our eyes.   —WP 124, 133–34

Goddess Traditions, Patriarchy, and Postmodern Science

In the goddess times, Chaos was honored as a goddess and was consciously (and unconsciously) incorporated into the culture. But when patriarchy took over, the stories changed dramatically, and the goddess Chaos became an enemy needing to be slain by masculine warriors. For example, in the Babylonian creation myth, the *Enuma Elish,* the story is told of how the goddess Tiamat is slain by a new god named Marduk. Marduk cuts open the belly of Tiamat in a very vicious murder scene. Marduk was celebrated as a hero, and rituals were held annually to celebrate his murder of the goddess. Parallel stories circulated in Greece where Apollo slays a female goddess who guards the shrine of Mother Earth and is considered the source of evil.

This same spirit of Chaos as the enemy—"kill the goddess"—is alive today in all acts of misogyny including religious fundamentalism and political fascism. These two movements, that so often go to bed together, insist that law and order take precedence over love, justice and compassion. Both are rigorously anti-women and misogynist. Both bolster patriarchy and yearn for a nostalgic past when, supposedly, the masculine ruled over creativity and kept all things in order.

Scientist Ralph Abraham, in his brilliant book, *Chaos, Gaia, Eros*, argues very convincingly that patriarchal religion—and then 18th-century modern science—carried on this antipathy toward the feminine and the goddess in the name of order and heresy-hunting which is based on a deep fear of chaos on the part of the masculine psyche. But with the discovery (better, re-discovery) of the positive role of chaos by scientific chaos theory beginning in the 1960s (and Abraham was one of the founders of chaos theory), Chaos was no longer seen as an existential threat. Within weather systems, ellipses of planets, within nature as a whole, chaos was recognized as an integral and necessary part of the creativity and unfolding of nature everywhere. Chaos seems part of all creative processes. She has returned as a goddess.

We need to dance a new but ancient dance that incorporates both order and chaos, respecting the power of each. With climate change and much else happening, we should all prepare ourselves for entertaining more chaos, not less.   —NU 100–101

Conclusion

The Future: A Letter to Young Seekers from Matthew Fox

Dear Seekers,

As an elder, I am pleased to be invited to write you a letter about our common spiritual seeking. Several stories come to mind: The advice from the late and admirable John Lewis, a lifelong fighter for justice and integrity, to not hesitate to make *good trouble*. Making good trouble is the mark of the prophet. And we all are called to be other prophets, just as we are called to be other Christs, other Buddhas, etc.

It is an axiom that we live in troubled times, but you of the emerging generations already know this to be true. And many of you are already rising to the occasion. You who have come of age in the time of climate emergency and its cousin, the coronavirus epoch, and of democracy in decline know how swiftly things can and do change. Society as we know it can come to a screeching halt almost overnight. It is important that we learn, even at an early age, the reality of mortality, finiteness, limits, not being in control. Mother Earth is bigger than any or all of us. She birthed us, but she is also being abused by the human agendas of the modern industrial age and is doing everything possible to wake us up.

We have the gifts and the talent to turn things around, but time is short and decisions will be made in your lifetimes that are irreversible. Not all solutions will come from the creativity of scientists and technology (though many will, as per the vaccines rolled out in record time against COVID).

Much has to change in the inner sanctums of our hearts and minds, our attitude toward earth and the values we commit to and teach one another, including our children and grandchildren. Our educational systems too often come across as void of values.

Recently, to my surprise, I stumbled upon an article on the internet entitled "The Redemption of Justin Bieber" in *GQ* magazine. Allow me to say that I do not read *GQ*, and neither do I follow Justin Bieber (though I've certainly heard of him and his fans over the years). I wondered if he, being a young man (twenty-seven years old), had something to say to the younger generation. I was struck by the title of the article, for redemption or conversion or waking up is a big part of my work as a spiritual teacher—indeed, I have often defined spirituality as "waking up." As the fifteenth-century Indian mystic Kabir does when he says, "you have been sleeping for millions and millions of years. Why not wake up this morning?"

In the article there is this brief passage: "Two things brought Justin Bieber back, ultimately: his marriage and his faith. What they had in common was that they were value systems that didn't depend on him performing in exchange for money."

Value systems brought him back from the brink of self-destruction generated both by his success as an artist and entertainer and from his wounds growing up in a broken family environment and the rest. And, the "exchange for money." Capitalism was killing his soul.

Another word for value systems is *virtue*. How to develop habits that carry on our values? And how to determine what our values are, how to winnow them and watch them evolve as we grow older and as culture reveals to us more of its dark side? How, for example, does climate emergency bespeak our values and call virtue out of us? Or the COVID crisis? Or the egregious shootings of black people by police? Or the rise of Black Lives Matter? Or regular mass shootings in schools and elsewhere?

Thomas Aquinas offers an amazing teaching when he says, "it is a great thing to do miracles, but it is a greater thing to live virtuously." Living virtuously—living out our values and fine tuning them as we go through life—is a miracle in itself!

A key value is the sacredness of Mother Earth. Have we lost the sense of the sacred as a dream I received twenty years ago told me? If so, we need to regain it, and the best way, as Thomas Berry instructs us, is to reconnect to the big picture, that is, to the cosmos for all its magnificence and eagerness to birth our planet earth, and with it so many marvelous creatures who accompany us on our journeys here. Birthing us has been quite an accomplishment and has been an impressive 13.8-billion-year endeavor. Extinguishing our very existence would constitute a refusal to say *Thank You*. Falling in love with earth and life and all our creaturely companions all over again and on a daily basis is the first response of Spirit working in and through us. The rest—good work and critical thinking and commitment to truth and justice and service and compassion—all flow from that.

Our calling in life, our vocations, flow from that. They are how we give back. Listen intently to your dreams, wrestle with them, and become educated, whether through hard knocks or school or both, to respond to your vocations.

Speaking of values, critical thinking is an important value, and a question raised by scientist Gregory Bateson fifty years ago haunts me still. He asked, "Are we rotting our minds from a slowly deteriorating religion and education?" This is a tough question to listen to and to respond to. But it is real. Religion that has fallen into a rabbit hole of anthropocentrism that feeds on fear and guilt and the ego ("Am I going to hell or heaven? Woe is me, the great sinner," etc., etc.) is a rapidly deteriorating religion that rots the mind.

An education that leaves out values is highly suspect and upholds the status quo and indeed rots the mind. It prompted Albert Einstein to say, "I abhor American education," because it ignores intuition where values are cooked—values do not come from the rational mind, he reminds us, but from "intuition or deep feeling which are the same thing." I call intuition *mysticism*—our being in love and in awe and in reverence and in gratitude. The Via Positiva. Thomas Berry talked about "academic barbarism" that trains people to kill the planet (never asking about values along the way of course). We need wisdom and not just knowledge.

Wisdom, as opposed to raw knowledge, is not afraid of exploring values, values that can unite people of wonderfully diverse backgrounds around our common humanity set in the context of sacred creation. If January 6, 2021, was a revelation of the shadow side of America, it was also clearly a report card on our educational system that seems to have utterly failed to deal with the pent-up anger of citizens as well as the ignorance of the virtues that are necessary to cultivate if a democracy is to survive.

Back in 1907, William James—whose classic work *The Varieties of Religious Experience* helped name the basics of healthy mysticism, which he called the "Yes faculty" in us, and who said there is a "germ of mysticism" in us all—was explicit that "democracy is on trial"! Democracy is still on trial, and to survive it needs a spiritual dimension and virtuous citizens. Is our democracy failing today because we have abandoned or distorted this value in both our religious and educational systems? Because lies and "misinformation" have replaced our efforts at truth seeking and truth telling?

For over fifty years my vocational fate has been to wrestle with both the religious and educational rottenness that Bateson points to. My effort has been to go to the heart of religion, which is experience or spirituality. James said that religion is primarily about experience. This makes it different from religion, which so often gets wrapped up in sociological structures and power games including rigid dogmatism. As a young man, I was blessed to learn from great souls like M. D. Chenu and Louis Cognet and others, and thanks to the former to learn of the creation spirituality tradition that holds so much promise in a time of nature crisis that we face today.

I have also been blessed to interact with and gather great spokespeople of that lineage such as Hildegard of Bingen,

Thomas Aquinas, Meister Eckhart, Julian of Norwich, Thomas Merton, Joanna Macy, Clarissa Pinkola Estes, and many more in a common conversation of how we deepen our souls and go to action on behalf of Mother Earth and a livable future. I have been blessed to undergo teachings and ceremonies with indigenous teachers such as Buck Ghosthorse, Rod McAfee, Sister Jose Hobday, Eddie Kneebone, and others. We are so blessed to have among us still the hard-earned wisdom of indigenous peoples.

The mystics stretch and expand our consciousness and take us to the edge. Heed John of the Cross's advice to "launch out into the deep." Do not settle for standing on the shore as a spectator. Become your own mystic and your own lover of this gift we call *Life*.

Another teaching from John Lewis in his good-bye letter was that young people should go out of their way to learn from their ancestors because "truth does not change." I urge you to do the same. Feed your mystical soul with the wisdom of these premodern ancestors, whether indigenous or medieval, for they were not anthropocentric but begin their view of the world with the wonder and holiness of all creation.

The latest biblical scholarship tells us that for Paul, the first writer in the Christian Bible, one "cannot be a Christian without being a mystic." Furthermore, Jesus's spiritual roots are in the wisdom (i.e., creation-centered) tradition of Israel. Heed the observation by poet Bill Everson: "Most people experience God in nature or experience God not at all."

The four paths of creation spirituality assist us to bring wisdom from the burning buildings of institutional religion at the same time that they alert us in ways to make our personal and communal journeys deeper and more useful to others.

A few years ago, I was having lunch with an old friend, cosmologist Brian Swimme, and he brought up his two sons, who were thirty and thirty-one years old, respectively. Knowing that Brian and his wife are practicing Catholics, I asked him: "Do your kids practice?" His response was striking: "Matt," he said, "I don't know anyone under thirty who practices who isn't weird." This pretty much affirms the religion question that Bateson was asking as well as the aversion of many young people to institutional religion today.

In addition to being blessed by studying the creation mystics over the years, (Carl Jung said, "it is to the mystics that we owe what is best in humanity" and that "only the mystics bring creativity to religion"), I was also blessed to establish an educational model that has been deeply vetted over forty-five years with adults and also with inner-city teenagers. This model incorporates the education of our intuitive brains along with our rational brains and acknowledges our wonderful bodies. "Wisdom is present in all creative works," Hildegard instructs us; and thanks to art as meditation, called "the way of the prophets," wisdom is possible. Our schools of creation spirituality have educated mystics and prophets (and martyrs such as Sister Dorothy Stang), scientists, artists, activists, engineers, politicians, educators, psychologists, social workers, and more who are serving the world generously and effectively. Thomas Aquinas assures us that "wisdom is able to direct us not only in contemplation but also in action."

Let us not underestimate the power of renewed ritual or ceremony to instruct about things that matter, including the holiness of creation and our relation to it. Our Cosmic Masses have demonstrated how we can work in an ecumenical way to enliven community celebrations that incorporate the body by way of dance, along with postmodern art forms of DJ, VJ, rap, and more—and in the process bring along traditional prayer forms into our postmodern age. Years ago, a young African American man came up to me following a Cosmic Mass in Los Angeles and said, "This would be worth committing one's life to." Yes, renewed ritual is worth committing one's life to.

Key questions for our time are these:

1. What does it mean to be human? Spend a long time researching and answering that ultimate question of value.

2. In this world where we are more and more mixing with
   people of other cultures and traditions, can our common suffering—such as climate change and the viruses it
   spawns as well as racial and economic and gender injustice—bring us together? Can the pictures of our special
   earth home taken from Jupiter 1 as it exited our solar system bring us together? Can we choose to not go extinct?

May you find and create forms of education and of worship
(ceremony or ritual) that honor the serious vocations each person is called to and contribute to the next level of evolution
of our species. One that celebrates diversity and existence itself
and brings joy alive and turns it back on fear and pettiness and
tribalism and sectarianism. That steps out of a rotten and deteriorating education and religion into a grand space as blessed as
the universe itself.

In *Painting the Dream*, David Paladin, a Navajo artist-sha-
man, talks about creation spirituality in these words:

> My native training taught me to believe that God was
> all. The ancestors and all of creation were a part of
> everything that we perceived. Everything that had ever
> been was us. God was in the food we ate and in the
> dish that held the food. God was a numinous Creator
> Spirit that bound us all together. It was our experience
> of everything in creation that was the Creator."

He also warned us that truth does not stand still. Truth is the
responsibility of people to share and to grow with the times:

> All great truths are only myths that exist momentarily
> in the evolving greater consciousness. Like individuals,
> they die, to be reborn fresh and glorious in the minds
> of each new age. They may bear a resemblance to their
> forebears, but each brings with it new features of its own
> and seeks to find its place and meaning in the dancing
> dream that is the cosmos.

Now we need to move on to new myths. We are taking quantum leaps, and our paradigms are shifting rapidly.

The concepts we form and practice today create the foundation for the cultural and spiritual growth of the future. We need to achieve more than a simple desire to live in harmony with each other. If we are to survive, we must creatively respond to the spirit of transformation.

If I were to offer a wish list for a new spiritual and religious consciousness that would contribute to the survival of earth and other creatures including us humans, it would be this:

1. Learn to calm your reptilian brain (i.e., meditate) and teach your children and other adults.
2. Meditate on the new cosmology just as much as you do on the Bible itself (which, after all, begins with a cosmology story in Genesis 1).
3. Marry the Divine Feminine and Sacred Masculine in yourself and the communities you work in.
4. Practice Deep Ecumenism, finding insight from all spiritual traditions as well as joint action for justice and healing and prayer.
5. Journey with the mystics—and become one yourself.
6. Journey with prophets—and become one yourself.
7. Journey with shamans and don't be surprised if you have more in common with them than you previously thought.
8. Values! Develop them, live them, practice them, and observe how they evolve also.
9. Let "the Common Good" be one of those values that you develop ever stronger in the public domain.
10. Contribute to the reinvention of education, worship, and work by bringing creation spirituality to them whenever you can.

Keep in mind what Aquinas taught: "The experience of God must not be restricted to the few or to the old." Build your lives and service on your experiences of God who is Justice and Beauty, Artist and Compassion, Flow and Energy and creative Mind of the universe. Do not be surprised if a shaman emerges in you asking for nourishment and attention—Thomas Berry observes that today our species "needs fewer priests and fewer professors and more shamans."

Expect adversity. Develop your inner warrior. Courage matters, and it is born of trust. Remember Julian of Norwich's advice: "The mingling of both well and distress in us is so astonishing that we can hardly tell which state we or our neighbor are in—that's how astonishing it is!"

Bon Voyage! Bon Travail!

Good journeying and good work!

In Hope,

Matthew Fox

Appendix

Twelve Principles of Creation Spirituality

1. Everyone is a mystic.
2. Everyone is a prophet.
3. The universe is basically good and therefore a blessing—indeed. Creation is an Original Blessing.
4. Human beings have to dig and work at finding our deep self, true self, spirit self. If we do not, we live superficially out of fear or greed or addiction or false idols or someone else's expectations of us.
5. The journey that marks that digging can be named in the four paths of creation spirituality that derive from a Jewish, biblical spiritualty like that of Jesus.
6. Everyone is an artist in some way, and art as meditation is a primary form of prayer.
7. We can and do relate to the universe as whole.
8. We are all sons and daughters of God, and the basic work of God (and us) is compassion and justice.
9. Divinity is as much Mother as Father, as much Child as Parent, as much Godhead (mystery) as God (history).
10. We experience the Divine in all things and all things in the Divine (panentheism), and this mystical intuition supplants theism (and its child, atheism) as an appropriate way to name our relation to the Divine.
11. There are many wells of faith, but all draw from one underground river of Divine wisdom. The practice of honoring and celebrating that diversity and wisdom is Deep Ecumenism.
12. Ecological justice is essential for the sustainability of life on Earth. —CNF 316–17

251

Resources for Creation Spirituality

—www.matthewfox.org
—Creation Spirituality Communities (CSC)
—Order of the Sacred Earth (OSE)
—www.dailymeditationswithmatthewfox.org (DM)
—The Cosmic Mass (TCM)
—Matthew Fox Legacy Project (MFLP)

MODERN SPIRITUAL MASTERS
Robert Ellsberg, Series Editor

Already published:

John Main (edited by Laurence Freeman)
James Martin (edited by James T. Keane)
Anthony de Mello (edited by William Dych, S.J.)
Thomas Merton (edited by Christine M. Bochen)
John Muir (edited by Tim Flinders)
John Henry Newman (edited by John T. Ford, C.S.C.)
Henri Nouwen (edited by Robert A. Jonas)
Flannery O'Connor (edited by Robert Ellsberg)
Karl Rahner (edited by Philip Endean)
Walter Rauschenbusch (edited by Joseph J. Fahey)
Brother Roger of Taizé (edited by Marcello Fidanzio)
Richard Rohr (edited by Joelle Chase and Judy Traeger)
Ronald Rolheiser (edited by Alicia von Stamwitz)
Oscar Romero (by Marie Dennis, Rennie Golden, and Scott Wright)
Joyce Rupp (edited by Michael Leach)
Rabbi Zalman Schacter-Shalomi (edited by Or N. Rose and Netanel
    Miles-Yépez)
Albert Schweitzer (edited by James Brabazon)
Frank Sheed and Maisie Ward (edited by David Meconi)
Jon Sobrino (edited by Robert Lassalle-Klein)
Sadhu Sundar Singh (edited by Charles E. Moore)
Mother Maria Skobtsova (introduction by Jim Forest)
Dorothee Soelle (edited by Dianne L. Oliver)
Jon Sobrino (edited by Robert Lasalle-Klein)
Edith Stein (edited by John Sullivan, O.C.D.)
David Steindl-Rast (edited by Clare Hallward)
William Stringfellow (edited by Bill Wylie-Kellerman)
Pierre Teilhard de Chardin (edited by Ursula King)
Mother Teresa (edited by Jean Maalouf)
St. Thérèse of Lisieux (edited by Mary Frohlich)
Phyllis Tickle (edited by Jon M. Sweeney)
Henry David Thoreau (edited by Tim Flinders)
Howard Thurman (edited by Luther E. Smith)
Leo Tolstoy (edited by Charles E. Moore)
Evelyn Underhill (edited by Emilie Griffin)
Vincent Van Gogh (by Carol Berry)
Swami Vivekananda (edited by Victor M. Parachin)
Simone Weil (edited by Eric O. Springsted)
John Howard Yoder (edited by Paul Martens and Jenny Howells)